S0-AFB-353

Wayward

T H R E A D S

R O B E R T B . G O L D M A N N

✡ JEWISH LIVES ✡

Wayward Threads

WAYWARD

THREADS

ROBERT B. GOLDMANN

NORTHWESTERN UNIVERSITY PRESS

Evanston, Illinois

3 1254 03530 6584

Northwestern University Press
Evanston, Illinois 60208-4210

First published in German in slightly different form under the title
Flucht in die Welt: Ein Lebensweg nach New York, translated by Mona
Körte. Copyright © 1996 by Fischer Taschenbuch Verlag GmbH,
Frankfurt am Main. This English-language edition published 1997
by arrangement with Fischer Taschenbuch Verlag and
Robert B. Goldmann. All rights reserved.

Printed in the United States of America

ISBN 0-8101-1501-8 (cloth)
ISBN 0-8101-1502-6 (paper)

Library of Congress Cataloging-in-Publication Data

Goldmann, Robert B., 1921–
    [Flucht in die Welt. English]
    Wayward threads / Robert B. Goldmann.
        p.   cm. — (Jewish lives)
    ISBN 0-8101-1501-8 (cloth : alk. paper) — ISBN 0-8101-1502-6
(pbk. : alk. paper)
    1. Goldmann, Robert B., 1921–   . 2. Jews—Germany—
Biography.   3. Jews—Germany—History—1933–1945.
4. Refugees, Jewish—United States—Biography.   5. Jews—
United States—Biography.   I. Title.   II. Series.
DS135.G5G55894413   1997
943'.004924—dc21   97-42191
                                                                CIP

The paper used in this publication meets the minimum requirements
of the American National Standard for Information Sciences—
Permanence of Paper for Printed Library Materials,
ANSI Z39.48-1984.

❖

Foreword

This autobiography literally grew out of occasional columns I had written in the *International Herald Tribune* while I worked in Paris for the Anti-Defamation League. The columns the editors most readily accepted and published were vignettes out of my past in Germany and, after my emigration, in America. My wife, Eva, to whom this book is dedicated, suggested that I write connecting tissue, which I did.

The book was first published in Germany, as part of a series of life stories edited by Professor Wolfgang Benz, within the broader topic of the history of the Nazi regime that has become a hallmark of the Fischer Taschenbuch Verlag in Frankfurt. So we are dealing with a kind of reverse order of events: the translated German book came first, and the present volume, as originally written and edited, followed.

The threads in the title are the three cultural influences that shaped my life: the German, the Jewish, and the American. They were wayward because in some periods only one or two were present, in others just one, and only in the latter stages of my work and life did they begin to move toward each other. The presence or absence of one or the other, the ups and downs in emphasis, were becoming less abrupt. The waywardness was giving way to a blending of these three strains, both at work and in the interests on which I focused my life.

My thanks to my German editors, Walter Pehle and Wolfgang Benz, to my gifted translator Mona Körte, and here, in America, to my insightful and superbly professional editor Ellen Feldman at Northwestern. They helped me tell a story designed to convey, through my family, how German-Jewish life and culture was killed even as it refused to believe this was what was intended.

What also emerges is how deeply unjust hindsight can be and usually is: German Jews were not any blinder than other minority groups who believed in a country and a society in which they had been a creative force and that had given them a feeling of belonging.

Much of this book is my story in America, the society that pulls in the migrant without exerting any pressure and that allows, perhaps even encourages, the kind of cultural experimentation that is expressed here in the many changes that eventually took shape as a pattern.

Robert B. Goldmann

I

I was sitting by our kitchen window, watching the blood flow on the cobblestones of the Stuckerts' courtyard. They were slaughtering a pig again. I was repelled by the rush of deep-red blood and the squealing of the victim. But I couldn't tear myself away. The thrill of the torture was greater than the disgust at sight and sound.

We were living on the second floor of 16 Hindenburgstrasse in Reinheim. The Stuckerts were our neighbors on one side—farmers like most people in town; the Stühlingers, who owned a notions store, were on the other. We had no business with them and didn't talk to either family. That's the way it was between Reinheim's twenty or so Jewish families and many of the Gentiles. There was nothing to say beyond a casual "good morning" or "good day."

My father was the doctor in town—*the* doctor, that is, for Reinheim and four villages in the vicinity, in the foothills of the Odenwald. My mother's parents lived downstairs and had lived there for decades. My mother had been born in that stone house, as had I. My father had "married in," and though he was the main breadwinner (my grandfather had a modest income as a grain dealer near retirement), Papi, as both my mother and I called my father, never seemed as close and legitimate a member of the family as my grandparents and my mother, and, of course, myself, the only child.

My horror at the sight of blood extended to a determination, when I was five or six, not to become a doctor like Papi. It hurt me more to see my father give an injection to my grandfather than it hurt Opa to receive it. To this day, I feel sorrier for the nurse who draws blood than for myself when she pricks me with the needle.

Watching something bad or unpleasant or ugly far away was all right, but when it came close, I withdrew to the safety of my room—

the place where no dangers lurked, where I was protected, where my mother wanted me to be. The safety and serenity I experienced there transcended any excitement on the street or in school or anywhere else where my mother was not present, or at least nearby.

Just as my room was my castle, Reinheim was our home, our anchor in a dangerous world. At least it was that for my grandfather, my mother, and myself, who had been born there, or, as in my grandfather's case, in Überau, which was about a mile from Reinheim. My grandmother had also "married in," having come from the hamlet of Romrod near Giessen, in a region north of the Odenwald known as Oberhessen. Both Oma Hilda and my mother, Martha, were forever alert to "dangers" on the outside, and the *Geborgenheit,* the cozy and warming safety of the house and especially the rooms in which each of us belonged, acquired the highest value and became my single most important source of contentment.

Reinheim was predominantly a farming village, but with a bit more commercial life than the smaller hamlets around it, for it was a station on the narrow-gauge rail line known as the Lieschen (little Liz) because of its almost miniature size and its slow, hesitant movement. The Lieschen connected the towns deeper in the Odenwald with the regional capital, Darmstadt. Our street ran across the tracks, where it met a highway leading to Darmstadt. Toward the center of town, in the Kirchstrasse, there were some lovely *Fachwerkhäuser,* the old houses found throughout southern Germany, the Alsace, Switzerland, and Austria, distinguished by dark brown wooden beams forming triangles and other geometrical shapes filled in by off-white paint. I think of those houses as giant *Linzertorten,* named after the Austrian city of Linz, filled with strawberry preserves and crisscrossed with strips of dough. The colors are different, but the structure is the same. Both are delicious, one to the sight, the other to both sight and taste.

Through the middle of Reinheim runs the Wembach, a quiet brook crossed by a few modest bridges and at some spots along Heinrichstrasse overhung by trees. Standing on one of the bridges and looking toward the center of town, I get the feeling of a peaceful, idyllic life that recurs every time I go to Europe and look along a river in similar gentle, unspectacular countryside: the Cher or the Indre in France, or one of those Kentish brooks that are so brashly misused by travel companies to attract customers. It's *Geborgenheit,* and I always feel a kinship with people who share my appreciation for it.

Almost everybody in town—as in Spachbrücken, Georgenhausen, Zeilhard, and Überau—was a patient of my father's. A slender volume of Reinheim's history, published in 1952, shows that "de Dokter," as he was called in the local dialect, had become proverbial. It tells of a group of Reinheimers having their beers in a local tavern, and one insulting another in fun. Whereupon the latter shouted, "Fellows, when this guy goes home tonight, ten Dr. Goldmanns aren't going to save him!"

Dr. Goldmann was the unanointed saint of Reinheim and its surroundings. Dr. Möllmann, who also lived and practiced in Reinheim, had much time for leisure. There was no love lost between him and my father, and between the two families, but there was much camaraderie between the jealous Möllmann and the Nazis in town.

This was just a personal and more pointed case of the undiscussed but clearly understood separate existences of Jews and non-Jews on all but the professional and commercial levels. We knew our place, and we accepted it as normal. Yet it was from this seedbed of communal separateness, despite some individual admiration and genuine friendships, that Nazism sprang. Only my father sensed this, indeed he knew it; the other Jews in town, all small-town people without the benefit of higher education and exposure to the larger world, who had an unquestioning sense of being at home in Reinheim and a deep commitment to Germany, did not. They refused to accept the evidence when it appeared before their eyes.

Hessian *Landjuden* (country Jews) were probably among the most assimilated in Germany's Jewish community of half a million. As small tradespeople, they were not part of the professional and intellectual community, as they were in the larger cities: Berlin, Frankfurt, Hamburg, Munich. They had lived in these villages for centuries. Within a generation or two after the emancipation, when Jews were granted citizenship in the mid-nineteenth century, they became Germans culturally; Judaism was only their religion. Having lived as tolerated usurers and tradesmen in the villages for hundreds of years, the emancipation seemed to set loose a pent-up need or demand for equality. And it expressed itself in a soaking up of German culture, a demonstrative eagerness to become like their non-Jewish neighbors. They seemed to say, "Thank you for letting us in, and in return we'll be more loyal and like you than you ever would have imagined!" Not that the non-Jews cared, but the Jews did. The Jews wanted so much for the non-Jews to appreciate Jewish acceptance of German culture.

Although cultural change in the villages lagged behind the pace of the cities, the *Landjuden* kept up with their urban brethren when it came to assimilation. My great-grandfather Frohmann was still called Mordechai, but his son, born in 1865, was Hermann. Oma's father was still Abraham, but she was Hilda, born in 1871. And our neighbor Steiermann, of my father's generation, born in the 1880s, was Siegmund. My mother's cousin, who emigrated to America during the post–World War I inflation in the 1920s, and who was born in 1900, was Siegfried. In fact, Siegmund and Siegfried, the Teutonic heroes of Wagner's *Ring,* became Jewish first names. When someone bore that name, one knew he was Jewish!

In my father's family, the pace was a bit slower. His father was Moses, and he called his son Jacob. But Moses's wife, my Worms grandmother, was Julie, well in line with Hilda and Hermann. And of course, my mother was Martha, and I couldn't be anything but someone like Robert, as the Steiermann youngsters with whom I played were Günther and Walter and Edith. It had happened within half a century. But it was not to last the lifetime of my grandparents.

In the late 1920s, four or five years before Hitler came to power, Anton Dieter, the Stuckert sons, and Appel, the butcher, were strutting around town with their swastika pins on their shirts or lapels, and the police chief, Slipzak, was smiling upon them. For my father, this was an omen. The other Jews didn't seem to worry.

Many people in town sympathized with the Nazis, but weren't active in the local party. They felt that, after years of inflation, changing governments, strikes in the factories in Darmstadt, it was time for law and order to be restored. Maybe, they felt, Hitler had the answer. Anti-Semitism in the social sense was endemic, but this was not what made Nazism attractive to most Reinheimers. As a general rule it helped Hitler, but one never thought of it in terms of specific people: Max Strauss, the butcher; Hermann Wolf, the notions store owner; or Siegmund Steiermann, who ran the gas station on Darmstädterstrasse. Their services were needed, and one respected them for being honest businessmen and good citizens, even though one would not invite them to one's home.

There was a story in those days about two Gentiles talking about their hometowns. One asked, "Tell me, do you have any Jews in town?" The other answered that, yes, there must be about three or four: the textile store proprietor, one of the lawyers, and the gynecologist. Maybe there were a few others like that. "What about you, do you have any?" he asked in return, and his friend, who lived in a larger city, responded, "Oh yes, we must have about three or four hundred!" That elicited a question from the first, "D'you need so many?" In short, the Jews were useful, and fine, as long as they knew their place. If they went too far afield, one had to let them know, and that would suffice.

When I was eight, my parents and grandparents attended a community ball, to which everybody, including the Jews, was invited. It was a community event, not a social gathering where one could select the guests. Oma was dancing with Opa when someone on the floor slapped her face. My father was furious; my mother, embarrassed, dissolved in tears. Opa's opinion was that they shouldn't have gone to the ball. But it was my grandmother who frightened me. She said nothing. Her face was like stone. Not a muscle moved. Only her eyes talked to me. I had never seen eyes like that before. They scared me because they told me that Oma wouldn't say anything, that she seemed to be talking only to herself.

Oma Hilda's favorite word was *vorsichtig*—careful. Everything had to be *in Ordnung* (in order), both in her household, which was a model of spotlessness from the dustless living room to the big iron coal-burning stove that never showed a speck of coal on or around it, and in the family's relationship with the outside world. Any kind of trouble made Oma uneasy, quite often panicky. The panic would express itself in less intense forms of that look after the slap at the ball.

Oma was tall, somewhat heavy, and always fighting high blood pressure. She wore her gray hair up in a tightly pulled bun, making her look more serious than she was, and strict, too, which she was not. Oma was gentle, patient, and loving with us all, and she dealt wisely with a routine-addicted, unimaginative, self-centered husband, who was devoted to *Ordnung* not out of anxiety but for its own sake. It was just as important for him that the files with his business papers were lined up like the soldiers in whose ranks he had served in the late 1880s as it was for their contents to be accurate, complete, and in correct sequence.

Opa was of medium height, a good deal taller than my father but slightly shorter than my mother. He sported a mustache that approached but did not reach handlebar proportions. He had a full head of hair and, in the style of the time, kept it short-cropped.

I developed a close relationship with Opa. This happened in the summertime, when he took me along on long walks to Gross-Bieberau and Niedernhausen, through the woods and on the paths that led over the fields of some of the clients whose grain he bought. My grandfather taught me about order, about the wonderful world of the military, and about Germany.

As we trudged through the woods and Opa explained the trail markers to me, he told me that Germany was best at everything. For example, Germany had the best marching music. How could the French possibly perform well on the battlefield when they had military music to which no adult person could possibly march? It was too fast, making French soldiers march in ridiculously small steps!

"What about other people, Opa?" I would ask, after a couple of years of European geography in the Volksschule (elementary school) in Reinheim.

"Ach," my grandfather would respond, "what about them? The English can't be trusted. The Italians always run away. And just look at those Poles! They never wash. *Polnische Wirtschaft!* ["Polish operation"—once a German pejorative term for haphazard, unprofessional management]." To this day, the images with which Opa filled my mind on those walks have left a mark. Experience, intellectualization, and countervailing influences have relegated Opa's stereotypes to the recesses of my mind, but they are still there, in spite of a long career focused on international affairs and the fight against prejudice.

But fortunately there was someone else who could give me a different view of things—my father. He entered my life later, in my adolescence, but he had an impact for which I have been grateful all my adult life. It took a long time, however, before I understood clearly and fully what he represented, and came to appreciate the values that had shaped his life.

My father was short and stocky. He was built like his mother, Julie: broad shoulders, short torso, and respectable girth. Both had eyes that could flash brilliance or anger, but only Oma Julie seemed angry most of the time. Papi wore a small mustache, and like Opa had full and short-cropped hair. He moved quickly and effortlessly, often taking two steps on the stairs at a time. His bursts of anger occurred rarely, but when they did, they seemed to release the power of a human volcano.

My father's father died when I was six years old. I remember him as a quiet, kindly man. I did not get to know my Goldmann grandparents well, because they lived so far away (today, Worms is a little over an hour from Reinheim by Autobahn). Moses Goldmann was a cattle dealer. He had moved to Worms from the village of Gundersheim on the Rhine, a rough equivalent to Reinheim. His profession and lifestyle were similar to those of my grandfather Frohmann in Reinheim.

It was Oma Julie, his wife, who had strayed from the paths of German *Landjuden*. She had been born and raised in a larger town, Bretten, in the *Mushterländle* (local dialect for model state) of Baden, in the southwestern corner of Germany, bordering on Switzerland and France and graced by one of Europe's most beautiful mountain ranges, the Schwarzwald.

Bretten and Baden were different from Hessen. My father used to speak with love, even admiration, of the region where he had spent most of his summers when he was a boy. He always said that "down there" people look out, not inward, across the Rhine, to France. Despite four years of service on the western front, as a physician in the Kaiser's army, Papi was a Francophile. It seemed that his service in France had made him more so. He was also proud of the fact that Philipp Melanchthon, whom he described as the philosopher of the Reformation, had been born in Bretten. Melanchthon had changed his name from the good old German Schwarzert (Blackearth).

Papi was open to the world. If he had prejudices, they entailed giving foreigners and other "outsiders" the benefit of the doubt, which of course put him in the opposite ideological and emotional corner from his father-in-law. And what Bretten and France had not done, the University of Heidelberg, and cities like Munich and Hamburg, where my father served his medical internships, did; they made of him the *Fantast* (dreamer) that my Opa in Reinheim, and sometimes my mother, called him.

Oma Julie never accepted her son's marriage to my mother. Not only did the Reinheim family clash with her views and ambitions for her son, but Reinheim itself was a place where her son had no business "getting stuck." It was all right for my father (Jacob to his mother) to accept an assistantship with a retiring general practitioner in Reinheim, as Papi had done in 1912, and there learn a great deal. But for a summa cum laude graduate in gynecology from Germany's finest medical faculty to go back to Reinheim after coming home safe and sound from four years at the western front—that was too much!

But back Jacob went, because he wanted to marry Martha Frohmann, one of the most beautiful girls in the region. I was never sure that it was mutual. It seemed that my mother had never forgotten her cousin Hugo Mayer, who had been killed in Flanders and whose life-size portrait hung on the wall in my grandparents' home. He was exceedingly handsome in uniform, sporting the Iron Cross First Class. Whether such a marriage would ever have come about is doubtful. But he had been killed before the very idea of their marriage could be seriously considered. Hugo was never discussed in the house, only hinted at by more distant members of the family in illicit chitchat.

To whatever extent it was true, it helped to explain the constant tension between my father and mother, the even greater tension between Papi and Opa Hermann, and my Oma Hilda's tendency to side with my father. Oma Hilda was a good wife, but there seemed to be little feeling between her and my grandfather. There was good chemistry between Hilda and my father, however, perhaps because both had "married in" and shared a feeling of not quite belonging. With the two men away most of the time, and with Oma Hilda minding her household and avoiding becoming entangled in the tensions among the other three adults, my mother became dominant in family life and decision-making.

Martha was an only child. I never found out why Oma Hilda had only one child, but I was told why I had no siblings. After my birth, when my mother was twenty-six, she developed gallbladder problems, for which she frequently visited Bad Mergentheim, where one supposedly could drink water and undergo other treatments to relieve this problem. In those days, I accepted the explanation. In later years, when I realized that Europeans had a spa for everything, whose efficacy many medical authorities—my father in particular—doubted, and that going to spas was as much a legitimation of vacationing and spoiling oneself as a response to serious medical advice, I wondered whether not having a brother or sister was really only due to Mutti's physical condition. Was it that more children would have been too much of a burden for her? Were the tensions between her and my father a factor? Was her lingering attachment to Hugo making her reluctant to involve herself fully with her own family, as she shared her affections equally, if not even a bit more generously, with the old folks downstairs?

I never asked about such things—not because I was afraid, but because that was the way things were. Questions were for school, restricted to certain subjects, and even then it was important to ask only when it was sensible, or to one's credit.

It was safest and most comfortable, physically and emotionally, to be in my room, doing my homework and reading, enjoying the feeling that I was doing what Mutti wanted me to do. Most important was to avoid trouble, and trouble was anything that could bring forth the dreaded words "how could you?!" from my mother. "Wie konntst Du?!" would be the greeting when I came home from school after a thunderstorm and I had gotten wet, even if the sun shone brightly in the morning and Mutti had not even suggested that I wear my raincoat and take my umbrella. If, on one of the frequent inspections to which my digestion was subjected, something was a tad off normal, the accusatory "how could you?!" would be pronounced in response to a question about what I had eaten, to which the answer might have been "three prunes."

Those three words became a menace, the worst that could happen, because my mother, who was my shield, my constant and constantly watching companion, wherever I was or whatever I was doing, was angry with me. I needed her as I needed to breathe. And though my mistake or failure to perform as I should have may have been minor in a another child's eyes, for me there was no little sin. "How could you?!" was pronounced for every infraction, and when I heard those words I was terrified. I trembled and awaited my punishment, be it in the form of words, a spanking, or, in the worst cases, being locked into the dark cellar.

Even as I craved the comfort of safety and the orderly and inconspicuous behavior that was thus rewarded, I felt special. I was not involved with the other youngsters as much as the rest of the class, or as much as the Steiermann kids were with other Jewish classmates or friends. In the sports class, I hovered at the edges rather than get into the thick of a *Völkerball* (volleyball) game. I didn't know then, but sensed, and now know, that I felt fragile, and would risk a "how could you?!" if I came home with a scratch, leading my mother to ask my father whether it required a tetanus shot.

Integrated into this family cast was Lisbeth, my mother's maid, whom Opa had discovered in Niedernhausen. Lisbeth was not another Stani, Oma Hilda's Polish helper. She was wise, intensely loyal, with a deep sense of right and wrong. Imperceptibly, she became an important and influential person in the household. She mediated many tensions, and I often looked to her to help out when a "how could you?!" had made me inconsolable, or when my parents had had one of their big arguments.

In the early 1930s, when the Nazis in town began to harass my father, Lisbeth would react with the spontaneity that overrides the fear of consequences. She was one of those people who don't know or care when they take risks. They seek the path of justice naturally. "Go home, you *schlechte Kerle* [ne'er-do-wells]!" she'd shout when some young Nazi rowdies would scream insults at my father. "The doctor is good enough to deliver your mother of you and your brother, and to be called at three in the morning to get on his bicycle and sew up the slashes you got in the beer garden! But in the daytime you're big shots, and you call him *Saujud* [Jewish pig]. You should be ashamed of yourselves! Go home and don't let me catch you again!"

Lisbeth was attractive, of medium height, rapid in her movements, and never minced her words. But every word she said in our home was respectful and loving, and tinged with the earthy humor that took the sting out of tension and rancor. Lisbeth felt she owed our family a debt she could never repay, although it was a happenstance we had done nothing to bring about: she met her future husband in our house.

Fritz, the slightly built carpenter and son of a well-respected family who owned a furniture factory and store that was renowned throughout the region, had a hobby: cars, motors, all things mechanical. His playground and "laboratory" were my father's cars and motorcycle. The motorcycle was abandoned after a while, after I had burned both hands touching the cylinder when my father had gotten off after returning from a round of patients. So Fritz concentrated on the Brennabor, first an open one, with the handbrake on the outside and a canvas cover against rain and cold, and later a closed version.

When Papi was called early in the morning on a snowy day and the Brennabor wouldn't start no matter how many times the enraged doctor turned the brass crank, my father would shout, "Lousy car, it's a piece of junk! Fritz must come!" And a call would bring Fritz within minutes.

Although Lisbeth gave indications that she had an independent and less neurotic attitude toward me than my mother, she had little choice but to follow Mutti's instructions, except in those subtle ways that I sensed but my mother overlooked. When Lisbeth gave me a little wink, my mother either didn't see it or didn't care, but it was immensely meaningful to me. It was the only way I could learn that tragedy, in the form of the cellar or some other punishment, might not happen, or that there was another, not opposing but possibly less severe, more bearable way of interpreting "how could you?!"

Still, Lisbeth was not immune to the excessive alertness of my parents to my *Anfälligkeit* (proneness to becoming ill), all the more so because my father was "de Dokter" who knew everything about such things. And perceptive as she was, Lisbeth would not second-guess him on this score, nor did she realize, although she may have suspected, that he was utterly unobjective in his diagnoses when it came to the many potential and likely assaults by a vast array of bacteria and other enemies on my "fragile" condition. When I had a cold, it was likely to be pneumonia, and my temperature was taken several times a day. My *grosse Geschäft* (bowel movement) and urine color were inspected at regular intervals.

When I was four or five years old, my parents' alarmist sense about my delicate health led to a pseudocrisis. There had been a dinner party, and I had gone to bed long before the guests had moved on to the *Herrenzimmer* (salon). But the noise of the conversation had kept me awake, and I got up again. Then I returned to bed and fell asleep. Long after the guests had gone, I woke up from a frightening dream in which the horses in the Kirchstrasse had jumped all the way to heaven and threatened to fall down right on top of me! I was in a panic, had gotten out of bed, and was walking around unsteadily. My parents heard me fantasize about the dream as I wobbled about. "Gleichgewichtsstörung! [Impaired equilibrium!]" my mother cried out in despair. My father did not contradict her, and seemed anxious and concerned. Plans were made to take me to the Elizabethen-Hospital in Darmstadt in the morning to check my condition. No doubt my parents were thinking of a possible brain tumor.

Lisbeth had been awakened by the commotion late at night, well after she had finished cleaning up, and came down to urge calm. Then she came close to me, and said, "I've got it! He drank beer!" Next I had to vomit, and the evidence became conclusive. I confessed that, when I couldn't sleep, I had returned to the dining room, which had not yet been cleared, and had drunk what was left in all the beer glasses.

I did not get punished that time, probably because my crime had been so egregious and brought such unpleasant consequences for me that it would not require a deterrent, and also because my parents were so relieved that I did not have a brain tumor after all!

The family's life played itself out in the two-story stone house, with a basement. When Papi married in, and moved his practice with him, a smaller building at one side of the yard was converted into waiting and treatment facilities, and an "Übergang"—a covered walkway on the second floor—enabled him to move back and forth between home and office. The onetime barn (all Reinheim houses were at one time farmhouses) was converted into a garage for my father's various vehicles.

Next to the barn, in the back of the yard, a stairway led up to the garden, which Oma tended with endless love and care, and which abutted the tracks of the Lieschen.

Finally, there was Blanka, our shepherd, who spent her life between her little doghouse and the confines of the yard. She had a lonely life, and no one much cared for or about her except to feed her. She was kept as a watchdog, but she did this job listlessly and unreliably—something that, with hindsight, I cannot blame her for.

It was a pleasant world, small, comfortable, and graced by the exquisite cuisine—German, to be sure, and kosher as well—of Oma Hilda. She was known as one of the finest cooks for miles around, and my mother learned everything from her. But by Mutti's own acknowledgment, she never approached the perfect balance of her mother's superb dishes, like her *Schmorbraten* (brisket), or her famous *Apfelschalet* (homemade apple pie, eaten steaming hot).

An annual highlight was our vacation in Norderney. Ah, how I looked forward to those trips north—the three weeks on the North Sea coast! As I anticipated and salivated, Mutti prepared and Papi worried, because it meant leaving his patients in the care of a young doctor, who might not work out. Not to be working was an enormous drain on Papi's psyche. The vacation did not relax him. Mutti took a long time to prepare, because to go to Norderney, one of Germany's Frisian islands, halfway between the North Sea coast and Helgoland, required a vast amount of packing. This meant above all a steamer trunk that could swallow up all the clothes for cold, cool, and warm weather; all our bathing gear, including several robes for each of us to change into when wet; hats for both my parents, in boxes that would protect them against crushing; and, of course, an entire mini-pharmacy for all possible and impossible contingencies.

I looked forward to Norderney because I loved the beach, but above all because I could spend some time with my father. And my mother did relax a bit, which meant fewer "how could yous." More specifically, I couldn't wait to go on our mid-afternoon walk, which included a stop at Café Hag, a café like no other because it was housed in a building shaped like a fat round coffeepot, with "Café Hag," the decaffeinated German coffee, written on it in the logo of the famous brand. There they had the best desserts in the whole world: to go to the counter and choose my piece of cake or pastry was one of the highlights of the year. My favorites were *Trüffeltorte* (chocolate with truffles), *Schlotfeger* (chimney sweeps, which were chocolate-covered cylinders filled with whipped cream), and *Mohrenköpfe* (chocolate-covered puffs filled with luscious, thick whipped cream that spilled over the edge).

There was nothing more delightful than to walk between my parents along the beach, which meant high above the beach on the reddish-brown, smooth pavement that sloped down to the sand. Those afternoon walks preceded the stop at Café Hag, so that not only did I feel the security of my parents' presence, but I could salivate as I dreamed of the *Trüffeltorte* that would soon melt on my tongue. But I betrayed no impatience, lest my mother consider it unduly hedonistic (*geniesserisch* was the word she used to describe undue longing for pleasure).

Mornings were spent on the beach. After breakfast, due preparations were made for the encounter with sand and sea: large baskets were packed with our bathing paraphernalia, which included several terry-cloth items for each of us so that we would never have to endure wet conditions outside the water. Of course, changing into dry bathing trunks was mandatory every time I came out of the water, into which I was accompanied by my mother. There were booths for changing on the beach, and there were the *Strandkörbe,* those wicker chairs with backs, sides, and tops that protected the (would-be) sunbather from the sun.

I loved the water, which compelled my mother to spend a fair amount of time in it as well. Papi, meanwhile, sat in a *Strandkörb* reading his favorite newspaper, the *Vossische Zeitung,* which he had no time to read at home. As he worried about the world, and especially about the rising strength of the Nazis, I let the surf spill over me, never letting go of my mother's hand, and trying to extend the time I could spend in the bracing saltwater. My mother was quite patient on that score, because the saltwater and the Norderney air would presumably be good for me.

We went to Norderney because it was decided that a sickly child with a flagging, desultory appetite needed the sea air to become hungry. We also went there because the island had a clean kosher pension, and my mother had been brought up to cook and eat kosher food, more for reasons of tradition than orthodoxy. In those days my father could not have cared less, having been around the highly nonkosher, heavily pork-oriented restaurants of Heidelberg, Munich, and Hamburg for years, and never having been urged by his liberal, worldly mother to observe the kosher laws.

It took many hours in Wagon-Lits accommodations to travel to the coast. The trip itself was exciting. It left such a lasting impression on me that, to this day, I still get a thrill out of rail travel in Europe. We would first go by car to Darmstadt (Fritz would drive us; the steamer trunk had been sent ahead as cargo). In Darmstadt we'd board the train, changing in Frankfurt to the D-Zug (fast long-distance train) and our berths.

A good part of the trip was made during the daytime, and at certain stops in large cities, like Münster or Hagen, I would be allowed a *Würstchen* and a *Brötchen* with mustard. This was another highlight, with what I never suspected would become addictive consequences. I am not sure that I like traveling to and in Europe because of the well-advertised and well-merited sources of enjoyment that the average traveler delights in, such as beautiful cities, gentle old towns, museums, and music festivals, not to forget highly developed eating. I think I like it just as much or more because I can get *Würstchen* as in the old days, and also forbidden large sausages that always looked so good but were "zu scharf" (too spicy), and, more important, pork (the ones at the station were beef, or so my mother ruled). To my shame and at the risk of my reputation, I must confess that, given a choice midday between a fine three-course meal in Paris, and two different *Würste* and fresh, warm *Brötchen* in Germany, I'd red-facedly pick the latter.

An important item of business in Norderney was my learning to swim. This was done under the supervision of professionals, in the Staatliche Nordseebad. A large indoor swimming pool, fed by seawater and agitated to simulate waves, was the learning and testing medium. With my mother at the teacher's side, I was gently guided with a ring around my middle, attached to a line held by the teacher. Gradually the tether was lengthened, and eventually removed. I took and succeeded in my test on July 29, 1932, according to a formal document signed by the beach captain and by Dr. G. Freyer of the private company that managed the State North Sea Spa Norderney. I was proud, my mother was proud, and so was my father, although he took it more in stride. But then he probably did not realize the agony of fear I went through in the process of learning, as seemingly towering waves threatened to gobble me up.

It was always a sad day when we would have to pack and leave this paradise of sun and surf, Café Hag and *Würstchen,* and go home to school, tensions, and "how could yous." It was also only a few weeks before the High Holy Days, which were for me then and remain to this day an experience to go through and get over with quickly.

We all went to the synagogue in the little alley behind Kirchstrasse, on the eve and the days of Rosh Hashanah and Yom Kippur. Opa went in his white *sargenes* (the garment in which religious Jews are buried and that is worn only on the Holy Days). The rest of us went in dark clothes.

I always felt downhearted about the High Holy Days, and still do today. It was too much of the same thing, too long, and though I had gone to Hebrew school, I understood little of the all-Hebrew service, which was conducted spiritlessly by Cantor Vorenberg. There was a musty smell in the small synagogue, as though people were breathing out their hungry feeling. It was bad enough on Rosh Hashanah, when we'd have breakfast at 7:30 or 8 A.M. and wouldn't get lunch until we returned from the synagogue sometime between 1 and 2 P.M. But on Yom Kippur! Then it was endless, and I kept looking at my father's watch to see how much longer . . . It's still this way today. And it's this way with most worshippers on that day, although it's easier to admit it and talk about it now than it was then. In those days, even to hint at boredom or unease or impatience was just another sin. Yet how could we repent our sins honestly if we were getting more and more unhappy about having to do so?

There was never a discussion of the meaning of the Holy Days, except the official version we got in Hebrew school. The rest just was done. The only questions were: Are the right prayer books ready? Is there one for everyone? Had the *sargenes* been washed and ironed? And off we went. In the synagogue, during the Torah reading and at other times when the congregation was in a listening rather than participating mode, there'd be conversation among the men downstairs, and among the women upstairs. There was a good deal of gossip, in which, of course, the little ones were not allowed to take part.

It was on Jewish holidays—the High Holy Days, and Pesach or Sukkoth as well—that my parents tended to have nasty arguments over lunch. My father would become angry at something my mother had said, and out would pour shouts and even insults—or words my mother took as insults. Oma would try to smooth things over, but generally to no avail, at least in the heat of the initial exchanges. Those were the times I felt deeply unhappy, lost, without the anchor that my parents, and especially my mother, were for me. She was always so certain of everything, knew everything, knew what was best. But when she cried, refused to talk to my father, and, as usually happened, began to feel ill and had to lie down, she seemed disabled, and I felt as though I were being tossed about helplessly, even hopelessly, on an endless and bottomless ocean. I'd run to Oma, or more likely to Lisbeth, for comfort.

Lisbeth would say, "Well, it'll work itself out again." But this was little consolation to me. She seemed so unconcerned, so unwilling to share my sense of crisis, even trauma. Of course, she did the only right thing: she diluted the drama, and that gave me hope, even as I felt she was not commiserating enough. Things eventually would be repaired via the medical route. Mutti would require, or say she required, medical attention; my father would find her weak or plagued by an especially painful migraine (she was given to migraine attacks even on normal days), and that would necessitate some communication. Out of those scanty technical exchanges normal contact would gradually develop again, usually with my father feeling bad and guilty, which my mother greatly enjoyed. She would smile a kind of triumphant smile that made me feel both bad for Papi and happy about Mutti's being in fine fettle again.

The one outbreak of almost savage anger by my father came after I had begun commuting to Darmstadt to attend the Ludwig-Georg-Gymnasium, a humanistic institution of higher learning to which middle- and upper-class children switched at age ten, because graduation from this level of schooling (there were various types of *Gymnasia* or *Oberschulen*) was required for admission to the university and the professional careers that were ordained for youngsters of our social class.

The Gymnasium, where I traveled via the Lieschen and a long walk from the Darmstadt Ostbahnhof to school, had a summer camp. It was at Dorndiel, not far from Darmstadt, in the countryside. I feared going there because I had never been away from home, except when accompanied by my parents or when I had gone to my Oma Julie's for a rare day or two in Worms. (Even this was not a happy outing; I missed home, my room, the *Geborgenheit* that only those four walls, that bed, and the house on Hindenburgstrasse could offer.) My parents, and Papi more than Mutti, insisted that I go to Dorndiel with my Gymnasium class. I tried to resist, my mother gently tried to support me, but Papi would not be deterred. I think he thought that I had to be "hardened." But I couldn't and didn't turn from clay into a piece of pottery just by spinning me around. Instead, I came apart. Once in Dorndiel, my craving for home turned into hysteria. I cried, demanded to be sent home, did not sleep a wink, walked around the night quarters, and woke up the others. I didn't care what I was doing, or that I was making a fool of myself in the eyes of the other boys or the camp director. I knew I was tearing wildly at whatever good standing I had developed among my classmates, but it meant nothing to me. All I wanted was home, home, home. "Ich will heim," I screamed over and over, until the director called my parents and asked them to pick me up.

They came the next day. My things were packed, and I was waiting, looking out for what then was Papi's third car, a brown Wanderer. When they came, they talked for a few minutes with the director out of my hearing. I didn't care what was said between them. I rushed into the backseat, waiting for the ride home to start. Mutti was upset but not angry. After all, she wanted me home as much as I wanted to be home, so she could only put on the act for my and, more importantly, my father's benefit, and it wasn't convincing. This, of course, made me feel better. But the real test was my father's reaction. He uncharacteristically said nothing on the ride. He just drove, but he looked fiercely angry.

When we arrived home, we went upstairs, my father still wordless, menacingly unlike himself. He directed me to the couch in the den. "Lie down," he shouted, "on your stomach." Now I knew what would happen, but before I could become scared and prepared for the inevitable, it was happening: a rain of blows. No instrument, just my father's hand. "You spoiled brat, almost twelve years old, it's a shame what you've done. I'll show you *Heimweh* [nostalgia]!" And more blows would come down, and more.

I was screaming. Mutti tried repeatedly to stop my father, but it seemed never to end. When it was over, we were all exhausted. Papi, too, was ready to let bygones be bygones. He could sometimes let out a burst of anger and then slip right back into his normal, encouraging, smiling self. My mother and I, though, were limp—she from suffering with and for me, and I from physical pain and the sting of shame and humiliation, from having acted in ways that made those "how could yous" child's play, in every sense of the word.

Then I was sent back to Dorndiel. I feared the hazing of my bunk-mates, but it wasn't bad. After the scene at home, nothing seemed bad. And if my father hadn't knocked the nostalgia out of me, he had at least anaesthesized me against its recurrence.

This experience taught me something. But it was not a cure, just a lesson. And lessons may be good for conduct, but not for how one feels. What I felt was that I wanted to stick even more closely to my room, my books, my homework, and to stay out of trouble, which meant out of any involvement that might bring trouble: unbecoming behavior, as at Dorndiel, or saying or doing something of which my mother would disapprove.

The Nazis were closing in by the end of 1932. It would turn out to be the last year we went to Norderney. Otherwise, there was little concern in our house. Only my father, with his democratic, Franco-phile feelings, worried, and he had worried for some time. But then, he was the *Fantast,* not to be taken seriously by the people who counted in our house, Mutti and Opa. After all, as my grandfather always said, Germany was "ein Rechtsstaat," and any government was bound by the laws of the state. As far as we were concerned, we were good and honorable citizens who minded our own business, so there was nothing to worry about. If something were to happen, it was bound to be our fault or that of some other Jews who didn't know how to behave properly.

I had absorbed the obsession with order from Opa. It fit in with my contentment at being safe and *geborgen* at home. Part of being orderly was to finish my homework before anything else, certainly before I could relax or listen to my favorite music—in those days Italian opera with their high tenors and coloratura sopranos—or any other pleasurable activity. Even as I wanted so much to be "regular," I felt special, deserving of attention. That's how I had been treated by my mother, and through agreement in absentia, with the exception of the Dorndiel incident, by my father as well, especially when it came to my "sickliness." So when I performed well at school, I wanted to be praised for it—so much so that I finished everything at breakneck speed in order to get my reward as quickly as possible!

My craving for attention manifests itself in many ways: in a crowd, or in an elevator with others, I lapse into German when I talk to my wife. In a social setting, I tend to be the maverick, arguing an alternative view to that current among the group. We've lost some friends, and certainly some dinner invitations, because I would set off violent arguments that marred companionship and envenomed reasonable discussion. My "specialness" also kept me from involving myself with fellow students, from acquiring close friends, and from seeking assignments in professional life that might have been exciting but also committed me beyond a point that was the "Stop!" dictated by compulsion. Only late in life did I take initiatives that called for independent and creative thinking and action. Even then, in the midst of enterprises I had launched, I would rush ahead to the point where all that I needed to do was done, and then it was up to others to respond.

Beginning in Reinheim, and increasingly as I went through life, I stored up anger. Why was I not praised for this composition? Why did Barry (a supervisor later in life) just take that news scoop I got in stride? He's unfair to me! "They have no idea what the issue is all about!" I'd come home screaming after a community meeting. "But I told them!" I'd yell. And I'd be proud at having shouted out my disagreement.

Order, duty, being in line—that was the message from Opa, the German message. Sickly, special, *Vorsicht*—that was Mutti's message. Although my mother did not realize it and would not admit it, it was the Jewish message in pre-Hitler Germany.

The Nazi regime was about to take over. Would the messages be tested? Would how we behaved make a difference? In early 1933, the first test would come, in the shape of an explosion.

❀

II

I woke up to a loud bang, a noise I had never heard before and that frightened me. I rushed out of bed in the middle of the night. I heard my parents talk excitedly, and then we all ran downstairs. My grandparents were also awake. The noise had been even closer to them. It had come from the yard, and my father was the first one to venture a guess: it was the Nazis trying to scare us. He turned out to be right.

In a deposition my father made to the local authorities in Germany after the war, he described the event this way:

> One night [in 1933] in our yard a so-called "cannonball" [a type of explosive used in fireworks] was exploded. I called Police Officer Slipzak for protection. It took an hour before he arrived, and all he did was to say that everything was quiet, and left. Soon after I was able to determine that Ludwig Appel [the butcher near our house and a leading Nazi] had actually done the job . . . I hold him responsible for the depression which at that moment overcame my mother-in-law, and from which she never recovered. Months of treatment in a sanatorium and almost two years of neurological and psychiatric treatment had no effect. My mother-in-law committed suicide on February 24, 1935.

Nazism hit us early, and with a bang—long before it directly hit most other Jews in Germany, especially those in large cities, where Jews were less prominent or conspicuous, and personal relationships, whatever their nature, less close. In a village like Reinheim, the Jews were easy targets, and the doctor, revered by the population, became the most obvious object of the small knot of haters and fanatics that made up the nucleus of the Nazi Party in the village.

In his deposition, my father gives thumbnail descriptions of some of them:

Police Chief Schmidt: He had distinguished himself for having helped train the SA [Hitler's brownshirt members] for several years prior to the Nazis' seizure of power. This although he had sworn an oath to protect the institutions of the Republic . . .

Slipzak: He helped the Nazis seize power [in Reinheim] by supervising and even helping when they harrassed Jews . . .

Appel: He maintained relations with a number of Jews, for business reasons. It turned out that he had been a member of the Nazi Party since 1928. He was outstanding for his cowardice: during the day he was the solid citizen, and after dark he committed his crimes . . . When Hitler took over, it was Appel who was in charge of having the black-red-gold flag [of the Weimar Republic] pulled down from the town's linden tree [the tree that had long been the "town tree" on which the national flag was flown and which was the center of open civic gatherings]. But he commanded someone else to do it, because he was too cowardly to climb the tree himself . . . I understand he has now secured some documents to rehabilitate himself. They should be disregarded. He is one of the most despicable people I ever met in my twenty-one years of practice in Reinheim . . .

George Stuckert: The son of our neighbors, he tried to have the Nazis seize my wife, by a vicious denunciation that was a lie. This attempt was foiled by our valiant and decent maid [Lisbeth].

Dr. Göbel: He was the mayor at the time. He tried everything he could do bring me under suspicion and to hurt me. When he could not find anything to support the suspicions he had spread, he got the police to arrest me on November 2, 1933, presumably out of frustration over the fact that our house had been legally and properly sold to an Aryan buyer. [My parents had by that time decided to move to Frankfurt to ease my grandmother's condition and to move out of the Reinheim spotlight. The house had been sold to a physician who had taken advantage of the Nazis' offer to "persecuted Germans abroad" to return and buy Jewish property cheaply. This physician had come from the Belgian border community of St. Vith.] This sale of our house had foiled the intentions of several Reinheim Nazis to get the house for themselves for virtually nothing. I was taken to the State Police prison in Darmstadt. My wife could not find out where I was . . . Only the thoughtfulness of the prison director permitted me to write to my wife. Four days later, I was released without any indication of the grounds of my arrest, and without a hearing . . .

My father wanted to emigrate then and there, but the Nazis, in another harassing move, had seized my parents' passports. My grandfather would not have left anyway. And that meant that my mother would not leave either. But most important was the condition of Oma Hilda.

Oma Hilda had ceased to speak. Her eyes looked past us. It seemed she had determined not to communicate anymore—whether by speech, eye contact, bodily movement, or any other possible means that could be interpreted by those in physical proximity to her as saying something. My mother was inconsolable. Opa seemed strangely detached, communicating little, albeit for very different reasons. I couldn't figure out what he thought or how he was affected. Father contacted neurologists and psychiatrists by the dozens. Shock treatments were considered for a long time, and eventually administered. There was no change.

I continued to commute to school, trying to concentrate on my work but feeling only tangentially involved with what was going on in my class. The heavy atmosphere at home was weighing me down. Also, once the Nazis seized power the Gymnasium was no longer the same. We Jewish students felt we were being treated differently. The other students were more reserved, and there was an occasional whisper behind our backs. This change bothered me less than it did my Jewish fellow students, because I was not dependent on friends at the Gymnasium, just as I was not in Reinheim. And there were few offensive words or acts at Ludwig-Georg. The students there came from decorous homes; it was not considered good manners to be crude.

On the other hand, the geography teacher did make openly anti-Semitic remarks. He did not voice them in class, but he'd say things in the hall, or the yard, within earshot of the Jewish students and others close by. "Why do we still have to put up with Jewish students here? This Gymnasium should be purged," he'd mutter. Once in the yard he called me over by saying, *"Judenjunge* [Jewish boy], pick up this banana peel that one of you *Schweine* [pigs, meaning one of us Jews] dropped." We dared not say anything in response. Nor did we hear objections, or even notice indications of disapproval, from our well-mannered peers.

The experiences of the months since Hitler's seizure of power had escalated Mutti's anxieties. It seemed that, with Oma not communicating, she was taking on her mother's even higher level of *Vorsicht* as an extra responsibility.

Early on, during the winter-spring term 1932–33, my mother had taken me aside to warn me of the potentially fatal danger of my saying the wrong thing and being overheard while I was out of the house, during the long day on the train and at school.

"They have spies everywhere, and if you say anything they could twist as hostile or insulting to Hitler, we could all be arrested and who knows what would happen to all of us," my mother warned me.

"But what could I say that would be so bad?" I asked, desperately trying to get guidelines from her, as the almost unbearable responsibility my mother had placed on me took my breath away.

"Anything you say could be used," my mother said, "so just stick to your school assignments and to the subjects in class. Don't talk about anything that has to do with Germany, or with any other people and their business, apart from what you have to or need to discuss about one of your subjects in class."

The injunction was so wide-ranging, so broadly defined, that I decided to document the subjects I had touched on in all my exchanges or conversations from the moment I left the house for the train to the time I returned to the house. I used a special notebook and devised a way to remember each exchange by noting a key word or phrase. When I arrived home, I'd rush up to my mother to go through the list of notes and check them with her to see whether everything was within safe limits: "brown jacket" (I had a new brown jacket and worried that mention of the color brown might be dangerous); *"Frankfurter Zeitung"* (my grandfather always brought it home on Mondays when he went to Frankfurt to the grain exchange—could this be a dangerous thing?). Everything was usually just fine, though occasionally accompanied by a suggestion to be even more careful.

The notebook became the equivalent of my room: it made me feel safe. And the new, extra burden under which I now labored made me even shier. I shunned involvements, relationships, not to mention commitments or friendships. I did not want to have to give anything, because anything I might give might get me in trouble.

The impact of the notebook and all it implied has remained with me throughout my life. Only in recent years have I gained some distance from it, but only intellectually. Emotionally, it is still locked in.

My father had thought and talked about emigration even before the Nazis came to power. But my grandfather, with his daughter tacitly or even openly echoing him, called the idea fantasy. Also, the Nazis had taken my parents' passports. And most important, Oma's condition made emigration unrealistic.

So it was decided that we'd move to Frankfurt, for two reasons: to get out of Reinheim and to make it logistically more practicable to provide treatment for my grandmother.

In mid-1934 we moved into an apartment on Eschenheimer Anlage, one of the park sections that ringed the inner city. The house in Reinheim had been sold, and the Ludwig-Georg Gymnasium, which had become an increasingly uncomfortable place for me, was now in the past. Lisbeth had decided to marry Fritz, and the pleas of many patients that my father should stay were to no avail.

"Herr Dokter," Kätt from across the tracks pleaded, "stay, please! Don't let no-goods like Dieter and Appel scare you away! We'll protect you, don't worry! We need you!" Others reacted in similar fashion, some more discreetly and cautiously, and my father felt bad about them. Of course, they didn't realize that there was nothing they could do to stop or even slow the anti-Jewish drive.

The car—a Wanderer—was sold. Fritz took care of that. Blanka, the old shepherd, was given away. And generations of Frohmanns in Überau and Reinheim had no succession: the roots had been deep; the loyalty to the land, both physically and ethnically, still deeper.

Opa seemed numbed by it all: his wife's absence except as a physical being; ending his professional life as a grain dealer; and leaving

Reinheim and the woods and meadows that had borne the imprint of his steps. For my mother, getting away was the priority. It was the only way to get back in touch with Oma. "We have to get out of here," she kept saying, and there was no one among us to contradict her. My father had no problem leaving a town that had so little memory of what he had done for so many. And then there was anger and resentment at so much in that house: Hugo's huge portrait, my grandfather's prejudices, my mother's anxieties and persistent echoing of her father's views.

For me, there was a new life ahead: no more commuting. The Philanthropin, the accredited Oberschule (Gymnasium equivalent) run and financed by Frankfurt's 25,000-member Jewish community, would be a new experience. And it was only a three-minute walk from our apartment! We could attend lots of concerts and opera without having to drive to Darmstadt. And in school, I wouldn't have to be so ultra-cautious anymore, since only Jewish students and professors would hear whatever "dangerous," "risky" things I might spill out!

"Never mind," my mother said when I voiced my relief at the new freedom. "It's less dangerous than in Darmstadt, but it's still not without risk. So don't talk too much, and get used to watching yourself. It's good for you anyway, for the rest of your life."

It certainly had an effect on me for the rest of my life. At the time, I accepted my mother's statement that it was good for me, as I accepted everything she said as valid and necessary. Later in life I came to realize that the constraints my mother's demands had placed on me had a high price—in initiative and creativity.

Meanwhile, I was getting used to the Philanthropin. I had to catch up on French, because that was the first foreign language of an Oberschule, which had a more "practical" curriculum and emphasis than Ludwig-Georg, where Latin was the first foreign language. I felt more relaxed in the all-Jewish atmosphere, but at the same time, I was unaccustomed to an all-Jewish environment. Physically, the school was similar to the Darmstadt Gymnasium—dark, with a broad central stone stairwell; large classrooms with an elevated, stagelike area at the front, and the professor's *Pult* (desk). Boys and girls sat together. I immediately became fascinated with Mathilde Rosenthal: tall, thin, with long blond hair, lovely blemishless skin, and smart, too.

Our professors, again all Jewish with the exception of the gym teacher, Mr. Stelzer, lectured and tested us just as those in Darmstadt had. Denomination made no difference when it came to applying deeply engrained methods of pedagogy! We made the usual cruel comments about them—Freudenberger's lisp, Schaumberger's wet *s*'s and *sch*'s, Rothschild's nose-picking, and Marbach's ears, attached at an almost ninety-degree angle to his head, became subjects of endless merriment. Only one faculty member escaped: Dr. Philipp, the German professor. His competence, modesty, and commitment to the work and to us as persons rather than "just" students made him a figure that commanded our respect.

Frankfurt turned out to be just fine: a lovely apartment with a view over the park and down toward the city center; a school that was a few minutes' walk from home where it was easy to feel comfortable; and stores and coffeehouses right in walking distance. For us, after the harassments and terror of Reinheim, it was ideal. That the mid-1930s turned out to be a "phony peace" for the Jews was not something we could or even wanted to foresee—least of all we "immigrant" Reinheimers, who valued the vastly improved atmosphere. My grandfather and mother had no patience with the Frankfurt Jews who were always expecting worse things to come. Also, the constant concern with my grandmother was enough for us all. We had no need for additional pessimism.

We had been in Frankfurt for a little more than six months when my grandmother began her climb from the second floor of our building up to the top, where the mansards looked down on the world. No one knows what time it was, but probably the middle of the night. She opened the window, leaned forward, and fell down.

That's how we reconstructed the event, after my grandfather noticed early on the morning of February 24, 1935, that his wife was not in bed next to him. He called out for her, woke us up, then we looked throughout the apartment, then out of the window: a crowd had gathered on the sidewalk in front of the building. The police and an ambulance were there. We all rushed down.

There was blood, nightclothes, a body inside them, and more blood. It was a heap of something unrecognizable as a person.

There was numbness all around me and inside me. Mutti had a stunned, faraway look. She sent me upstairs, but I didn't go. My grandfather, then sixty-nine years old, looked lost and said nothing. It was my father who started to talk to the police and moved closest to the body.

"How could she get up there? How could she do it?" my mother screamed after a minute or so, when what happened had begun to sink in. "How? How?" she kept on shouting.

Grandfather remained silent and continued to seem distant. It was getting cold, and we all had just flung coats over our nightclothes. My father took command, as he always did and had to do in a crisis, and sent the three of us back upstairs.

Mutti continued to scream "How? How?" I still had trouble taking in what had happened, and what was happening now. My confident, strong-minded mother was slumped on a chair, crying and screaming; my grandfather was speechless. I felt lost, with nobody to ask, to hold on to, to help me understand. That was Oma? I had only glimpsed the sidewalk scene. I wanted to know, to talk, to hear someone say something I could understand. But nobody was there to do it. And I was old enough, at fourteen, to be told and to understand. Finally, my father came back up. He gave Opa and Mutti some medicine, and he talked to me. He reconstructed what had happened on that stairway, and then at the window on the top floor. And he told me that it had been too late: Oma's depression had gone too far and too deep for her to be pulled back from what such people often do.

He did not have to explain what depression was, because that topic had been discussed ever since my grandmother ceased communicating that night when we heard the bang in our Reinheim yard. My father also had to make the arrangements for the burial, because my mother, even after recovering from her initial reaction, was unable and unwilling to do it, and my grandfather remained aloof. I did not see tears. He said little beyond "I looked, and she wasn't in bed."

Oma was buried in the Neue Jüdische Friedhof. Every time I visit Germany (my return trips began in 1955), I visit her grave, and the scene on the sidewalk returns to my mind. Every time I make it a point to walk by the house where we lived, and then the one we moved to because we wanted to get away from what had become a reminder of horror. And every time I approach the sidewalk in front of the Eschenheimer Anlage house, I step off into the street . . .

So we moved again—but again not out of the country. We still had not gotten our passports back, but the real reason was that now "we can't leave Opa alone" and Opa refused to consider leaving. It wasn't just faith in the "Rechtsstaat," although even Oma's suicide had not completely shaken it. It was his fear, at age seventy, of going to a country that was so different, that scared him, where he didn't know the language, and about which he had strong prejudices (although he would never concede that he had a prejudice, not even opinions; what he thought was the way things were).

My father's sister and her family—the Grafs from Nuremberg—had by then emigrated to New York. My father felt and said that they had done the right thing. But this had no effect on Opa. He had little but scorn for Julius Graf, my Aunt Flora's husband. "He's always traveling and has those crazy ideas," Opa's would say. He was similarly critical of anyone who did not share his "straight," "sensible," "responsible" views. These were euphemistic adjectives for what might most charitably be called small-town, petit-bourgeois, crotchety romanticism. It was an attitude that precluded all discussion, both at home and in the larger society.

We found an apartment on Scheffelstrasse, which bordered on the backyard of my school. No doubt that was a major reason why we, that is my mother, chose it. It was fine with me, too. It limited, indeed almost eliminated, the chances of my talking to anyone on my way to school. That meant I didn't need the little notebook anymore.

Oma's death remained a dark cloud. But life had to go on. My father continued to practice medicine, and he drew new patients by the week. I enjoyed school and evenings at home, often with some fellow students who loved classical music, and we listened to the nightly radio transmissions from EIAR, the Italian network, of live opera performances from Italy's great houses—the Reale in Rome, La Scala in Milan, or others in Florence, Naples, and Venice. My operatic education, at least in the Italian genre, dates from those evenings at Scheffelstrasse 13.

Even as my mother and grandfather found release and relief in Frankfurt after the experiences of Reinheim, and even after Oma's death, something different and important was happening to my father and, by extension, to me: he became Orthodox, a committed

Zionist. His zeal to catch up on what he had left undone as a Jew drew me in as well. He couldn't change my grandfather's habits, nor did he try to affect Mutti's feelings, except to demand and get strict kosher cooking. But he could recruit me.

Since that time, Jewishness has played a significant role in my life. It all started with our going to the Börneplatz synagogue—Conservative in the Frankfurt context, but Orthodox by current American standards. The rabbi there was Dr. Jacob Hoffmann, a Hungarian-born scholar in both Jewish religious and German cultural heritage. This brilliant, stylistically exciting, but temperamentally calm orator became my father's idol and advisor.

Soon Hebrew lessons were added. Aaron Lischner, a young Hebrew teacher, came several evenings a week to give Papi private lessons. And I was sent to be tutored by a Talmud scholar, Rabbi Donath, to study the complexities of the great rabbis' teachings in the Mishnah and Gemarrah. This was in addition to the regular religion class in the Philanthropin and the Saturday-afternoon extra study period in the Talmud-Torah school attached to the synagogue.

Here I was, an outcast from the society I had been educated to be part of and whose values I was taught to admire, thrust into the culture that had meant very little beyond formal rituals on rare occasions in our home. Who was right? Opa or my father? Where did I belong? I wasn't sure what was happening. Still, even as these questions bothered me, one thing was clear: after Reinheim, Frankfurt was just fine. The continuing pressure of the Nazis on the Jews that was felt strongly and ominously by the Jews who had lived in Frankfurt all along meant little to us. We had gone through much worse in Reinheim. So the SA were boycotting Jewish stores for a day or two and smearing disgusting slogans on the windows. So firms were "Aryanized"—the big department stores on the Zeil, like Wronkers, Tietz and Carsch on the Hauptwache. We could not get that upset about it.

After all, we had our Kulturbund. Players who had been dismissed from Frankfurt's orchestras and opera formed a Jewish orchestra and chamber ensemble, and we enjoyed music among ourselves. So what was so terrible about living and earning a livelihood in a well-to-do, culturally respectable, well-organized, and Jewishly lively community of twenty-five thousand?

More important, we had our own excellent Oberschule in the form of the Philanthropin, where I could get my *Abitur* (certificate of maturity entitling me to go on to university studies). What more could we want? "Compare this paradise to Reinheim!" Mutti and Opa seemed to be saying. But not my father, who drifted farther and farther away from his wife and father-in-law as he steeped himself in Jewishness and Zionism and found his identity there, which meant he had chosen to be a Jew over being a German.

I was so busy running from school to Rabbi Donath to Talmud Torah, doing my homework, and meeting my commitments to my school friends that I had no time to think about anything larger than my own personal life. I walked by the *Stürmer-Kästen*—those wooden frames protected by chicken wire behind which the pages of Julius Streicher's anti-Semitic paper, with its horrid cartoons of Jews, were displayed. But this, too, became "normal"; I hardly paid attention to them.

I was also becoming infatuated—with Mathilde Rosenthal. She was the daughter of a distinguished Frankfurt physician, but more important for me, she was magnificently beautiful. She wore glasses, but that didn't matter to me. She was also unattainable, or so I felt, having been made to feel that way by fellow students and by my mother. I walked by her side for a minute in the Philanthropin yard and was elated that she responded to me, no matter how trivial the subject I had raised. Eventually, I walked her home to Bockenheimer Anlage, and those were moments of supreme happiness. But there wasn't much time, the response was cool, and so there was little more than those fleeting moments of barely flickering hope, and fantasy . . .

Hitler became stronger, Germany more powerful, the race laws were promulgated. But so what? No one in our family and no one we knew had any intention to marry, even to consort with, non-Jews beyond professional or everyday needs. In Frankfurt's large, active, intellectually and artistically well-endowed Jewish community, this Nazi policy to exclude us from a society governed by uncultured and intellectually, socially, and morally unacceptable people who claimed to be good Germans had little or no impact.

Life was gray and brown and black in Frankfurt in those days. And the swastika, black, white, and red, was everywhere. Gray were the stone and inside walls of the Philanthropin. Brown was the omnipresent SA. And black was the SS. Gray was also the color of Jews' lives. It was the most common shade of men's clothing. It was also the feeling of life: an uncertain midpoint between the black despondency of some Jews and the knock-on-wood-that-something-worse-hasn't-happened attitude of others.

Even as we felt good about our submersion into the Jewish community, concentrated on work, school, synagogue, and friends, we had to work hard at maintaining our sense of normalcy. Every time Hitler took another step against the Jews, it was the last in my grandfather's and mother's eyes, and in the eyes or all those who preferred to focus on the diminishing bright spots of life rather than uprooting themselves.

Only much later, with the benefit of hindsight and the knowledge of the ultimate horror none of us wanted to have, did I realize the almost invincible power of roots. Routine and familiarity are to the soul what food is to the body. Fear of losing these things makes us turn away, makes us dismiss or rationalize any evidence that argues for change, even when that evidence spells ultimate danger. By the same token, I came to admire all those who, without the compulsion of extreme persecution, chose to tear up roots and start life anew elsewhere: the "economic refugees," as they are often pejoratively referred to these days—the Irish; the folks from Apulia and Calabria; the few Jews, like my mother's cousin Siegfried, who left inflation-ridden Germany in the 1920s to seek opportunity in America; and today, the Pakistanis, Indians, Koreans, and others.

So as the Nazis marched by singing the Horst Wessel song about how "the blood of the Jews spews forth as the knife cuts deeper," as we walked by the now familiar *Stürmer-Kästen* with their horrid Jewish caricatures and bloodthirsty articles, looked across the street as the non-Jews walked up the steps of the Opera House from which we had long since been barred, we stayed on, making our ghetto of "Germans of Jewish faith" comfortable and endowing it with the glory of normalcy that screamed conviction but could not drown out doubt.

The reoccupation of the Rhineland was the first "foreign" success of the Nazi regime. It went so smoothly that it was difficult not to admire the operation. My father never took his mind off the threat to the Jews, as well as to Europe. But Papi's views mattered little to me, for two reasons: he had never involved himself in my upbringing, except on specific occasions, like that summer camp thrashing; and I had little time, between school, homework, private Talmud lessons, and, yes, now also violin lessons, to think about issues beyond my own and the family's immediate concerns and responsibilities. The result was that what my grandfather and my mother had planted in my mind and soul remained my frame of reference: order, smoothness, acceptance, duty. And should anything go wrong, it was "how could you?!"—my fault. That left little if any room for questioning authority. And though Hitler was intellectually unacceptable and had made it clear that he was determined to rein in (not yet destroy) the Jews, he *was* the government. He *was* authority. Where, then, was an order-admiring, authority-revering, German-feeling, anxiety-filled teenager who had the Talmud stuffed into his brain to find his moorings?

What was I thinking or feeling at the time? A lurking danger? I always felt that. About our lives? Yes. Everything I said and did could get us into trouble, and trouble might well mean death. Why? Because we had to be especially careful, as Jews. All we could do was be careful. At the time, it seemed that the Germans either were right, or had the power and we could do nothing about it, or both. And so the tefillin in the morning, the synagogue, the Talmud and Hebrew—the center of my father's new life and, by his orders, my new burden—became identified with the *Fantast* image that Opa and my mother had attached to Papi. The real world and the one that counted was the place we lived in, the law that governed us and had to be obeyed. Whether we approved of, liked, or disliked those laws was not an issue. The point was to obey them and thereby assure ourselves of security, or at least survival. The answer to the "moorings" question, for better or worse, unclear and never articulated, lay here, in the existential dominance of the German, and the troublesome, not quite real Jewishness that was inevitably ours as well, and that my father inexplicably made so conspicuous.

An incident in the mid-1930s illustrates the priorities that governed our lives and, in my case, feelings and images. My mother found out that my father had deposited several thousand marks abroad, as a safety net in case we should be forced to flee. It was against the law and punishable by high fines, possibly death, to export currency without official approval, and Jews never got such approval.

"Is it true?" Mutti asked. My father tried to make light of it and evade the question, which made my mother even more frantic. "I want to know whether it's true", she came back, "because it would mean that you, without asking me or Opa, decided to jeopardize all our lives."

"Don't exaggerate," was my father's quite casual response, as he continued to try making light of the subject, in the vain hope of calming my mother. Instead, his comment was taken—and rightly so—as an admission of guilt. What my father had done as a small measure of protecting our family was seen by my mother as an irresponsible act that endangered us. Rarely were Mother's and Father's opposing views more tellingly illustrated: who we German Jews were, what was right and wrong, what was safe and risky, what was good and bad—all were at odds in this case.

The result was foreordained, given the prevailing priorities. No vote was needed, because all such issues were two to one for the "legal," orderly side of Opa and Mutti, I, of course, didn't get a vote. With a heavy heart, my father requested the return of the funds by the same circuitous route he had used to move them out, making us "clean," and enabling my mother to sleep with just the usual dose of sedatives rather than the extra measure she needed before the money came back.

What made matters worse for my mother was that she could not talk to anybody about it, least of all Opa. He would have raged against my father, had he known about the *Schiebung* (illegal transfer), a word to which he attached special opprobrium. It was part of the Jewish stereotype, a staple in *Der Stürmer,* depicting the money-grabbing international capitalist engaged in enriching himself by illegal deals that robbed decent Germans of the fruits of their labor. A *Schieber* was worse than a murderer in the Nazi lexicon: a person who used his gun or knife either was mad or had courage; a *Schieber* was a criminal who acted in secret, a coward who tried not to take responsibility for his crime. He was slimy, "typically Jewish." I have no doubt that this image of the Jew, which Nazism did not invent but merely developed, was a nightmare for people like Opa and my mother, who felt that too many Jews had acted in ways to buttress this notion, and for whom meticulous observance of the laws was the highest of all duties, no matter who had made them or how they had been made.

For me, school became increasingly important as the work became more demanding and only a little over two years remained until the *Abitur,* the final examination that was the crowning event of higher education, the passport to university studies, which were synonymous with life. My relationship with Mathilde became stronger, at least on my part, as we took walks to discuss literature, especially during the weeks when we read Goethe's *Faust* with Dr. Philipp. I felt enriched and confident in talking about *Faust* with Mathilde after I had gone on one of my occasional and adulatory walks with Dr. Philipp. I never forgot a word he occasionally used to describe changes in pace in Goethe's writing: *Akzentverlagerung,* shifting of rhythmic emphasis.

We were by now learning French and English, the latter with a new "auditive" method, stressing pronunciation over reading, but our "real" education in the sense of *Bildung* was German and history, especially German. Here we penetrated into the deeper layers of literature, felt and not merely read what was on the page, tasted the sweetness of romantic poetry, the fervor of Schiller's passion for freedom, the complicated meanings of the second part of *Faust.* Shakespeare was revealed to us in the famed translation of Schlegel and Tieck, which even knowledgeable non-Germans consider miraculously close to the original, both in meaning and in capturing the pithy perfection of Shakespeare's verses.

In 1937, Hitler's forces marched into Austria. The wild enthusiasm of the crowd on the Heldenplatz in Vienna still rings in my ear with the thin sharpness of even the best radios of the day. And as Hitler advanced, more of my fellow students and their families moved out, many to the United States, but also South America or Palestine. But not us. School and all the different private lessons continued, with singing instruction replacing the violin hours that I had unsuccessfully spent under the strict but not unattractive eyes of Fräulein Schnerb. Ancient Herr Würzburger became my new music teacher, it having been determined that I had a fine singing voice, a bass, that merited development.

The new "crisis" came soon enough. This time, it was the Germans of western Czechoslovakia who wanted to "come home." Their leader, Konrad Henlein, made widely broadcast speeches lamenting the persecution these oppressed but proud Germans were suffering at the hands of a cruel Czech government. I remember my father laughing heartily at this Nazi propaganda. "Die armen Deutschen werden von den grausamen Tschechen unterdrueckt! [The poor Germans are being oppressed by the cruel Czechs!]," he said, laughing at this joke of "poor Germans being oppressed." "That's as if I were accused of biting that ferocious dog in the Stühlingers' house! You'll see, Hitler is starting the campaign for swallowing up the next country! We really have to get out of here! There'll be a war, and what happens to us then?"

"Don't be silly," Mutti would say to Papi. "He can't fight all the Western Allies! And besides, we shouldn't even be discussing this! Who knows when you'll say it outside the house, and that'll be the end of all of us. So let's mind our business, and not talk about leaving before Robert has made his *Abitur,* anyway."

There was still a year to go to the *Abitur.* And the crisis atmosphere in the East was heating up steadily. Then came the negotiations with Britain, and eventually the Munich conference and settlement, giving Hitler the Sudetenland and yielding Neville Chamberlain's triumphant "peace in our time" statement on his return from Munich to London.

"You see," Mutti said to my father, "I was right again. The Allies stopped Hitler, and he had to accept their conditions."

"How can you say that?" Papi would say. "They gave him what he wanted and they think that's the end! Can't you see that it's only the beginning? They're entirely blind, and blinded by their fear of Stalin and communism!"

My father was most indignant at the Poles for having sided with the Nazis and gotten a silver of Czechoslovak territory around the little town of Teschen. He cursed the Rydz-Smigly government, and especially its foreign minister, Beck. "They'll get it in the neck next. They just don't know it yet," he'd exclaim.

My grandfather would not even debate the issue. In his eyes, my father was being unrealistic, as usual, and it was altogether too dangerous to discuss the subject. My mother would respond, also as usual, that Papi was talking about things he didn't know anything about. "Of course you understand all these matters!" she would say sarcastically. Then she'd repeat the customary "be realistic and be careful about the way you talk" message.

On we stayed. In November 1938, young Ernst vom Rath, a middle-level diplomat at the German embassy in Paris, was murdered by a Polish Jew named Herschel Grynszpan. By this deed Grynszpan wanted to call the world's attention to the growing menace of Hitler, particularly his policy to persecute the Jews.

Today's reader may well ask why on earth this fellow had to commit such an act to call attention to something everybody knew about. It's a question that can be entertained, understood, and, yes, excused only by the wisdom of hindsight. For in the fall of 1938, most Europeans—not even to mention the far-off, isolationist Americans—either did not realize what was going on in Germany and what Hitler was planning, or they didn't think it was too worrisome, or they didn't mind the Jews being given a little kick in the posterior lest they get too cocky and take over everywhere . . . Wasn't it enough for France to have a Jewish prime minister (Leon Blum), and for Germany to have had a Jewish foreign minister (Walter Rathenau)?

If my grandfather and mother thought the way they did, why shouldn't the average German or Frenchman be excused for faith and optimism? As for anti-Semitism, how often I had heard my mother say, "Is it really necessary that Herr Goldschmidt heads the Deutsche or Dresdner [or whatever] Bank?" How often she had told me, when, to reward me, she had taken me to the coffeehouse in Darmstadt after I had gotten a good mark in class and showed my enthusiasm over a piece of *Trüffeltorte*, "Psst, not so loud! People will think Jews can't behave! That just makes more anti-Semitism!"

Yes, in a sense, Hitler was our fault! He was there because too many Jews had not been told, or had not observed, the rule of "how could you?!" What Mutti was saying, without realizing it, was that to be good Germans, which of course was mandatory, we had to be quiet, even silent, Jews.

My mother changed her mind abruptly and dangerously on the morning after Kristallnacht, November 10, 1938.

We had been glued to the radio, had been on the telephone all day November 9, when the Nazis broadcast warnings that "die spontane Volkswut" (the spontaneous rage of the public) at the murder of vom Rath was expressing itself all over Germany. The customary anti-Semitic rhetoric escalated to ever higher decibels and ever more obnoxious invectives. It was *Der Stürmer* all over the airwaves. And we were frightened.

The mass arson of synagogues all over the country had been forecast (which was merely another word for ordered), as was, of course, the "spontaneity" of popular rage. In the evening, we could see the fiery glow of the Friedberger Anlage synagogue in the gray autumn sky. We knew that our own synagogue on the Börneplatz, and all the others, were burning, too.

We felt, and were, defenseless. For the first time, our nakedness in the face of battalions of SA and SS, armed with all kinds of sophisticated, rapidly firing weapons, was stark, clear, and cold in our minds. The discussion of the past five years stopped; the red sky had put an end to it. The threat and fear of things to come had become real. Suddenly, the meaning of "realistic" had changed radically in our family: my grandfather had fallen silent, forced to accept that he could no longer rely on the Rechtsstaat to protect him, no matter how "recht" he was conducting himself. And my mother had become an enraged protester! It all revealed itself on November 10, after a night that had not been for sleeping.

We were in our bedclothes but had spent the night with our robes on. Since none of us could sleep, we periodically got together in the living room to try to figure out what might happen. We had heard rumors that all Jewish men would be arrested and shipped to concentration camps. But perhaps it wouldn't be all. Perhaps they would not take physicians, because they were needed. "Needed to treat Jews? Don't be ridiculous," my father would say in response to such speculation by Opa.

"We have to be prepared for anything," Mutti said, signaling her changed expectations.

"If they come," my father said to me, "and if they take you, too, do everything to stay close to me, understand?"

Back to the bedrooms we'd go, and I could hear my parents talking, as my grandfather stayed uncharacteristically silent.

The feared dawn was breaking. We did not have to fret long before the doorbell rang. My mother went to answer it, with me trailing behind. An SS man, in his odious, neat black uniform, and a Schupo, a regular policeman in a blue uniform with black helmet, stood before us.

The Schupo spoke, calmly and politely, "I have orders to take Dr. Goldmann to the police precinct. Please have him get ready." Meanwhile, my father had joined us, and he went to get dressed without saying anything. The SS man, too, remained silent.

But not my mother. "I know what you are doing!" she screamed at the policeman, who had introduced himself as Roeth. "You are going to take my husband to the concentration camp!" Utterly and completely out of character, breaking a pattern of caution and anxiety that had guided both her and my life, and stifled any attempt by my father to resist or emigrate, my mother spewed venom and insults at the two representatives of authority at our door.

As Roeth attempted to calm her, assuring her his orders related only to the police precinct, she sneered, "You are lying, and you know it! You are all liars! You want to destroy us all! While you are at it, why don't you take him as well?!" she shouted, pointing at me.

I felt as though I had been thrown into the mouth of a lion, but I dared not say a word. I was too stunned, too scared, too torn away from the footing I had firmly and confidently stood on all my life to know or say anything. Here we were, in our nightclothes and robes, with the synagogues burned to the ground, my father getting dressed to be taken to an unknown and likely terrible fate, and my mother was screaming at the people who had limitless power over us, against whom there was no defense, no protest. And surely these people didn't need any suggestions volunteering others, like me, for arrest!

My father had heard my mother lecturing the officers. How could he miss those decibels? He came to the door, dressed and with his overcoat on, and suggested that my mother have me go to bed, because, he said, he had found that I had an elevated temperature the night before and was probably coming down with the grippe.

I understood what he meant to say, and fortunately, Mutti did as well, despite her seemingly uncontrollable fury. My father sought one last, albeit probably hopeless way, to protect me from arrest.

Roeth agreed readily, saying that my mother would be well advised to follow her husband-doctor's advice. Besides, he added, he had no orders concerning me. "How old is your son?" he asked.

"Seventeen," my mother answered, adding gratuitously and continuing to curry danger, "but since when would that make any difference to you people?"

"Oh, no, Frau Doktor," Roeth said, "these orders pertain only to Jewish men above the age of eighteen. So please don't worry about your son, and let him go to bed and cure his grippe. I'm sure Dr. Goldmann will return soon."

At this point, my father kissed my mother and me good-bye (Opa was still in his room), suggested with a look and a gesture that my mother calm down, and went off with the two officers. The SS man had not said a word.

We called Opa, reported on what happened, and I was sent to bed. My mother had fallen silent, as if from deep exhaustion. Opa said nothing. His lifelong faith in the Rechtsstaat must have been shaken, if not completely shattered.

I felt lost in our own home. Here we were, sitting like broken reeds, not knowing what to do, what would come next, where we would be tossed by whatever wave would sweep over us, maybe to swallow us up for good . . . But why was Roeth so patient? What could possibly be behind his seeming solicitousness on this day of the public's "spontaneous fury"? It was cold—both in the room and in our minds and feelings. Nothing seemed to matter anymore. Yesterday my mother was concerned with everything being clean, dusted, and orderly. What did it all mean now? Would Papi go to Buchenwald, the concentration camp that rumor had mentioned as the place the Jewish men would be taken? What would they do to him there? Would they come for me after all? Would I find him when I got to Buchenwald? Would we be able to help each other?

We didn't have much time to dwell on these morose meanderings. A bang at the front door made us jump up. In came a posse of some fifteen to twenty toughs, shouting anti-Semitic invectives. "Jewish pigs, damned exploiters, now you'll get what you deserve!" screamed the leader, as they ordered us into the kitchen, slammed the door, and proceeded to tip over the furniture in the dining room. We knew that's what they were doing, because we could hear the large china cabinet fall, and the glass and china crash to the ground. We heard wood crunch, more glass and porcelain crash to the ground. And the shrill sound of breaking glass was always mixed with the shouts of "More, more, over there!" and similar words of discovery and mutual encouragement.

We were soundless and motionless, by now also emotionless. What did it all mean, anyway, after Papi had been taken away? We'd all be dead soon . . . so what did furniture matter? These were our thoughts as we waited in the kitchen, in those few minutes of destruction that seemed like hours.

Suddenly, there was quiet. The kitchen door opened, and the leader said, "You can come out now. We are done."

We looked out on a sea of shards and jagged pieces of china and crystal. The name Kristallnacht (crystal night) was not accurate in our case; it should have been Kristallmorgen (crystal morning). What the name really, but inadequately, signifies is the burning of the synagogues, which did occur at night, and the arrest of Jewish men. The broken glass was an anti-climax, the destruction of replaceable and reparable material items. I have long felt that, even as it may sound more spectacular and descriptive to an unknowing audience, the name downgraded the deep human and cultural wounds that were struck that night and the next morning—struck at Germany's large, vital, loyal and confident Jewish community by Germany itself—yes, not just by Hitler or the Nazis, but by Germany. For the German people had by then not only accepted but embraced their Führer. But was it really that simple? Had it all come crashing down with the glass and the furniture? The ideals engraved on the opera house: "Dem Wahren, Schoenen, Guten [To truth, beauty, and goodness]"? Faust, with his daring and confident wager on man's decency? The ideals of the emancipation, derived from the French Revolution and its German epigones, which had inspired Moses Mendelssohn to make his wager with the German people?

We got a glimmer of hope a little later that morning. Less than an hour after the wrecking crew had left, the doorbell rang again, even though anyone could have walked in without announcing himself after the vandals had broken in. My mother went to the door, and I could clearly hear the conversation from my bed. It was Roeth. I sneaked out to look and saw that he was in uniform, but he wore a regular hat instead of the helmet. This meant that he was off duty.

"So now you've come for my son, right?" my mother said, but less angrily and more sadly than before.

"No, Frau Doktor, please believe me. You keep him in bed until he is well again," said Roeth. "No, I've come to pick up the checkbook. Dr. Goldmann said that you have no access to the account, because you don't have signature authority. So he wants me to bring the checkbook to him so he can sign checks, and I'll bring them back to you. That way you can draw money when you need it."

"You want me to believe that?" my mother asked, getting angrier by the word. "So now you want our money, too, and you make up this phony story!"

"No, no", said Roeth, "please believe me, I am telling the truth. The doctor asked me to do this—nobody else, I swear it."

At this, my mother went to get the checkbook, and I heard her shout, "All right, take it, nothing makes a difference now anyway!"

I heard Roeth say how terrible he felt about what the mob had done to our apartment, and he apologized for this "schreckliche Unrecht" (terrible injustice). My mother did not acknowledge his apology, and Roeth left.

As we surveyed the wreckage of our home and began to figure out how to bring some order into chaos, the doorbell rang again. It had been less than an hour since Roeth left, and now he was back. To my mother's stunned surprise, he delivered a checkbook filled with blank signed checks. Finally, Mutti was convinced he was telling the truth. For the first time she was polite to Roeth. "Thank you. I'm sorry I shouted at you," she said. But Roeth merely countered that he understood, that Mutti shouldn't think twice about it. By this time, I had gotten up to join the scene at the front door, because there no longer was any need to feign illness in front of this man.

"Frau Doktor," Roeth said, "please give me some extra pairs of socks and some underwear, and put them in a small valise. And also make some sandwiches, please. It's not clear when Dr. Goldmann will be released, although I don't think it will be too long. But I want to take him provisions, just in case. He didn't ask me, but I think it's better to take precautions."

Roeth must have known by then that Buchenwald would be my father's and the other Jewish men's destination. He did not deny it when my mother asked him about it. He just said he didn't know for sure what would happen. Obviously, he wanted to console Mutti, but also not to lie.

We made contact with Roeth after the war, and visited him. He had been upgraded to a high position in the Frankfurt police department, in part perhaps because of the voluntary testimony my father, and probably others he had helped, had provided to the postwar authorities. But as we discussed it over the years, and as I confirmed when I visited Roeth in 1955, there was no way to repay or adequately honor him or other "just ones" like him, so sublime was their sense of decency. Nor did this rare breed of people have any expectation of recognition or reward. It was a small group of men and women throughout occupied Europe who did what they did without the feelings of courage or heroism that the postwar generation has attributed to them. They were the real heroes of the war because they did not do it for the recognition. They were uneasy when honors were bestowed on them—not because they were shy, but because they did not know what the fuss was all about. The absence of a feeling of courage is the mark of their decency's incandescence.

That's how Roeth responded when my wife and I called on him in the Polizeipräsidium of Frankfurt in 1955. He was the one who could not cease thanking my mother for the food and clothing packages she had sent him and his wife at the end of the war. Never did he realize that those packages were a terribly meager response to the unforgettable errands he had run so matter-of-factly seventeen years before. "The true hero is the one who doesn't know that he is one," said my father.

That morning, though, the significance of Roeth's actions did not register with us. All we could think about was: where is Papi? And my mother still expected me to be picked up. But she had become a different person. Just as her mother turned catatonic, noncommunicative from one moment to the next, that night when the *Kanonenschlag* exploded in our Reinheim yard, she made an almost complete about-face when those two uniformed men appeared at the front door.

As the days wore on and it became a certainty that my father and thousands of other Jewish men had indeed been deported to Buchenwald, Mutti settled down. But she didn't revert to her former anxious self. She remained angry, but converted her feelings into determined planning: for emigration, and for the repair and purchase of new furniture, china, and other household goods that had been destroyed, plus my father's medical equipment that the mob had smashed. We would need that in America, and we'd have to buy it here without worrying about the injustice, what it would cost, or any other problems that would normally be of concern. We'd also have to pay our share of the huge "reparations" that the Nazi government had assessed all German Jews, as a collective punishment for Grynszpan's act.

My grandfather had not been "converted" to the reality my mother had now accepted and on which she based her planning. But he was less confident about the Rechtsstaat. Joining my mother and me in the wait for my father's return, Opa had to face facts that only days before he would have dismissed as wild. For what we were thinking about was not just when my father would return, but whether he would come back at all. And if he did, what condition would he be in?

My daily routine had stopped. The Jewish-staffed and Jewish-run Philanthropin had suspended operations; Talmud, singing, and dance lessons stopped. Everything seemed to have stopped, and the only people we could talk to were those whose husbands, fathers, or brothers had been taken away. All this did was multiply rumor and speculation, and create depression.

My mother also talked to the HAPAG (Hamburg-America Line) man, a person who had become an important figure in our household in the sporadic discussions about emigration. He was a source of information not only on travel but on the waiting situation for an American immigration visa, and, as long as we all exercised care, on the political situation. Herr Halder had become a person to confide in, and since he was the only non-Jew and the only person in a quasi-public institution we were in touch with, he became an authority. In fact, as my parents recognized later, he was another of the decent people who had taken the hunted Jews to heart far beyond the requirements of his duties as a travel-agency executive. There was also Herr Beutel, our tax advisor, but he stuck more closely to his professional responsibilities than Halder, who consciously and sensitively did what he could to keep our spirits up without ever taking advantage of his position and our utter helplessness.

So we cleaned up, planned, dreamed of America and of Uncle Siegfried, my mother's cousin in New York, and of the Grafs on 149th Street, who would be our affidavit sources. In those days following November 10, America was becoming a beacon of hope, but it was shrouded in a veritable fog of "ifs," the biggest of which was Papi's return. Another was my *Abitur*. Yes, in the wake of Kristallnacht, my mother was planning our emigration around my *Abitur!* There was also the if of the American visa. The German quota had long since been oversubscribed, and waiting lists had been set up for those who had the necessary papers, of which the affidavits from American citizens were the most important. There was no way in those days to assign unfilled or underused quotas, like those of Britain or other un-occupied countries of the world, to the desperate needs of the Jews of occupied Europe. America's sensitivity to the plight of the victims of persecution, and of the refugees, developed only after the war.

My mother hardly ever slept, and I dropped off from sheer exhaustion. Then, one glorious day in the second week of December, Papi arrived. He was one of the first Jews to come back. Our joy was endless. We hugged and kissed him, almost loving the bad smell that he exuded from weeks of bad or nonexistent hygiene. I still have that smell in my nostrils. It was a mixture of the air in an unventilated toilet and the ugly, thick odor in our cellar in Reinheim, where the coal, the potatoes, and old furniture were stored.

After the initial joy, we realized how Papi had changed: his head had been shaved, and he was thin. His cheeks seemed to have caved in. His nose seemed so much longer, and his body, which was always a bit on the stout side, was only part of what it had been before November 10.

"Thank God," said my mother, and both she and Opa hugged him.

"Now tell us what happened and how you got out," my mother said. But Papi first wanted to take a long bath, which he said he had not done in all the time he had been away. And before that, he wanted to get rid of his clothes. "Throw them away or burn them!" he said to my mother.

To this day, I know next to nothing about what happened in Buchenwald in those four weeks of November and early December 1938. My father said so little about it. We asked, he responded time and again that all that worried him was what was happening to me, and that he was always looking for me. The only other comments he made were that he managed to skip away from most of the blows the guards tried to rain down, and that many people disappeared into the ditch that served as the inmates' toilet: one had to be agile and well-balanced to climb out on the narrow bar over the ditch, and back again.

The change that had come over my mother that morning when she screamed at the arresting officers was now showing itself to be deep and sustained. She had become businesslike, less emotional, but also a lot sadder. Her sadness now was not the despondency that reflects anxiety, with its depressive, hopeless manifestations. It was the healthy, normal response to the bleak reality we were facing. Instead of being paralyzed by fear and anxiousness, leaving all difficult decisions to my father, Kristallnacht and the ensuing weeks had made my mother calm down, had steeled her, as though the irrelevancies of anxiety had been burned off by the fire of experience.

Now realistic planning for emigration began. New furniture and medical equipment was bought. Arrangements were being worked out with the Grafs, my father's sister and her husband, in New York, to help us financially while we waited for our U.S. immigration visas in England. Passports were rechecked and validated for emigration.

My grandfather watched and listened to all this without much comment. What he did make clear was that he would not join us, but would stay on in Frankfurt. If we were really going to leave, he would look around for a room in some pension where he could stay and spend his remaining years. He was seventy-two at the time. He no longer objected to our plans—how could he and face my father after Papi's return from camp?—but he stuck to his guns about his own future.

My father recovered quickly. He had spent his life bouncing back from reverses and interruptions of his career. He had completed his last internship in 1912 and come to Reinheim on the basis of an advertisement placed by a retiring physician seeking an assistant who would take over his practice. The young Dr. Goldmann—he was twenty-five—rented a room from an elderly lady in the old doctor's neighborhood and started work. He had specialized in gynecology at Heidelberg, and this expertise came in handy in communities that did not have or did not believe in hospitals for the common procedure of giving birth.

But it lasted only two years. When the war broke out in 1914, Dr. Goldmann was called up for service as a physician with the rank of lieutenant. He spent all four years at the western front and was never wounded. He served at Verdun, in Flanders, wherever the battle raged, taking care of wounded and sick soldiers. He ended his service with the Iron Cross Second Class. And, to his mother's dismay, he returned to Reinheim. By now the old doctor was ready to retire. Dr. Goldmann took over the practice, and began seriously to court the Jewish community's most beautiful and eligible young woman, "die Martha."

They married in 1920, I was born in 1921, and things went well at the Goldmann-Frohmann house on Darmstädterstrasse—for fourteen years, until 1933. That's when we packed up to go to Frankfurt, and my father started over again in a new and very different community—different because it was a large place, with plenty of specialists and hospitals and a different professional style; and different, more importantly, because the Nazis were in power. And though initially it was easier for us because of the absence of unwanted prominence, as Hitler tightened the screws, my father's life became increasingly difficult. But one would never know it from his calm and quietly committed life and work style. If he found it difficult, he did not let on. Instead, he added to his daily workload the responsibilities of strict religious observance and Jewish and Hebrew studies.

Four years later came Kristallnacht, and the realization even in our family that we had to save ourselves, if we still could, by emigration. As it turned out, my father started practicing again in New York in 1942—the fourth start in thirty years. And his resilience was undiminished. War, harassment, Buchenwald, and a new country with a different language, customs, and professional practices had not diminished Jacob Goldmann's single strongest trait: to be a *Stehaufmännchen,* the little man who keeps getting up from the floor. In my father's case, it was not just professional resilience, but the ability to absorb punishment without either apology or complaint. I believe he punished his adversaries by shaking off their blows and resuming his work and his responsibilities. He did not mean to punish them, which is why he succeeded all the better in doing so.

Now, toward the end of 1938, my father had shown most convincingly that he could be neither defeated nor discouraged. Within a few weeks, he was leading the effort to get us out of Germany, by now no longer having to contend with arguments or sniping from my grandfather, or sullenness in my mother. She was with him, as, of course, was I.

I would have liked to go to England immediately. For by December I had my passport and the necessary permits from the United Kingdom to spend my waiting time for the U.S. immigration visa there. All of us, and I especially, were worried about another Kristallnacht at any time. I would have wanted all of us to leave as soon as we had the required papers—never mind the furniture, equipment, and other concerns that cluttered my parents' minds. What was essential was that my grandfather would be taken care of—at least as well as one could take care of Jews in those days, as he had irrevocably decided not to join us.

It wasn't that simple, however. Important considerations needed to be weighed. No hasty, panicky departure would be contemplated. In this situation, my father was at one with my mother, and I, of course, had to accept their judgment. "The *Abitur* first" was my father's decision. I had to finish the Philanthropin and get my certificate of maturity, which German students and their families saw as the passport to a career and a life worthy of any "good" family's sons and daughters.

"But the school has been closed for weeks since Kristallnacht, and some teachers were hurt and can't work. Who knows what will happen, and whether there will be a final examination?" I asked.

"You just study and work for it. The school will reopen shortly, and I am sure there will be an *Abitur*," my father answered. "Did you go to school and work for good grades to give it all up as if you had never gone?"

It didn't take much to convince me. Even the questions I asked were articulated hesitantly, without too much conviction, against the background of the all-enveloping respect I had for my parents' judgment. It wasn't an intellectual difference. How, after all, could I, a seventeen-and-a-half-year-old, consider myself smart enough to question my parents' wisdom? A deeply engrained and carefully nurtured attitude allowed only hesitant suggestions of a difference of view or feeling, lest the feared "how could you?!" with all its chafing guilt be brought on.

And so my parents purchased new furniture and medical apparatus for export, and paid all the extra taxes and special payments that entailed. And I went back to my room to cram for the test that might never come. . . .

Well, my father was right: the Philanthropin did reopen. Dr. Marbach, our Latin professor, sat at the *Pult* with scars and bandages on his face. Other teachers had slight limps or new glasses, adding to the changes in faces that had become smaller, thinner.

But an *Abitur* there would be! Even though there were only eight of us left to take it. Even though Director Albert Hirsch could not be sure that this Jewishly administered but publicly accredited institution would still receive the imprimatur of the State Education Authority.

How could we even imagine that we—a Jewish school with a German curriculum—would still receive official approval in 1939? The very speculation seems grotesque. And yet, as it turned out, it wasn't. Because the culture that fed the reasonableness of the expectation, or at the least hope, also brought on the Schulrat, the State Education Authority's supervising administrator: the Philanthropin had not yet been disaccredited, so it warranted official supervision of its *Abitur*. And so Herr Dr. Seidel came to us on March 29, 1939, with a shiny swastika button in his lapel, ready to sign and put the swastika stamp of the Oberpräsident (chief of administration) of the Province of Hessen-Nassau on our diplomas.

But our oral examination that day did have to undergo changes. The swastika did make its impact on the custom, which was for professors to examine students according to a subject selection that had been agreed upon beforehand and that had guided the preparations of the *Abitur* candidates.

"These students will not be examined in the subjects of German and history," proclaimed Dr. Seidel. "Jewish students are by definition unable to grasp and unworthy of dealing with these topics. Instead, the students who were due to be examined in German and history will be tested in physics and chemistry."

I felt as though the end had come. Not only had I prepared for German and history; I was a virtual illiterate in the two sciences and had not touched a book of chemistry or physics for months, ever since we started to cram for our designated subjects!

But Dr. Narewczewitz, a reasonable and fine teacher with a gentle sense of humor, handled matters well. The questions were easy, albeit phrased in complicated language (in the hope, which was justified, that Seidel knew little about science). When our answers lacked conviction or were incomplete, Dr. N., by superbly suggestive facial or body movements, encouraged us and, through additional questions, brought out what had been missing.

We ended up with our fully certified diplomas, with one exception: Seidel had put a black stamp over the word "official" on the first page of the diploma. Yet on the third page was Seidel's signature, next to that of Dr. Hirsch, and the Oberpräsident's swastika next to the stamp of the "Direktor des Philanthropins."

I had my "passport to life," or so I thought. When I submitted it to the admissions office of Columbia University's (evening) extension services, however, I was given only twenty credits, because I had studied under the Nazi regime, which had watered down the German educational system. That was in mid-1941, when America was not yet at war, and when my protestations that I had attended a Jewish-run school, which had not been influenced by the Nazi doctrine, fell on deaf ears. The old German saying that "was nicht sein darf, kann nicht sein" (what is not permitted to happen can't happen) seemed to have its echo in the bureaucracies of other countries.

I was now ready to leave for England. It seemed that the experience of Kristallnacht and its aftermath had also changed, perhaps matured, my feelings. I was eager to go. My obsessive nostalgia was gone. When a few years before I could not even stand to spend a night only a few miles away from home, I was anticipating crossing the border. The only thing that worried me was when my parents would follow . . . how long it would take for the furniture to be packed, for the shipment to be cleared. And there was the underlying concern whether they would come, and the fear of another Kristallnacht. But I was excited when my mother packed my suitcases. (I couldn't possibly do that right, at eighteen! After all . . .)

I crossed the German-Dutch border at Emmerich on May 8, 1939, traveled via Hoek van Holland to Harwich, and arrived in London the following day.

❖

III

When I got off the train in Paddington Station, I glimpsed Eva Metzger, a second cousin whose parents had left Mainz for London in the early 1930s, and ran toward her. I was excited by this big station, the bustle, and above all by sounds of English being spoken. The "ohs" and "nows" and "afters" sounded just as exaggerated in my ears as the twisted vowels Dr. Plaut, our Philanthropin English professor, had asked us to imitate so insistently and endlessly!

Vast crowds milled around Paddington, and Eva and I had to work hard to push our way through them with my two suitcases (the Nazis had taught us to forget steamer trunks). Eva steered me to my first experience with a train that ran under the street—way down. It was my introduction to a mode of transport on which I would spend a good deal of time over the next fifty years!

In we went, changed trains at Euston, walked through endless and sometimes frighteningly low-ceilinged and narrow-walled passageways to another train that took us to Golders Green. That's near where my mother's cousin Harry Stern, his wife Lotte, and their daughter Hanna lived, and where I was fortunate to find my home away from home.

To this day, Golders Green still feels like home—less than Reinheim, not so much less than Frankfurt, and almost even with West 100th Street, where we came to live after our arrival in New York.

Golders Green! Similar to Washington Heights in upper Manhattan, it was soon dubbed the Fourth Reich. One heard more "Guten Tags" and "Danke schöns" than their English equivalents. And since it was raining often, the careful German Jews always wore their raincoats, which were a good deal longer than those the Londoners wore. The story went that an indigenous Golders Greener had decided that the German refugees wore such long coats because they wanted to deprive Hitler of as much cloth as possible so he could make fewer uniforms . . .

I was received warmly and graciously at the Sterns. Their welcome, the close family feeling that we all enjoyed, Harry Stern's many jokes, and Lotte's raised eyebrows almost made me forget Frankfurt.

I knew I could not stay at the Sterns for long, because they were living in tight quarters themselves, on Middleway in Hampstead Gardens. So the first thing to do was to look for a room, or rather two rooms and use of bath and kitchen, where my parents—who were due in June if everything went according to plan—and I could stay. After a few days, I found accommodations with Mrs. Webb, an elderly widow, who had just the right kind of place for us to rent in her little house on Cumbrian Gardens, off Pennine Drive near Cricklewood. Kilburn and Cricklewood were sort of German-Jewish islands, or in today's terminology, settlements, in outlying districts of Golders Green's Refugeeland.

I moved in with my two suitcases, unpacked, and explored the huge bed with a massive pillow the likes of which I had never seen or even imagined. Until my parents came, I could luxuriate in this vast space of comfort and peace. Yet it wasn't quite peace: as the excitement of the new began to wear off a little, I became worried and impatient about my mother and father. Telephoning was expensive, letters took several days, and communication with Germany was not made easier by the fact that Britain seemed inevitably headed toward a clash, possibly war, in the spring of 1939.

My parents arrived by plane on June 18, a little over six weeks after my departure. So we were together again, except for Opa, who had rented a room in a pension in Nesenstrasse, not far from where we had lived in Frankfurt. We worried about him and still thought he ought to leave Germany. We tried to cajole him, to manipulate him out of Germany. We knew we had to use flawlessly legal means or he would not consider leaving at all. So we started thinking again about the nice HAPAG agent, Herr Halder, and our accountant, Herr Beutel. They would be our "accomplices." Opa was more likely to listen to them than he was to his daughter, and certainly more than to his "Fantast" son-in-law!

First, though, Father and Mother had to get used to Britain. Their acclimation process was fast and smooth, just as mine was. How they loved and admired those two little rooms at Mrs. Webb's! They acted as though they had never lived in that big house in Reinheim, or the seven-room apartments on Eschenheimer Anlage and Scheffelstrasse! No, the little house on Cumbrian Gardens was a dream castle, its two rented rooms the most comfortable of homes, and Mrs. Webb's bathroom and kitchen just perfect! How Hitler had taught us, almost overnight, to embrace and love what is real, to shed pretension, and to see each other in a new, more honest relationship of love and caring. It was as though everything nonessential had been melted down, transfigured. We now looked at life through a different lens. My father did not experience this change, because he never cared about elegant rooms and the earmarks of class and profession. This was one of the roots of his resilience. My mother, spurred by the will to survive, had come to share his values and the sources of his strength.

Since that time, I have had a low threshold of tolerance for immigrants who find fault with the country that had received them, with those who demand assistance without exploring every possible avenue to self-reliance. In later years, when I had professional responsibilities in the social service field, the term that most infuriated me was "dead-end jobs." As a friend of mine used to say, "There are no dead-end jobs, only dead-end people."

Despite our renewed strength, it was nevertheless awkward and just a touch humiliating to live on money that the Grafs had deposited for us. Yes, it would soon be repaid, but how soon? We found out that if I volunteered for military service in Britain, I might get permission to work. I did. Since we were only due to stay in the United Kingdom for a few months, I was not accepted for the service, but as a volunteer I was rewarded by the issuance of a temporary work permit. I found a job as a delivery boy at Frohwein kosher butchers in—where else?—Golders Green. The Frohweins, German emigrants themselves, had built up a nice business, and they needed help, especially on Thursdays and Fridays, as the Sabbath approached, and before Jewish holidays, to deliver all those kosher chickens, breasts of veal with pockets for stuffing, *Braten* (roasts), and, most important, the *Flanken* (brisket). The *Hausfrauen* were determined to follow, with fewer frills but all the essentials, the culinary habits formed in part by religious requirements, in part by tastes honed by generations.

During the week, the carryout trade was less active. And the bills were smaller: more cold cuts and frankfurters. The women preferred to take the smaller packages with them instead of having to pay the delivery boy a tip. The tip was the all-important item for me. I could barely wait for Friday, when I'd get lots of nice coins, sometimes even a pound, and would proudly empty my pockets at home. The earned money would reduce our withdrawals from the Graf-supplied account. With each of us having been allowed only ten marks in cash when we left Germany, this English cash, which on any given Friday would be more than the equivalent of ten marks, was indeed something!

In those summer months of 1939, we entertained ourselves by meeting friends, most often joining the Sterns. (The Metzgers were nice, but a bit snobbish, and we felt more comfortable with Harry and Lotte.) Harry kept on pouring out his seemingly endless stream of good jokes, and I did imitations of people's speech, particularly their accents (with my own superimposed!).

It was on one of those summer Saturday afternoons that I performed one of my Hitler imitations, mimicking one of his perennial harangues from the days just before he came to power: "Vierzehn Jahre sind vergangen . . . [It has been fourteen years since the day when Germany experienced the worst humiliation . . .]." The windows at the Sterns were open, and it was quiet outside. My voice was loud, which was an integral part of the imitation. When I paused, a voice came from the street: "I say, is the bloke talking again?" Harry looked out, and it was a policeman. I immediately got my "how could you?!" reaction, true to type. A policeman had heard? What would happen to us?

Harry calmed me down. He had told the bobby what had happened, and that British guardian of the peace had actually complimented me on my performance: "Jolly good job," he'd said. What a relief! And what a lesson in how policemen can handle their job. What was more remarkable to me was that this sense of humor and calm was maintained as tensions grew between the British and German governments. The peace that Neville Chamberlain thought he had brought home from Munich some ten months earlier looked shakier from day to day, as Hitler started rattling the sword at Poland.

For us, the danger of war raised two questions: what would happen to my grandfather, and how and for how long would we be able to stay in touch with him? And would we still be able to cross the Atlantic once we had received our U.S. immigrations visas, due sometime at the end of 1939? These were constant sources of worry. But it was a different kind of worry than what we had felt in Germany. We were in a free country. And while we were foreigners and restricted in what we could do, we were treated as guests: we were not ostracized, insulted, faced with having our windows smashed, or in danger of being dragged off to a camp and possibly death. Also, our worries were attenuated by humor, both in the family and in the community.

Fourth Reich–style jokes and good-natured self-denigration abounded. It took a little time before some of us realized that Piccadilly was not a toy, and that one could go to Oxford Circus without having to pay an entrance fee. And why did the English know what we were, even if we didn't open our mouths? "It's those long raincoats," said one refugee. "But they recognize us even when we don't wear them," said the other. "It's because we also walk with an accent," responded the first. With war approaching, it was a mixture of gallows humor and relaxed gratitude—with the latter dominant.

As days went by, we spent more time by ourselves and less with the Sterns. Harry was busy with his job in a business downtown, and my father was studying English, especially medical English, as a first stage of preparing for the state board examinations he would have to pass in America to practice medicine. I, of course, was riding my bicycle, delivering the kosher goodies to Frohwein's faithful customers. I was always happiest when I had deliveries to make to the people who had been in London for several years; they were the best tippers.

My father continued to observe Jewish rituals and to go to a nearby synagogue on weekdays as well as the Sabbath. I went on the Sabbath, but I was beginning to ease up on my observance. For so long I had felt pressed into religious participation, and now I had a reason to be "excused": my job. It was the beginning of a distancing process that would continue to develop. My father understood, or at least made me feel he did. I think he was hurt by my slackening interest in the Jewish religion, but he did not show it, for fear of burdening me.

In those tense weeks, Winston Churchill was sounding his warnings in Parliament. My father and most German refugees we knew were pinning their hopes on this man, who was criticized, even insulted, by many important British voices in politics and in the newspapers. "Why can't they understand?" my father asked in frustration, speaking of Churchill's critics. Some refugees, understandably paranoid, viewed Churchill's opponents as pro-Nazi. And some undoubtedly were, since they saw Stalin's Soviet Union as the principal threat to Western interests. Also, they either did not know, did not believe, or found it inconceivable that Hitler, who, after all, had done quite a job rebuilding the German economy, would do the horrid things he was accused of doing. How could Germans be so uncivilized?

But there was also just a mite of understanding for someone who dampened Jewish prominence a bit. After all, weren't the Jews really up there everywhere—in business, in the theater, everywhere? But to hurt them physically, to put them in concentration camps, that of course was intolerable. But then, aren't Germans, after all, Germans? They never had really learned proper behavior. Even when they behaved right, it was oh so rigidly correct.

This genteel prejudice and musing about manners was rudely interrupted on September 1, 1939, when Hitler attacked Poland. Britain and France had no choice but to declare war. If there was ever a case of mixed feelings, we experienced them that day. What a relief that there was finally armed opposition to Hitler! The decision we had argued for, prayed for, yearned for—a Western "stop" to the Nazis—had been made. But what would happen to my grandfather? Now we were cut off from him. Would we ever get him out of Germany? How would we communicate with him? How could we find out whether he was well? Or whether he was still alive?

Their questions aside, my father enjoyed a sense of "just retribution" about the quirks, reversals, and sheer madness of the politics that had triggered the war. "Those two criminals, they deserve each other!" he would say of Hitler and Stalin. It was Father's deep and unfailingly principled insight into the sameness of totalitarian dictators, and about the irrelevance of left and right when it came to inhumanity, that has guided me ever since. It has guarded me, even as I followed Father's basic left-progressive inclinations, from ever blurring the line between Social Democrats, or their equivalent, and Communists following their leader as he committed atrocities, such as the pact with Hitler, in the name of the "ultimate goal."

He had a special gripe against the Poles—not just because they were perceived as hopelessly anti-Semitic, but because of Teschen. What father found unspeakably despicable was that, as part of the price of carving up Czechoslovakia a year before, the Poles had gotten their piece of flesh, a very small piece, in the form of a small corner of Czechoslovak territory on the Polish border. It was the Rydz-Smigly-Beck government's reward for siding with Hitler. "If they didn't know they would be next," Father would say, "they are stupider than I think they are. If they thought they could appease Hitler and get a few square kilometers in the process, they are as abominable as I know they are."

To listen to my father, both when he commented on events after reading the paper and when he discussed them with Harry and others in the refugee colony, was to get an education in politics and ideology. There is nothing like soaking up lessons taught by personally experiencing history and having a wise and loving father interpret it for you. Those lessons have stayed with me throughout my life. They have stood me in good stead, both professionally and personally, particularly in moments of crisis.

My mother had little patience for her husband's intellectual and emotional involvement with what was going on around us in Europe. She was worried about her father. She needed my father's support, and his help. We needed to try to find a way to contact my grandfather via New York. There, my mother's cousin Siegfried Flörsheim, related to the well-known shoe company owners, who had emigrated to America in the early 1920s, was available. He got in touch with Hermann Frohmann in Nesensstrasse, and got word back to us via telegram. (Wasn't it true what the Nazis and the Communists said about us—that we were a bunch of no-good cosmopolitans? To which my father answered, after himself jokingly posing the question, "Thank God!")

Opa was fine. We didn't get much detail, except that he was still in Nesenstrasse, that he was in touch with the two links to the non-

Jewish world, Halder and Beutel, and that there seemed to be indications he was considering leaving, if it was still possible. Siegfried strongly encouraged my grandfather to do what he could to prepare for America. Siegfried had secured affidavits from the Flörsheims for Opa some time ago, and had brought other required documents up to date for the application for an immigration visa.

My mother's next worry was how we would get to America. We had bought passage on the Cunard line, with the date of passage and name of the ship left blank, pending information about the day on which we were due to get our immigration visas. But by October the Nazi U-boats were roaming the seas and sinking British and French ships. "So we are supposed to save ourselves and start a new life, and instead they'll kill us after all, in the ocean!" said my mother. She had shed much of her anxiety, but her pessimism was as strong as ever. And events were not helping my father, or the Sterns, who had a delightfully sunny outlook on life, to ease Mutti's deepening worries.

"What can you do about it, you old worryhead!" Lotte would say to my mother in her Heidelberg dialect.

"But you take it too easily," Mutti would respond. "How can you not worry? If we'd stayed in Germany, at least we'd still be together!"

"You know that's crazy!" everyone would respond. My mother by now would have realized she was merely voicing her anxiety. Still, she needed to unburden herself repeatedly, and we all knew it and understood it.

There was little time, and no money, for romance, but for a while I did hang on to Mathilde Rosenthal, who had emigrated to London with her mother after her father died in Frankfurt. I was still infatuated, but her response remained short of encouraging. We had good conversations, in the style of the "Abiturienten" with their unseasoned literary enthusiasm, articulated in the stilted jargon that was borrowed but awkwardly carried from truly *gebildete* ("cultured" does not quite cover it) people like Dr. Philipp.

My infatuation cooled in part because of logistics: Mathilde lived in Earl's Court, in the West End. It was a long way from Golders Green, both literally and hierarchically. There was no substantive difference in our families' degree of assimilation, but there was a class difference unrelated to our common Jewishness. In this case, it was the higher standing of a distinguished specialist like Mathilde's father. Whether Jew or Gentile, one did not entertain relationships with people on lower professional levels. It was an almost unconscious behavioral habit, which was why it was little affected by emigration.

My parents humored me about Mathilde. They sensed that nothing serious was going on, and as long as I did my Frohwein job and attended to my share of the household chores, and the costs did not exceed an Underground fare and a cup of tea, they were relaxed about my infatuation. Had my mother objected, as she did in later years in different situations, the relationship might have become complicated because of the tensions that would have developed.

Mathilde later fell in love, married an Indian, and moved to the Subcontinent, where I never heard of her again. Her mother stayed on in Britain, where she, like the Sterns and thousands of other German Jews, sought and eventually recieved admission as permanent residents. They and their children became British subjects, and while the parents, like mine, never lost their accent, even with that glorious British passport in the safe deposit box, the children did. Hanna Stern was a little girl of four or five when her family moved to London, and she speaks without a trace of an accent. She still manages German, but with just a touch of English coloring.

In later years, when we were living in New York, the story went around about a German immigrant who stayed on in England and was eminently successful in business. His was an exceptional experience, which filled all other German refugees with pride and admiration. His accomplishments were so extraordinary that they had contributed to the war effort, in return for which he was awarded his British citizenship much earlier than customary. Toward the end of the war, Herr Siegmund Grünthal even received an honor from the queen, which led to innumerable celebrations in the refugee community of this commercial Wunderkind's genius.

One day, so the story goes, after the end of the war and as vast changes transformed what had once been the British Empire, Sir Siegmund was taking a walk in Regents Park, dressed in striped trousers, cutaway, bowler hat, and swinging a Phipps bamboo-handled umbrella. Herr Blau from Golders Green, still wearing one of his Berlin suits, a bit worn but lovingly cared for by Frau Blau so it might last longer, came walking from the opposite direction. He recognized Sir

Siegmund immediately. After all, hadn't there been dozens of photos of him in the refugee press? And a few times even in the venerable *London Times?*

"Forgive, Sir Siegmund," said Blau, putting out his hand, "but I must stop to tell you how much we admire you in our community. You are our pride, our role model." And the breathlessly enthusiastic oration went on and on.

The converted Briton listened patiently, without showing emotion or even a fleeting smile. Which prompted Blau to ask, "But Sir Sigmund, with such success and such satisfaction, why do you look sad?"

"Who can be heppy?" said the famous man. "Ve chust lost India."

The deeper truth of the joke is that all of us identified with Britain, both because we had been given a haven and, more important, because the British people told Hitler "no," meant it, and made good on it. A new kind of assimilation was beginning. The German Jews had been ineluctably grounded in Western values. When Hitler cut them off from the deep roots they had struck into German culture, customs, and tradition, that which Europeans shared became the base for striking out anew toward assimilation. While the cultural oneness that Jews had achieved in pre-Nazi Germany was never accomplished in Britain or in any other European country, Jews did find a way to fit into British society.

As winter approached, there was still no action outside Poland, which had been conquered in days, and on the high seas, where U-boat warfare was in full swing. What would come next, we kept wondering. There were as many theories as worried Jews.

In those fall months of 1939, nothing happened. Hitler neither attacked any other country nor was he attacked. The British dubbed it the phony war. Perhaps Hitler was still hoping to get away with Poland. With Austria, Czechoslovakia, and Poland under his sway, he was now the head of Europe's most powerful country by far; perhaps now he'd stop.

"Nonsense," my father would say about such theories. To begin with, he argued, if it were so, it would be nothing to be hopeful about. "How can one hope that a madman who wants to kill all the Jews, who mercilessly bombs cities like Warsaw and other Polish towns, and who sits with vast military power in the center of Eu-

rope—how can one hope that things stay that way?" It was his response to those who, like Mutti, still had close relatives in Germany
or conquered Europe, and thought no further than that everything
should stop and not get worse. "Maybe he'll calm down," Mutti
would say.

Despite my father's political sense and merciless analysis of Hitler's unstoppable determination to conquer the world, he, too, had
hopes. He hoped and prayed, literally, for Hitler, his war machine,
and the Nazi Party to be so thoroughly destroyed that the ideology
he preached and the hate he spewed would be forever discredited.
"The time to stop him was when he marched into the Rhineland,"
Father would say time and again, "and even before! The German
people should never have let him come to power! And those Austrians! They had a chance to watch for four years what Hitler's rule
meant. And not only did they not reject it; they loved it and couldn't
wait for the Führer to come to Vienna!"

Father would clinch his analysis with a point that none of us accepted, except for Harry Stern who always echoed or added to my
father's arguments: "The longer the West waits, the higher the price."
Many of us wanted to believe that the West was just waiting to grow
strong enough to smash Hitler.

Father did not want to feel disappointed by Franklin Delano Roosevelt, who was the hope and later the hero of all German refugees.
He had understood the Nazi threat earlier than the British and the
French did, or at least earlier than their governments did, Father used
to say. The Lend-Lease Act and other Roosevelt efforts to join America's productive strength to that of the British and French made Roosevelt a modern Moses.

Of all the teachers I have had, my father was the greatest. For the
measure of a great teacher is not just what he knows, but how convincingly he communicates his knowledge. This in turn depends on
the strength and vitality of his values, and the inner need to articulate
them. People like my father teach so well because they don't realize
that they are teaching. They teach just by being what they are.

All one heard on the radio or read in the newspapers conveyed
German strength and confidence. Western words, by contrast,
sounded hollow and seemed to spell vacillation. Some of our friends,
and especially British people quoted in the papers, believed that the

British and French governments would resist Hitler and make good on their declaration of war. For us, only action meant anything, and there was little of that. But we couldn't convey doubt about the honesty and honor of Britain, because we were the British government's guests, and one didn't insult one's hosts. So we were careful about what we said where we could be overheard.

My father, though he disagreed with Allied policy, or at least was impatient with it, did not chime in. He had abiding faith in the courage and determination of Winston Churchill. For the rest of his life, Father would get a small lump in his throat whenever the conversation turned to Churchill. That name meant strength, persistence, and honor. He would never put up with a word of criticism of the Briton, and he was deeply shocked when the British people defeated him at the polls after the end of the war. He said, "I would have thought they'd show this man their appreciation, and keep him on." Father did not understand the British well enough to grasp their understanding of democracy and the public interest. But he could be forgiven for his views. We'd only lived in England for a few months—and most of that time among people just like ourselves.

The High Holy Days had passed—for the first time we observed them outside Germany, even though we attended synagogue in the German-Jewish district. What was missing, painfully so for Father, was Rabbi Hoffmann of the Börneplatz. But then, there was no more Börneplatz synagogue, just as there were no more other such large and venerable houses of Jewish worship in Germany. To Father, this was less important than the rabbi, and his message and his style. To be sure, Judaism does not require large and heavily ornamented settings for communal prayer. Four walls, a place for the Torah, and a lectern will do. And my father did not mind the simple shuls of England and, later, New York, where he felt more comfortable than in the large synagogues with choirs, not to mention organs! What was important was a man up there who had both knowledge and convictions, and who knew how to articulate a religiously rooted sermon in language that made it meaningful both in biblical or prophetic and in broad humanistic terms. In his view, only Jacob Hoffmann knew how to do that.

For me, the week leading up to the High Holy Days was a treasure trove. I worked hard those few days, delivering heavy loads of pre–Rosh Hashanah meat and poultry, and then later, the chickens and *Flankens* that were the mainstays of the *Anbeiss* meal, when the twenty-four-hour Yom Kippur fast was broken. My tips were no more generous than on regular Sabbath eves, but there were more of them.

Shortly thereafter, with my income a welcome windfall, we moved to a sublet on Hendon Way, renting two rooms with a larger kitchen and a bath of our own from a couple who worked as jugglers. It gave us more space for just a fraction more rent, and the big advantage was that the Singers, our landlords, were away much of the time, giving performances around the country. They didn't mind having their place looked after, and we enjoyed their absence.

It occurred to me later on that people take things for granted very quickly. Here we were, in June, so proud of our new home at Mrs. Webb's—a pride grounded as much if not more so in a feeling of safety after escape from danger as in the attractiveness of the rooms we had rented. And by September we had already become interested in something more comfortable!

Came the winter, and still no hostilities. "Strange war," Father used to say. "Be glad," Mother would answer, with her father in mind. Papi stopped right there, because an answer would have hurt Mother. One of the good things about the events leading up to emigration and of our new and frugal life in London was that we were growing together. In Germany we had lived apart—my father always out or busy in his office, my mother tending to the home, and myself either at school or Talmud Torah or violin instruction. In London, except for the period when I was working at Frohwein's, we lived together in two rooms. And where one might have thought that this would create tension, it led us to make the best of things. And making the best of things both physically and monetarily meant that we had to get along. We did, and in the process we became a better family. Most important, where there used to be tension between my parents, especially on Jewish holidays, there was none during that fall of 1939. I enjoyed the new atmosphere, especially knowing that I didn't need to worry about a loud argument at dinner before Yom Kippur or at lunch on Rosh Hashanah.

In January 1940, we got our American immigration visas. In those days the words "your number has come up" was the most joyous news one could receive. Now that we had visas, it was time to find passage. We found it on a medium-sized Cunard liner, the *Scythia,* which was due to sail from Liverpool on February 22.

We had ample time to say our good-byes. I had become accustomed to London. I had learned to ride my bicycle on the left side of the street, become used to saying "Lovely day, isn't it?" before the postman could say it, and even exchanged some of my German accent for an approximation of British English, less exaggerated than what Dr. Plaut had drummed into us.

We didn't get to know many British people. There was Mrs. Webb, of course, our later landlords, the Singers, the postman, and the store people where my mother went shopping. Without much conversation or special effort, these people made us feel at home, safe. This feeling of safety probably predisposed us to feel pro-British. As distant as we were from them in language, customs, and traditions, we felt close to them in a shared hostility toward the Nazis. Even though the bombing had not yet started when we left, British sailors and passengers on British ships had become victims of Hitler's submarines, and Britain made convincing preparations for resistance to any Nazi attack.

My father was so buoyed up by being among people who opposed Hitler that he worried little about the trans-Atlantic hazards. My mother was anxious, but she had learned not to be too vocal about it. I was excited. The *Scythia* was not a luxury liner; it was a medium-sized, rather sad-looking ship, and the people who crowded its decks, with their well-worn German clothes and suitcases, made it look sadder still. We boarded on a cold, gray winter morning in the busy but weary-looking harbor of Liverpool.

Many people traveled as cheaply as they could—the equivalent of steerage. Somehow, my parents' relationship with the HAPAG's Halder in Frankfurt yielded us a ticket that was convertible in part for Cunard. In wartime that convertibility counted for little, but it was enough to get us, with some London-saved pounds added, a small cabin at the water line. We were told that the time of our voyage was uncertain, since the route was being determined as we proceeded, in light of orders from Navy craft who were escorting the convoy of which we were a unit. We knew beforehand that this meant zigzagging and other time-consuming maneuvers. "And still, it doesn't mean we're safe," my mother said, true to her irrespressible pessimism.

"So should we have stayed home, or in London, where we couldn't stay, or what?" my father would respond. The answer was that habitual lifting of the right eyelid that said, "I know, but it's still no good . . ."

Neither the grayness of Liverpool, nor the cold, nor the frugality of the accommodations and the crowds that spilled into the narrow hallways could dampen my excitement. We were crossing the ocean, we'd sail under the protection of the British Navy, but, above all, we'd go to America. America! New York! Now that we were heading there, the Wild West stories and the gangsters that Opa used to warn of dropped from memory. All I could see in my mind were the towers of lower Manhattan, of which I had seen so many postcard pictures and photographs. And Times Square! I couldn't wait to see all those lights. And Roosevelt. Maybe there'd be a parade, and I'd see him! And surely I could hear his speeches over the radio, loud and clear, and not just patches over the crackling shortwave!

What saddened Mother, beyond her fears of an unknown future, was her father. As we were sailing across that ocean, made more fearsome by dark clouds and seemingly endless periods of heavy waves, we were moving farther away from Opa every hour, every minute. She had learned not to talk about it too often, because she knew that my father was burdened by his responsibility for the family and by an indeterminate period of study and no income. Mother and I would have to earn the money for our needs. And I was no longer Robertche. I had already earned money in London and become a different person. The diminutive had dropped sometime during that winter, and neither of us seemed to be fazed by it. It was quite natural.

Mother also thought of Oma Hilda. We were moving away from her as well—from that grave in the Jewish cemetery on Eckenheimer Landstrasse that conjured up such horror. Would Opa still be able to visit it? Could he still go up there in the tram? After all, he had been taking those iodine pills for more than ten years, and my father had written all kinds of prescriptions, just in case . . . Both the Frohmanns and the Florsheims had hypertension . . . It could happen. And then? Would Dr. Binsack still be permitted to care for a Jew? Would there be a hospital where Opa could be admitted if necessary? "We have to get him over," Mutti kept saying. "I'll work at two jobs if necessary, but we have to get him over. Can you imagine what might happen once the war really breaks out?"

My father understood, and consoled Mutti. He understood. It was refugee conversation. All those passengers had their own burdens and regrets and worries about the future.

Refugee conversation also included deep bitterness about the Germans. In London and on the way to New York, I heard merciless condemnations of neighbors, colleagues, the German people as a whole. My parents joined the discussion, but with a difference: Father always condemned individuals and the political leadership; he did not chime in when some of our fellow refugees swore eternal rejection of everything German.

We were free to speak now, without worrying about being overheard. The horror of the Nazi evil had registered and fastened once we were out of Hitler's clutches. There was also the bitterness of disappointment in those refugee voices: they had been rejected by a culture of which they had felt a part, had to give up values and customs they had been proud to admire and share. We had been Germans, after all. Our mainstream organization was the Central Association of Germans of Jewish Faith. We spoke German, just like the non-Jews around us. And now we had to put a good deal of that life behind us.

My father, perhaps because he had never shared that sense of complete assimilation of so many German Jews, did not feel the need to throw out Goethe, Kant, and Heine along with Hitler. In fact, he used to quote Heine to underscore that everything was not so perfect in the old days. "Keine Messe wird man singen, keinen Kaddish wird man sagen," he used to recall ("No mass will be sung, no kaddish said," was a Heine poem about his feelings of not belonging). Yet Heine was a German poet; Freud was a scientist in the German cultural tradition. And so, just as my father had kept his head about our Germanness, he was not ready to abandon a cultural heritage that was rich, and could not be shed anyway, even if we wanted to. Perhaps this is a reason why, in later years, I could never join in the wholesale rejection of Germans and Germany.

The *Scythia* sailed on, and the farther into the ocean we went, the colder it became. What we realized later was that we were not just going west, or zigzagging within moderate limits on a southern latitude; we were going northwest. That cold had the effect of making the quarters even closer, and our contact with the patient but very overworked British crew occasionally became tense. One couldn't blame those stewards and officers. Unanswerable questions were pelted at them all day and evening—in heavily accented, often unintelligible English, or, when the passenger was upset, in German. "How long still?" "Wirds noch colder?" "When we turned just now, was it a U-boat?" "But we didn't turn, ma'am," was the answer to a lady who undoubtedly had unconsciously extended her concern about a submarine attack into a fact to which the *Scythia* had presumably responded. One fellow passenger was overheard to say, "If these *Engländer* weren't anti-Semitic when we started out, they surely will be by the time we land." My mother smiled and agreed. After all, it was always safer to worry, even with a smile. Jews practiced defensive humor, not gallows humor.

Close quarters, heavy seas, and unanswered questions notwithstanding—or perhaps because of it all—my father continued to adhere to his strict observance of religious customs: tefillin in the morning, silent grace after meals, afternoon and evening prayers. On the Sabbath, it was easy to get a minyan, a quorum of ten men, together, and to get an officer to approve the use of a small salon for services. I joined in on the Sabbath, but did not join Father in the everyday rituals. I was giving way to feelings that had become stronger over the months since we left Germany. I was not comfortable with what I felt was just too much ritual. It wasn't the time or the effort it took to complete all the required chores. It was the deeper questions that concerned me: Was God really interested in all these minute details of observance? And were there really different Gods who called for different kinds of beliefs and prayers?

I didn't go too far in asking these questions aloud of my father. I hinted of at some of them, because they bothered me. But I realized that it might hurt him to push deeper, toward the core issues that touched on faith. And he did not reject or dismiss my little stabs of doubt, or make me feel guilty about having them.

It was the beginning of a new phase in my life, one where I followed a different direction from that of my father. Mother did not interfere, if only because she did not share Father's post-1933 immersion in Orthodox observance. Father's insight and tolerance, and Mother's detachment and preoccupation with her father's future, converged in enabling to grow, to develop and shape my own views. A year earlier, I probably would have not let myself think as independently as I did on that voyage, always fearing that thundering "how could you?!"

After more than a week on the cold, gray, angry Atlantic Ocean, we saw land. We were told that we were approaching Halifax, Nova Scotia. I remembered something about Nova Scotia from our geography lessons in the Philanthropin. Dr. Freudenberger had taught us about Canada. We had made cruel fun of his lisp when he talked about the Hudson Bay, which he pronounced as "Hootthone Bye." Dr. Freudenberger dwelled on northern Canada quite a bit: he must have liked the images of its rugged, inhospitably cold land. So I remembered "Novah Thcoscha," too. And now here we were.

We all went on deck to get a look at the land, but it was too cold to stay more than a few minutes. "My nose is freezing off," my mother said. "Do you think it will be just as cold in New York?" Yes, even in that cold yet delicious moment when we had almost completed our voyage and were on the threshhold of a new life, Mutti was worrying about the future.

"No," my father answered. "New York is south of here, a long way south, so it won't be so cold."

"Ja," my mother answered, "aber weiss es auch der Hund?" This is a proverbial German response to someone who gives reassurance without having convincing evidence: someone had been warned about a dangerous dog, and was reassured that it was safe to go into the house because the owners were highly responsible people and knew what to do. "But does the dog know it, too?" goes the response. Mother often used this or similar expressions to put the damper on my father's optimism and willingness to take risks. In this sense, the instincts of my parents complemented each other nicely.

I was excited. Yes, it was icy cold. But we were in America, albeit not yet in the United States. When we left Halifax after a few hours, sailing toward New York, excitement caught hold of the other passengers, too, even though they showed it in the more sedate ways to which both upbringing and the experience of the last couple of years had accustomed them.

The *Scythia* was awfully slow. It seemed that the closer we came to New York, the more slowly the ship was moving. It was our anticipation, our expectations, our worries, the by now high tension in this refugee group that made the imperturbably steady engines of the old ship seem laggard. And then, on a beautiful March morning, we glimpsed the postcard that had become real.

Manhattan island! There it was. It was still cold, not as cold as in Halifax, but very cold indeed. Yet we didn't pay attention to the temperature now. "Vaal Shtreet!" somebody cried out. Everybody tried to show how much he or she knew about New York, both to show off and to persuade themselves that since it wasn't entirely unfamiliar, there was no need to be frightened.

Even my mother was smiling, at least for a moment letting go of her worries and her guilt feelings about her father. My father was calm, showing little of the emotion that had gripped most of us, especially the younger people. He knew he would have to force himself to stay home and let Mother and me work until he could resume his medical practice. Would he be able to pass an exam that he had studied for thirty years ago, plus all the new things he had to learn, and in English? Or should he change careers and drop medicine? No, he couldn't and shouldn't do that. Medicine was his life, not just his profession. He didn't say so, but his life said so.

The Grafs would be waiting for us at the pier. They had made it possible for us to save ourselves and to come this far. But there was little love lost in this relationship. Father and Flora had never been close, and Father did not want to be dependent on her. He felt more comfortable with her husband, Julius. Julius was a generous, cosmopolitan man, a man with whom Father could enjoy talking.

There was also tension between Oma Julie, who was living with the Grafs, and my mother. They had had little to say to each other on the few occasions when they met in Germany. But here, at least in the beginning, we'd all have to stay together. My father was on his wife's side. The issue of how this would be handled had come up several times during the voyage, and Father always was completely supportive of Mother, even though they disagreed or were out of harmony on many other matters. It reassured me, because it helped cement a relationship that was my anchor to life.

We were docking. Everybody had moved to one side of the boat to catch a glimpse of the welcomers on shore. We were landing on one of those wooden piers on the West Side; the buildings at the end of the pier didn't look too clean. And where were the Grafs? Eventually, Papi spotted his sister, who had pushed her small frame to the front row of the crowd on shore.

Admission and customs proceedings were simple, and we were soon united with Flora and Julius. Father and Mother asked lots of questions. There were some procedures to be taken care of about the luggage, which we would get later. We were here. That was accomplished. But every time something has been accomplished, at least in the culture in which we had been reared, it was not a cause for rejoicing, but for worrying about what would come next. As we left the pier in a taxi for West 149th Street, "Vaal Shtreet" had been left far behind us. Some very ordinary, not very clean houses bordered the streets we were riding through. We wondered what was in store for us.

sia, Sweden, Spain, and Portugal. And those were either Hitler's allies, or they carried on a forced-smile neutrality vis-à-vis Germany.

Grandfather kept writing us long letters on the thinnest airmail stationery imaginable. Only his perfect handwriting made them legible. They had been opened by both sides—the Nazi censors, who had reclosed them with swastika-stamped tape; and some British authority, since the letters had to go via Portugal, and the British were close enough to Lisbon's government to have access to the mail that passed through from Germany. With all this roundabout routing, Opa's letters said little. They were long, two pages of closely packed writing, but the contents were trivia about the weather, his room and food, when he was planning to wear his heavy coat. He did give indications of contact with his advisors, but they were so guarded that they told us little about possible travel plans. One letter had a postcript: "By the way, I feel fine." That was Opa: the details first, the headline last.

By summer, I had become accustomed to the routine at work and felt at home there. But the process had a price: I was paid back, cheaply and gently enough, for German Jews' attitudes toward Eastern European Jews when we lived in Germany. The entire work crew in the cutting room at 498 was composed of Eastern European Jews, while I was the "Yecke," their pejorative term for a German Jew. The term derives from the German word *Jacke,* or jacket, and has an important social meaning: German Jews wore jackets, while Eastern European Jews worked in shirtsleeves—a class and cultural distinction. German Jews were "higher class," but also snobs; they dressed and acted like Gentiles, and either neglected or played down their Jewishness. Most important, they treated Eastern European Jews with contempt and whenever possible avoided contact.

I did not fully realize all this when I started work at David Crystal, Inc. But the snide comments of the cutters soon began to make sense. In Reinheim there were no *Polacken* or *Ostjuden,* and in Frankfurt they lived in the eastern part of town. My grandfather's views of *Polacken* were those of many, probably most, German Jews toward the unassimilated immigrants from Poland and Hungary. They wore beards and forelocks, and we had and wanted nothing in common with them, except our religion. They were as different from us as they were from Gentiles, and we resented that in *Der Stürmer* all Jews were caricatured as *Polacken.*

"All they do is make it worse for us," Grandfather would say, "with their *mauscheln* [talking Yiddish-accented German], those clothes and beards and *peyes* [forelocks], and their loud and boisterous behavior." Mother would agree, but Father indicated he did not, pulling up his right eyebrow and tipping his head sideways. There was no point in arguing with Opa on his many articles of prejudiced faith.

Even in the mid-1930s, we maintained our separateness from the *Ostjuden,* while the Nazis proclaimed, through vicious caricatures, the unity of the Jewish people. Ours was a deeply engrained attitude that should not be seen as pure, ill-willed prejudice designed to serve our self-preservation at the cost of people who were our brothers. It was that, but it was more. It was a way to celebrate our assimilation, to ensure the triumph of Jews who had become Germans by sealing themselves off against Jews who resisted the march of progress, the blessings of enlightenment, and the security of integration into one of the great cultures, if not *the* great culture, of the Western world. In those years, we could not allow those Eastern intruders to make things worse by shoring up Hitler's stereotyped view of the Jews. After all, Hitler was a passing phenomenon. The culture we shared with the Germans would not allow him to stay very long as chancellor. We German Jews had accomplished what no other Jewish community had ever achieved. We would not, we could not abandon our history-making assimilation without a clear signal that we had nothing in common with those people.

All this history informed those looks, remarks, and "come here, Yekke" summonses from Mike Claw and Siegel and Plotkin at the long cutting tables. But my supreme test was the hazing they had decided to visit upon me, in what would become my card of admission to the cutting-room community.

My job was to assist Jack Scoppelli, the head of the stockroom. The stockroom wasn't really a room, but a long, narrow space along the wall opposite the windows of the cutting room. Here all the rolls and bolts of cloth were stored. The storeroom housed what at the beginning seemed an endless, unlearnable variety of materials, patterns, and colors. Each roll or bolt had a label with the various numbers that designated it, plus the color. The colors bore romantic names, which sounded less so in the pronunciation of head cutter Mike Claw and his men. One of them would call out "tvenny-niny faw, B, vistaria," or "fory-toity-dree, Amarric'n beaudy," and we'd zero in on the desired piece of goods, take it from the rack, and deliver it into the metal cradle that allowed the cutter to pull the length needed for one garment onto the table and impale it on nails at the other end. Then the cutter would place as many layers on top of the first as the order called for, lay out the pattern as it had been worked out by Mike Claw to yield as little waste as possible, turn on his machine, and steer the rapidly rotating blade through ten, twenty, even forty layers of material with the ease of a spoon through whipped cream.

Joe Calabrese had made the pattern, based on Mr. Morgan's design. Mike had laid it out on the material, often calling Calabrese to see whether a minor change could be made to save material without altering the design. Sometimes they'd argue, with tempers and accents flaring. It was an exchange that bore resemblance neither to Dr. Plaut, nor to London, nor even to the English I heard on New York radio stations. "But it-a wont werka," Joe would shout, and Mike would answer, "So make it voik!" He'd point to a piece of pattern, move it just a few millimeters, and ask, "Nu, dis voodnt voik?" Joe would reluctantly say, "per-a-haps-a," and the problem was solved.

I had worked at David Crystal's for a little over a week when Mike Claw called me. "*Yecke*," he said, "go to Mister Dreddy and ask him for the goods stretcher."

"The goods stretcher?" I asked, looking for an explanation, because this was an important assignment: going up to the paneled area of the showrooms to talk with Vincent Draddy, the Irish son-in-law of David Crystal and an exceptional phenomenon in this almost all-Jewish field of business.

"Yeah," Mike answered impatiently, "how often d'I haff te say it? The goods stretcher. Go awready."

Dressed in my shirtsleeves and wearing a lint-speckled apron, I hesitantly proceeded to a place I had never been to before—that rarified, elegant world of blond, tall, blue-eyed Mister Draddy; equally blond, but more suave and sophisticated-looking Mr. Morgan; and those heavenly women, the models, just a glimpse of whom made working in the garment center worthwhile. Into this world strode the aproned *Yecke*.

I gently knocked on Draddy's door. "Who is it?" he asked. I opened the door, found him seated on a chair opposite two distinguished-looking ladies. They were buyers. A frown came over his forehead as Draddy asked, angrily, "What do you want?"

"The goods stretcher," I answered.

Draddy jumped up, and screaming "get out of here!" pushed me out and slammed the door.

This was it. I was fired, I was certain. "How could you?!" was screaming through my head, coming simultaneously from mother and myself. My job was gone! How and when would I get another one? It was all my fault!

As I was trudging back slowly, I realized that I had fallen for a cruel joke. How could I not have realized it before my fatal knock on Draddy's door?!

When I approached the cutting room, there was complete silence, an unusual state of affairs among the always shmoozing cutters. As soon as I entered the room, an avalanche of laughter descended on me, burying me in shame, humiliation, anger, and self-accusation. I felt like crying, but managed to stave it off. That would give them more satisfaction.

As the laughter died down, Mike called me over. "Come, *Yecke,* I vonna tawk te ye. It's awright, vas jost a joke."

"But Draddy was so angry," I said. "I'm sure I lost my job, and I need my job."

"Naw, you dint lose your job, Robert," Mike said, for the first time calling me by my name. "Draddy knows it's a joke. You're awright . . ."

I did not lose my job. Instead I gained the respect of the cutters. I was still a *Yecke,* but they had cut me down; I still held my head high, just not too high, as stubborn and incurable *Yeckes* would. In those days, we were fair game; the full measure of Nazi persecution we had experienced had not yet registered with American Jews.

Our fear of saying the wrong thing had become an instinctive reaction. Yes, we were in America now, and we could say what we wanted without having to worry about the Gestapo. But our instinct of looking around before we said something in a public place was still with us. This became comically clear one summer day on the sidewalk of Seventh Avenue, as the lunch-hour crowd squeezed forward, sideways or diagonally, to wherever they were heading.

At the beginning of the summer, a new man had joined the stockroom crew. He was George Agree, a freshman at UCLA whose father had found him a summer job at Crystal's so he could get work experience. George and I became lifelong friends. But in those summer days at 498, we were just becoming acquainted. We found ourselves instantly drawn to each other: he because I was a recent immigrant from Nazi Germany, the kind of person he had read about but never met, and from whom he wanted to soak up firsthand information; and I because here was someone with whom I could talk about music or literature or American politics—all things I didn't think the cutters cared about or cared to discuss with me.

George was intensely, sympathetically, and thoughtfully interested in what made us refugees from Hitler's Germany tick. His family was not religious. But they were consciously and openly Jewish. This Jewishness minus religion was a new experience for me and was to have a decisive influence on my life. George was also a political person—in those days not professionally so, but one could have foreseen that he would make politics his central interest in life.

One hot day in the summer in 1940, at lunch hour, George was once again talking politics. It was a few months before the election, and Roosevelt, our hero, was running for a third term. George was always critical of Roosevelt for not leading the country more actively to join the Allies in the war. At one point, he shouted out, "Roosevelt stinks!" which triggered my accustomed reaction: an instinctive frightened expression as I looked around the crowd on the street. Before I could say anything, George laughed out loud. He said he had deliberately shouted to see how I would react. And I came through for him!

Politics was not the only thing American I was learning. The summer of 1940 made a baseball fan of me. This was to make me different from every German refugee I knew, and I am sure virtually the entire German-Jewish immigrant community. Even today, more than fifty years later, people who came here in the 1930s in that soccer-attuned wave from central Europe can't understand why Americans like baseball. "*Merkwürdig* [strange and weird]," Herr Nussbaum, a family friend, would say after having been taken to a game, "these players just stand around doing nothing, and the public gets all excited and screams as if something were happening!"

I knew better. Jack Scoppelli had taught me. In that hot stockroom, Jack would talk forever about the Yankees. Soon they had become a symbol for me: America, winners, heroes . . . In the course of talking about the previous day's game, Jack would explain to me what it was all about. He was determined to make me a fan, partly because, apart from girls, that was all he cared to talk about; he also needed someone to talk to who understood the game, so that his comments would be duly appreciated, even contradicted, so a discussion, or maybe even an argument, would ensue to serve as entertainment.

So I learned about baseball from a teacher who was determined to make me understand not just the rules, but the wisdom and lack thereof of different strategies and managerial decisions. And though Jack was an ardent Yankee fan, with Joe DiMaggio the equivalent of Beniamino Gigli in my cultural ballpark, he would not hesitate to criticize, even consign to temporary hell, the great and legendary manager Joe McCarthy for having given a hit sign when a walk was "the only thing he coulda and shoulda done . . . the joik!"

After a few weeks of indoctrination, and once I had demonstrated in our discussions under the wisteria and vermilion bolts that I had caught on, Jack invited me to join him at Yankee Stadium on a Sunday afternoon. I shall never forget that first baseball experience, which sparked the flame of fanship in my *Yecke* soul! It was a game against the Chicago White Sox, with Johnny Rigney as the opposing pitcher. The remainder of the Sox lineup has long since escaped me, but the Yankee team will always be with me: Babe Dahlgren at first; Joe Gordon at second; Phil Rizzuto at short; Red Rolfe at third; and that never-to-be-equaled outfield of "King Kong" Keller, Joe DiMaggio, and Tommy Henrich. Pitching was Spud Chandler and catching the great Bill Dickey.

Jack had prepared me well. DiMaggio, Chandler, Dickey, and Rizzuto had all become heroes in my mind. And here they were in the flesh! And all these people understood what was going on! I made a quantum leap forward that Sunday toward becoming part of the American community, of the culture in which sports—whatever the country—plays such a significant and characterizing role.

I joined in shouting approval with every strike Chandler threw. The trouble that day was that it wasn't one of the great Spud's best days. But for such situations, the Yankees always had "Fireman" Murphy—the best relief pitcher in either league—to put out the flames.

The trouble was that Ruffing had permitted too many runs to score, and though Murphy stopped the Sox, Rigney blanked the Yankees. Jack was crestfallen, because he wanted the Yankees to win for me, to nail down my commitment. He didn't need to worry. I was a dedicated Yankee fan from that day on, who listened to the play-by-play on the radio whenever there was a chance, usually on weekends. Eight years later, long after I had left the garment center, I converted my Prague-born wife into a Yankee fan, as we both discussed what was happening in our incongruously accented English.

My attempts to explain baseball's fascination to my parents and friends remained unsuccessful. "Will ohne baseball gluecklich sein [I prefer to be happy without knowing baseball]," my father would say, implying that he had other priorities and worries. It was a variation on Walther von Stolzing's comment in the *Meistersinger* by Wagner after he had passed the singing test of the master guild ("I shall find happiness without any masters . . . "), and it was the perfect choice of words to articulate the culture gap.

That widening culture gap had implications for my sense of Jewish identity. There had never been any question about my being both German and Jewish, until the experiences of the 1930s began to raise questions. The Nazis had told us that we were not Germans; and my father told me I was Jewish, and sent me to Rabbi Donath to provide extra food for my supposedly Jewish-starved mind and soul. Amid all the things that happened and the conflicting influences, both public and private, that confused rather than focused the issues, I went to my lessons, as a required routine rather than a desired or needed source of knowledge. Up to the Kristallnacht crisis, we continued to listen to our favorite music, to read our Goethe, Schiller, and Shakespeare, and didn't have time, or didn't care to think about, those identity questions.

By the time we arrived in America, the issues still had not been resolved in my mind, and there was no time to think about them. Our focus was to earn enough money to keep ourselves housed, clothed, and fed, and to get Grandfather over if we still could get him out of Germany. Father continued his religious observances, but I had long since ceased to attend synagogue regularly, and had not any Hebrew or religious lessons since we left Frankfurt. Now George Agree and his parents seemed to be showing me a new way: Jewishness without the synagogue, or at least without the synagogue as a requirement for Jewish identification.

George and I discussed this new kind of Jewishness, and George's family and I had talks about Zionism, Jews in America, and above all, America as a society. Things began to fall into place when I looked at all those different kinds of people in the subway, the streetcar, or on the street. They were all Americans—white, black, brown, Chinese, blond . . . Not that the race theory of Hitler had left any favorable or deep impression, but there was something sharply and appealingly contrasting in this infinite variety of New York that, just by being there, challenged and contradicted all that the Nazis were talking about.

So how did Jews fit in?

"Just like all the others," George would say.

And his father would add: "Robert, here you can be Jewish and American and Zionist and atheistic—whatever you decide is right for you. This is what America is all about."

What I saw and heard was both confusing and exciting. And what seemed beyond question was that it was in our interest, not just as Jews but as people, to support this outlook. Wasn't it in our interest as a minority to stress our humanness and our being part of a world community above our "specialness" as Jews? Wouldn't it advance everybody's sense of security and comfort if we could get rid of all the things that divided people and build up those that united them?

It was my tendency, once I had grasped something, to go all out. So it was with my sense of who and what am I. Somewhere I had heard or read about an organization called the Society for Ethical Culture. I got their literature, and it seemed to answer a lot of questions. Ethical Culture promoted universal ethical values, the breaking down of religious, racial, and other walls in the interest of values that everyone could make his own.

Wouldn't that be just the right thing for me? That it was not the lesson to draw from what America was all about did not become clear to me for some time. I did not understand that what was different about America was that it tolerated, indeed was made up of, differences rather than was committed to wiping them out. No, I had to go all out. Perhaps it was also a reaction to my years of suppressed resentment of being steeped in heavy Jewish lore—from Hebrew to

Talmud—by my father. Then, while we lived in Germany, I was afraid to rebel; now that new priorities, new influences, a new world had changed everything in our lives, the way seemed open to new directions. The requirements of making a living and other day-to-day necessities made it easy to stop participating in what I hadn't liked, without making a scene or openly defying my father. But it took some time before I actively pursued my new ways. Ethical Culture seemed interesting, but not yet ripe for my commitment.

What I also heard at the Agrees, as well as from refugee families in our acquaintance, was merciless condemnation of Germany. The same attitude, albeit in more measured language, colored the editorials in the newspapers—the *New York Times, Herald Tribune, World-Telegram,* and several others that then still competed for the New York reader.

My parents felt the same bitterness, with a difference: my father had no mercy for the Nazis, but this did not affect his sense of the cultural heritage that, along with his newly acquired Jewish identification, was his intellectual and spiritual environment. Father never said so specifically, but his feeling was that one did not throw out Goethe with Hitler—that to do so, in fact, would give Hitler a victory.

We spoke German at home, even though with time American expressions for which there was no ready German equivalent—"ze subveh," "a sandvitch," toast, and soda—slipped into the interstices of German sentences (*Untergrundbahn, Butterbrot, Rösterbrot,* and *Sprudelwasser* began to sound artificial and came to mind less readily after a few months). As time went on, this trend accelerated, to the point where German became a mere frame for English words and phrases.

What made Father and me different from most Jews, both refugee and indigenous, was that we did not feel hate or contempt for everything German. My father would hum his favorite tune—Walter von Stolzing's "Am stillen Herd" from the *Meistersinger*—while American Jews who never were physically close to Nazi persecution refused to attend performances of Wagner's operas. We did not discuss this; we just felt it. This sense of sharing in the German culture, even as I became legally and culturally Americanized over the years, has remained with me. I have never regretted it. Rather, I feel I have benefited from cultivating it: it has made me feel qualified to discuss

German-Jewish issues after the war and throughout the ups and downs of the Federal Republic and, finally, reunification, realistically and with constructive objectives for both Jews and Germans.

In those early American days, the issue did not come up too often or as heatedly as in later years. We were what we were, argued lightly and occasionally, mostly worried about making ends meet, getting Grandfather over, and letting Father study. The things that were happening to us that were significant for the long run and for finding our way culturally and socially were developing imperceptibly, like a plant's growth. One could only see what was going on after months or years had gone by.

Mother and I were highly sensitive about our accent in English. What surprised us was that nobody seemed to mind. And we realized, in a sort of double-take caused by our almost complete preoccupation with ourselves and how we would be perceived by others, that many, if not most, "Americans" spoke with an accent. So what was this being American all about? It wasn't people looking like Roosevelt or Cordell Hull, whose picture we had seen so often before we came here, although it was fine, perhaps even good, to look like that. It wasn't people speaking American English, like Al Grobe on WQXR, the classical music station in New York, although that sounded nice, and it would be nice to speak like that. It certainly wan't people looking like Old Surehand who was fighting the Indians in Karl May's books, certainly not in New York, although there probably were people like that in the West. You could be and were American if you were black or white, Chinese or Puerto Rican, and if you spoke with an accent that even many Americans, native or naturalized, had trouble understanding. Was this really so? Hitler would go crazy here!

It was much too early for me to grasp the theoretical underpinnings of this society. George had talked about it a lot, and I continued my contact with his parents, who were my first unintentional tutors about America, after he had returned to school in California. But the people and things I saw every day made an impact that I discerned later on. And the seeds of learning that George and his family had planted were growing. They are the roots of my intellectual development as an American.

Fall and winter came, and New York became gray again, after a hot summer the likes of which we had never gone through in Europe.

But nothing physically uncomfortable mattered. Even the dirt on the streets, the elevated trains clattering infernally on Third Avenue, and the puddles on the street corners were fine. Indeed, if only Grandfather were here, all the dirt and noise and exhaust mixed with hotdog odors would be pleasant to the senses. The war still seemed to be in a state of suspense. But there was no longer any way to dredge up hope that it could end this way, or that it should.

Not only was Grandfather's life at stake, but we had not had word from the Wassermanns in Paris. Gertrude was another of my mother's cousins, married to a lace importer who had emigrated to Paris, where he had business connections. We read that the Germans had also pounced on the Jews in France and other occupied countries. What might have happened to the Wassermanns and their daughter, Ilse? For a while, they had tried to help us from Paris, and now and then my father cited them as having had more sense than we did for leaving early. We never heard from them again. We recently learned from the Washington Holocaust records that they had died in Auschwitz. Their fate demonstrated the futility of trying to figure out events, all the more so with a regime that did suicidal things which turned out to be triumphs.

Everything that had happened and was happening led us to think and act in terms of immediate needs—today and tomorrow and for Opa. That meant working for my mother and myself, studying for my father, and saving money, literally nickels and dimes.

All our clothing was German-bought. We had packed as much as our luggage could accommodate. It made us instantly recognizable on the streets of New York, as it had in London. They were good clothes, and they lasted a long time. It wasn't until the mid-1940s that we had both the need and the money to buy clothes in New York. The transition was gradual. The suit and tie I wore for my passport picture in Frankfurt were still serviceable six or seven years later, when I was working at the Voice of America on Broadway and 57th Street. One of my American colleagues there said one day, "Hey, Bob, why don't you buy yourself a suit instead of wearing that German straightjacket!" Eventually I did, but to this day I hate to go shopping for clothes. "I have enough," I tell my wife, pointing to my fifteen-year-old suits and jackets of good quality. And I still use two pairs of shoetrees I brought from Frankfurt, vintage 1939.

On February 8, 1941, a telegram came from HAPAG-Frankfurt announcing that Hermann Frohmann was due to sail on the Portuguese ship *Angola* on March 25. This meant that he had his American immigration visa and transit approvals through the Iberian countries. It also meant that somehow the Germans had approved his travel through Germany and France. But would it really happen? Could it happen?

Mother was constantly speculating about all the mishaps, the traps, the duplicity of the Nazis, perhaps even of the HAPAG! Her cousin Siegfried Flörsheim, who had been the key to the papers for Grandfather, was trying to reassure her. My father's and my attempts to relieve her anxiety were unsuccessful. "You just want to make me feel good," Mother would say, "but you have doubts, too. I know it." There was no way to provide reassurance to someone so certain to reject it. After all, feeling good was irresponsible in such a situation; only anxiety could yield a defense against *Übermütigkeit*.

It wasn't all neurosis on my mother's part. It was also the memory of my grandmother's suicide. Everything had to be done, in practice, in silent prayer, and in the avoidance of sinful expectation, to prevent another tragedy.

A month and a half to sweat it out! And who knew what Hitler would do in those six weeks that would foil Grandfather's trip to Portugal? Toward the end of February another HAPAG cable came: Hermann Frohmann would not sail as previously advised, but would leave on April 15 with the ship *Nyassa*. This really set my mother off. "All lies!" she shouted.

"No, Halder wouldn't do that," Father said. "I am sure everything is in order, just that the ship in March may have been overbooked. Don't forget, this is the only escape route left, and I am sure there are thousands of people in Lisbon trying to get on the next steamer to America. He'll come, don't worry."

It was all speculation by Father, but, it turned out, he was right. There was lots of wheeling and dealing going on in Lisbon in those days, with the shipowners in the market for the highest "geito." Bribe is too coarse a translation; "lubricant" is more accurate—something to make things work properly that otherwise might encounter a hitch. "Don't be silly," Mother would say. "You always think of those explanations—the Portuguese taking advantage of an old German

Jew. Why should they?" My mother's response was a convergence of several strands of thought and feeling: things were bound to go wrong; things were either black or white; Germans were all-powerful, and all others, including the Portuguese, had nothing to say.

The worrying out loud, our attempts to respond helpfully, work, the winter weather—it made those February and March days of 1941 miserable. The sky seemed darker gray, the tall buildings in the semi-daylight of winter depressing—not at all the same as they had been when we approached the harbor a year earlier.

We had by then acquired a secondhand radio, a table model. It didn't sound like the Agrees' Harmon-Kardon, but it was a lot better than a home without music. Father and Mother didn't listen much, he because he studied compulsively and she because she was busy worrying, so I had it pretty much to myself. WQXR became my source of beautiful sounds, my combination concert auditorium, opera house, and recital hall.

Before that time, my knowledge and interest had been centered on opera, Italian opera specifically, because this is what we had listened to regularly in the evenings at home in Frankfurt. WQXR introduced me to the lied, chamber music, and symphony. Lieder and chamber music were not my favorites at that time (they became highest priority in later years). It was those symphonies, played by great orchestras in America and Europe, under conductors who became my new heroes—Toscanini, Beecham, Furtwängler—that grabbed me: first those of Mozart, then, more gradually, Beethoven's, and finally, with an impact that they have never lost, even as I passed into middle and older age, the four of Johannes Brahms. Darmstadt was my introduction to music; in Frankfurt, EIAR, the Italian radio, and, for a short while, the Jewish Kulturbund, developed my involvement and my caring; the table radio on West 100th Street helped me to acquire a solid base of taste, a frame of reference for how styles and scope changed and grew—in scale, harmonies, volume of sound, from the filigree perfection of Mozart to the vastness of Brahms' Fourth.

I was lying on my cot in the kitchen, listening, looking out the window at a big sumac tree. To me, it was a *Lindenbaum* from one of those romantic German poems. On a bright Sunday, a Mozart symphony, the tree, and the sun did wonders for me.

Finally, we received definitive word that Hermann Frohmann had embarked on the *Nyassa* at Lisbon on April 15. Mother believed it and was relieved, but only for a moment: A Portuguese ship? How seaworthy was it? What route would it travel? How long would the voyage take? There were no solid answers to these questions, but the best guess was that it would take in excess of a week. Opa arrived on April 25. He came down the gangplank with his solitary suitcase, age seventy-five, and there was a since unequaled sense of fulfillment: the family was reunited.

Grandfather looked grayer than New York looked that April day. His full head of hair was unchanged, but his face looked much older, with more creases. He looked paler, terribly tired. His clothes were rumpled. He was a contrast to the way he wanted to look, the way he thought it all important for people to look to deserve their peers' respect. Fortunately, he did not know it.

We took a taxi for this important trip. The conversation on the ride was general, above all relaxed. Mutti was crying, and Father and I (Mother and I had both taken off from work) were happy, sitting on the two jumpseats of the Checker cab, leaving the backseat to Grandfather and my mother.

It was only six days until my twentieth birthday, and it was the best present I could get. At 100th Street, Opa was impressed with the apartment. He was overcome by the size of the room, and even though we had written to him that this was the only room there was—aside from kitchen and bath—he was happy. We had some tea and cake, and Grandfather was introduced to his new quarters: a corner in that grand room, separated from the rest of the space by a secondhand screen from Columbus Avenue. My parents had their bedstead in the opposite corner, near the window to the sumac. Their window was at a ninety-degree angle from the one in the kitchen through which I got my glimpse of the world.

An overflowing feeling of contentment filled that room in the greystone after Grandfather had washed up and sat down in the one big easy chair we had bought on Columbus. The strain of suspense, of waiting, of the voyage showed, but his eyes radiated relaxation—the first time Opa could feel genuinely secure after more than two years of inner struggle. Alone in his pension in Nesenstrasse, he suffered the pain of his waning faith in things he had believed in all his life. He came to realize that his and every Jew's life was in danger, that Germany's military victories were Hitler's victories, and that one could no longer identify one's own hopes with those triumphs. As Nazi terror mounted and the Rechtsstaat became the laughingstock of Joseph Goebbels' cruelly clever speeches, Opa had to do something that was previously inconceivable: hope for Hitler's, and thereby Germany's, defeat! He who was so proud of his service in the Kaiser's army, for whom Germany and German military tradition and discipline had been deeply rooted sources of respect and loyalty, had to hope for the victory of France and England!

He didn't spell it out (Opa wasn't a man of sophisticated thought or speech), but even on that first day some of what he had gone through and of the new thinking he had developed came through: "Well, it kept getting more terrible all the time," he'd say, or "Beutel [the accountant and loyal advisor] put the fear of God into me . . . that I'd have to get out as soon as possible."

For the next few days, we went out of our way to give Grandfather a chance to become accustomed to his new surroundings. We did not encourage him to go out, lest too much that was new and unfamiliar upset him. After all, he was seventy-five, and he had long suffered from hypertension. We did not encourage him to talk, but rather left it to him to open himself up. It was clear he needed to speak. For Grandfather, who had never been loquacious, these early days developed into a story with many strands: how he traveled, how he was helped, and what life was like in Frankfurt during eighteen months of war.

He had his passport since August 1940, with the restriction that it was valid only for emigration to the United States. Grandfather was able to get the all-important document on the basis of papers that showed that it was only a matter of time before he would receive his U.S. immigration visa. Along with his passport, he got his *Sichtvermerk,* the approval for departure showing that he had met all the tax and other obligations he had to the German state. This was marked "to the U.S.A. via Königsberg, Lithuania, and Soviet Russia." At that time, after the fall of Western Europe, travel through that part of the continent was barred, and only the trans-Siberian railroad was available. That would have meant taking a ship from Vladivostok across the Pacific.

But across this *Sichtvermerk* is a big stamp, *Ungültig* (invalid), followed six months later by a new one marked "for crossing the border to Spain and Portugal." Grandfather explained that sometime in the second half of 1940, after the German occupation of France had settled in and the borders brought under control, the Nazis reopened travel through the West, and his advisors counseled him to take this much less arduous route.

It was only when we heard Grandfather tell his story and looked at his passport that we realized how little, if anything, he was able to decide for himself, and that whatever room for a would-be Jewish emigrant's decision there was had to be left to his advisors. Thus, Opa's fate was in the hands of a hostile government and of two advisors whose loyalty to their client and passenger led them to piece together a way out of the Nazi vise. "You see, I just did what they told me to do," Grandfather said, with the tone of both resignation and confidence in Beutel and Halder.

What they told him saved his life and led to an exit that only a few German Jews were still able to gain. One thing was certain, and that was Grandfather's decision: he would only leave legally, in accordance with the requirements of the regulations that permitted emigration. And his advisors concurred. This, too, was fortunate. For had Grandfather been counseled to cross a frontier, such as to Switzerland, at night, with the aid of people who were not in good repute, he would have refused. And had there been no legal way out, he would have gone the way of the six million. It was a heaven-sent gift that he was spared this fate, and the quandary that he would have resolved in a way that would have led to tragedy.

By the end of 1940, when Nazi power in the West had been consolidated and the frontier into Spain brought under German control, the authorities reopened travel through France. Halder then got Opa a new *Sichtvermerk*, dated January 24, 1941, that permitted him to travel via Spain and Portugal, and to do so within a three-month period, until April 23, 1941. The American immigration visa—the most desired commodity for a European Jew in modern history—was stamped into Grandfather's passport by Vice Consul A. John Cope, Jr., at the U.S. Consulate in Stuttgart on March 17, 1941.

Grandfather told his story over a period of several days. He was tired, stunned by the newness around him, gripped by a gamut of emotions, from being with us and being safe to being unsure of what lay in store for him, how he would find his way in such a totally different environment, missing his friends left behind in Nesenstrasse. He seemed numb, groping, anxious. He liked to wear an old cardigan and keep his pocket watch in his vest. His strong nose had shrunk a bit, his color had become less pink, and he seemed thinner, even smaller. And so gray—in his face, his clothes, his mood. Opa was always a bit stooped. Now he was more so. "I have a regular hunchback, no?" he would say, telling us in his way that events had taken their toll, had pushed him down.

The tale of Hermann Frohmann's escape from Nazi Germany continues: Upon receipt of the U.S. immigration visa, Grandfather had to travel to Berlin to get his transit visa through Portugal from the Portuguese Embassy there. He did so, on March 29. From Berlin, the Reichsbahn took him to Düsseldorf, where the Spanish consulate responsible for the western half of Germany issued its transit permit. Date: March 31. With that, Grandfather was set to go.

HAPAG had provided the rail ticket to Lisbon, and both Halder and Beutel accompanied Grandfather to the Hauptbahnhof. Grandfather told us how he boarded a train, went to his assigned seat, and that Beutel helped him stow away his suitcase. What Grandfather didn't realize until later was that he was traveling on a train under the aegis of the Wehrmacht. Soldiers kept passing through the corridors, as Hermann Frohmann, with a big red J for Jew on the first page of his passport, with swastika stamps all over the pages, and those three life-saving visas, rode to freedom through occupied France! After two days, the train reached the Spanish border, and that passport got a new stamp. Opa was too tired, too bewildered, too numbed by the mind's spontaneous defense against the excessive, unmanageable impact of too many conflicting feelings, to understand that it would once be seen as special, perhaps even historic: it's the rectangular, black imprint of the Grenzpolizei (German border police) customs post at Hendaye, on the Bay of Biscay. Date: April 3.

So the normally slow and deliberately moving Hermann Frohmann got his last visa in Düsseldorf on March 31, and was in Hendaye by railroad on April 3. After two more days of train travel through western Spain, he crossed the frontier into Portugal at Fuentes de

Oñoro, west of the city of Salamanca, on April 5. He arrived in Lisbon on April 7, which means he was riding the rails of Germany, France, and Iberia for a week.

Grandfather did not describe his trip as a complaint. He was matter-of-fact about it, and some of the details of his frontier crossings he did not even know about or was too exhausted to ask about. They are recorded in that passport, whose pages speak volumes about the cruelty, the contradictions, the pedantic demands and performance of bureaucracy amid massive illegality, and the marginality, almost irrelevance, of a human being in that grotesque environment.

A Jewish organization received Grandfather at the Lisbon station and quartered him in a room for a week, until the sailing of the *Nyassa*. He did not tell us much about the week in Lisbon, except that the food was not tasty, which meant he was not used to it, and that the few Reichsmarks he was allowed to take with him did not permit him to buy anything.

The *Nyassa* took on passengers on April 15, her sailing date. Normally it was plying the route to the then-Portuguese colony of Angola in Africa, but Hitler had made trans-Atlantic refugee traffic more lucrative, and Lisbon had become the primary port of departure. Stray Jews who were still able to get out all headed for Lisbon, like pins strewn over a wide area attracted by a magnet. There were enough of them—mostly illegal arrivals in Portugal who had paid substantial sums for steerage—to make it good business for Portuguese shipping companies.

By sailing time, the ship was loaded to the gills, mostly with steerage passengers. Grandfather, who had purchased a regular ticket through HAPAG in Frankfurt, had accommodations in a cabin. When we asked him about food, washing and toilet facilities, and service, he responded with a blank look. "We were happy to be on board. As long as we weren't hungry and there was water, everything was fine," he said. What had happened and what we didn't grasp was that conditions in Germany had become so much worse, and the fear of death so much more immediate, during the two years since we left Germany that our questions had become irrelevant.

After a week, Grandfather had caught up on food and sleep, and was perking up and turning from past to present. He was so happy with his bed behind the screen, and began to explore things in the immediate neighborhood. When one might have expected this routine-bound, ultra-conservative seventy-five-year-old to complain, or at least suggest discomfort with lack of privacy, tightness of living conditions, and other personal needs or desires, his criticisms centered on trivial items that were not "as at home." "The electric plugs are all different," he would say. "They are not rigid, they can be bent one way or another. How can they possibly work?" Or he would be struck by the "holprige Trottoir," the sidewalk with little bumps and holes in it, which took the place of the even little square stones in half-moon patterns he was used to, or else the cobblestones of Reinheim, where Opa knew each one by heart. "Even the doors don't shut as tightly as at home," he'd tell us.

Grandfather had been saved from what he had finally come to recognize as a terrible fate, and for the rest of the thirteen years he lived in New York, he never uttered a word of personal complaint. But the cultural difference struck and bothered him. He felt at home in his eight square feet behind the screen, but he couldn't understand how things could work when doors didn't fit right, or streetcars were not washed every day, or paper was gathering in the gutter and nobody wielded a broom.

The next big event was Hitler's attack on his ally, Stalin. "You see, that's what I told you," Papi would say. "There is no difference between these dictators. Left, right, makes no difference. Today they are allies, tomorrow enemies—all they care about is power, and they'll do anything to hold on to it. And the best way to hold on to it, in their minds, is to extend it." But Father believed that the attack on the Soviet Union was Hitler's biggest mistake. "They are not smart enough to understand," he said, referring to the Nazis, "that extending power can also mean weakening themselves. That's what happened to Napoleon. But that's another typical dictator's trait: when a predecessor failed in an 'heroic' venture, it's a challenge to the next one to do better. They're all crazy mystics and romantics, right along with their bottomless ruthlessness. They won't face the facts that made a previous attempt unsuccessful."

For my mother, the assault on Russia was another reason to count her blessings. "You see," she said to her father, "it's a good thing you went through France and Spain. You couldn't go through Russia anymore even if you wanted to! Thank God for the French route or you'd never have gotten out."

As fall approached, so did school and university semesters. We had talked for some time about my completing the presumably few courses it would take to get my bachelor's degree. We had found out that City College was excellent and free for qualifying applicants. But my parents felt that the cachet of a renowned institution like Columbia would be important, even if it cost something. We'd get the money together somehow. I agreed, and while the inclination to choose Columbia was discussed in pragmatic career terms, there was a little German-Jewish snobbery in it, too. Perhaps more than just a little.

One afternoon after work in August 1941, I took the streetcar up Broadway to 116th Street. I had previously explored the campus and found out where to go for registration in the university's extension courses, which was then the name for the evening classes that later acquired the more respectable sounding title School of General Studies. In my folder I carried that hard-earned *Abitur* diploma from the Philanthropin, which would make it possible for me to get my degree with little if any extra work. I proudly laid it before the admissions official, who reviewed it with care, and then dropped a bombshell: I would get at most thirty credits for the *Abitur,* which would mean that I would have to earn another eighty-five or ninety to get my bachelor's degree. I was shocked into momentary speechlessness. Before I could protest, explain, or whatever I might have said, the official volunteered his rationale: "After all, you studied under the Nazi regime, which distorted and devalued the German education system. We can't accept this diploma as though it had been issued by a serious, politically independent institution!"

By now I had found my tongue. "But I studied in a Jewish-run school, which carried on the tradition from before the Nazis and could not possibly adopt Nazi ideology without hurting, denouncing, and denigrating ourselves as Jews!"

"Sorry," he said. "Your diploma has the Nazi stamp on it, and was approved by an official of the regional education ministry. To us this means the authorities approved what you had been taught."

"But look, please. On the front page, the word *öffentliche* is crossed out, meaning the Nazis had dropped our accreditation!"

The man across the desk was unimpressed. And I did not have the initiative or courage to question the judgment of authority—and he *was* authority, like anyone sitting across a desk. I had not yet progressed far enough in my acculturation to question this tenet of my upbringing.

The passport to life had shrunk to an almost useless piece of paper! The arguments we had and the risks we weighed in deciding to wait for it in Frankfurt were a joke! That the Philanthropin was a Jewish-run school didn't count. That the Nazis had put their stamp on our diplomas counted. One must have lived through the capriciousness of dictatorships to understand what happened in the Philanthropin that March day in 1939. My admissions officer, fortunately for him, had not. I had, but I was on the wrong side of the desk.

I registered for one course, or three credits, which is all I had money for. I chose Spanish, because languages were the field in which I seemed to have a modicum of talent, and, besides, it might become useful in a hemisphere where half the people spoke that language. I started my treks up to 116th street in September 1941. I received my bachelor's degree in June 1948, stepping up the course load as our resources increased. With the finish line beckoning, I became more eager to cross it.

What I did not know in those early days was that at that time, during the 1940s, Columbia's Spanish-language faculty was probably unexcelled in the world. Spain and several Latin American countries had dictators or juntas who had either expelled or prompted some of their finest intellectuals to leave, and it was New York's gain. A whole new world of Spanish and Latin American thought and literature opened up for me, quite aside from language competence, under such teachers as Angel del Río, Francisco García Lorca (brother of the poet who fell in the Spanish Civil War), Federico de Onís, and Arturo Uslar Pietri of Venezuela.

But what happened to my English was equally important: to a degree beyond my expectations I became competent, more articulate, and immeasurably surer of myself. I had superb professors, who taught me so well that I grasped and never forgot the rules about the use of "who" and "whom."

On those early evening streetcar rides to Columbia, I had another learning experience. One of the conductors on the route was an Irishman, Jim Healy, in those days close to retirement and clearly more interested and involved with literature than with the start-brake lever in the streetcar. He was a delightful and instructive source of knowledge on everything from Shakespeare to Joyce: delightful because he spoke with a gentle brogue and in colorful, articulate English; and instructive because he truly knew whereof he spoke.

As I resumed my schooling, my father was plowing through the medical tomes that were to prepare him for his professional examinations. He felt ready for his first attempt in the spring of 1941. He had applied in the states of New York and Ohio, which at that time admitted noncitizen immigrants to the state board tests. He failed in New York on a minor technicality. He passed in Ohio, which made us happy, although Father had not given up on New York, where we preferred to live because of friends and relatives in the city. Still, Ohio was insurance, and also made Father more confident about another try in New York.

He succeeded in New York on the second try, and received the document authorizing him to practice on April 15, 1942. It was Father's fourth start as a physician: the first was Reinheim, 1912; then again Reinheim, 1919; then Frankfurt, 1934; and finally New York, in English (!), 1942. Now it was a matter of assembling the money for basic office equipment and furniture, and finding a place we could afford that would accommodate the practice plus the four of us. Father was confident that, once established in an office, he would quickly develop a clientele to repay the loan his sister had made to us and the rent for a larger apartment. We had put away enough money for furniture, found an apartment at 240 West 98th Street, which another refugee doctor, who had been practicing for several years, was vacating for the fashionable East Side, and moved in during the summer of 1942.

In the meantime, Grandfather had become remarkably well adjusted to his new surroundings, greatly easing his daughter's worries about him while she was absent at work. I had received a raise, too. I'd now be making fifteen dollars a week. Things were looking up.

Equally important, while all this had occurred to us as a family, America had joined the war, in the wake of the Japanese assault on Pearl Harbor. For Father, still awaiting his credentials to practice in New York, the American entry into the conflict was as important as our family fortunes, judging by the amount of thought and discussion he devoted to it. "Now Hitler is finished!" he would say when the headlines proclaimed the now rapidly developing U.S. war effort. My mother did not argue, and Grandfather, whose attitudes were changing quickly, said he agreed with my father. This was unheard of. Grandfather was being absorbed into America, and when he agreed with my father about the Allied victory to come, he spoke more as a patriot than an observer, more in hope than from conviction.

At 240 West 98th Street, where my parents would live until my father died in 1961, we were joining that stream which for 150 years had engulfed the United States and made the country more fruitful: the immigrants. We needed the country to receive us and make us safe; what we realized only later was that the country needed us as well. It seemed to be a perfect fit—so rare in the history of people and the growth of nations. There was no pressure to assimilate, to speak English, to be like the "regular" people. Everybody was different. By the time one got one's naturalization certificate, one had already become American.

❖

V

I f the room on 100th Street was safety and comfort, the apartment on 98th Street was sheer luxury. Sitting today on the twelfth floor of an East Side building with three bedrooms, of which my wife and I use only one because our children have long since flown the coop, I am amused at the elasticity of human perception. Upon arrival in 1940, that greystone room was heaven. With a certificate to practice medicine reactivating Father, the family now saw 100th Street as a humble beginning, something to be left behind though not looked down upon. There have since been many upward jumps in my life. Yet to this day West 100th and 98th retain a glow of contentedness and serenity in my memory: 100th was safety; 98th was security. Scarsdale, Chevy Chase, Bergen County, N.J., and the Upper East Side can't compete with those "early American" feelings.

As a doctor's apartment, our home on West 98th was on the ground floor of a building occupying half of the block between Broadway and West End Avenue, and the entire block from 98th to 97th streets, with a back entrance on 97th. Our apartment looked out on 98th, where we could see Thomas's drugstore, which became my father's prime source of supplies and prescription handling, on the northwest corner of Broadway and 98th. The building boasted a large and luxurious hall, with marble walls and floors, and majestic elevators, decorated with brass appointments, opposite the entrance. Although we never used the elevators, Fritz, the most social and congenial among the operators, became a family friend and a source of largely unwanted information about family dramas in the building.

At the entrance to our apartment hung an American-style shingle: JACOB GOLDMANN, M.D., General Practitioner. It was a fraction of the size of the German physician's *Schilder*—large squares with the doctor's name in black letters on a white enamel background, all framed in shiny aluminum, conveying importance. But that small metal shingle on New York's West Side was so much more important! Neither the one in Reinheim nor that in Frankfurt had been as hard-won. "Well, we've done it!" Father said, when the sign had been placed, and there was pride and satisfaction, and just a touch of a quiver, in his voice. Grandfather shed a tear, and once inside Mutti embraced her husband, which had not been a frequent occurrence, at least in my presence. Warmth had been restored to their relationship, and Grandfather, without realizing it, had shed his negative feelings and prejudices about his son-in-law. This, too, America can take credit for, and the best part of it is that America seemed to take it for granted. It never asked for praise, even recognition.

The new home of Dr. Goldmann and his family consisted of a long hall, which served as waiting room for the patients; a large room off the hall, which served as Father's office; the big room looking out on 98th, our living room, and at night my parent's bedroom; and another room for Opa and myself. Once again, the screen split the room: Grandfather took the part with the window and I slept near the door to the hall. A windowless kitchen and a bathroom completed our accommodations. We had little more living space than on 100th Street, because close to half of the apartment was taken up by father's office needs. But here my parents had their privacy, after each evening converting the living-room couch into their bed.

With work and school taking up most of my time, I spent few waking hours in the apartment. Opa and I had always gotten along, and now we did even more so. Later, when I became familiar with the phrase "plenty of room," voiced by the operators of crowded elevators squeezing in a few more human sardines, or by streetcar conductors, or by passengers pushing themselves into a subway car, I thought the expression could occasionally be applied to our home, especially when patients used our one bathroom during office hours, or when Mother was preparing dinner, Grandfather was using the living-room table, and I needed to do homework. Sometimes I would sit opposite Grandfather, but he did not care for this arrangement when he was reading his *Staatszeitung,* New York's German-language paper, which he liked (or needed?) to spread out in all its standard-size glory.

The big change in life's routine came for my parents: at age fifty-five, Father was practicing again, after three years of professional inactivity, which for him had been unremitting suffering, though he never complained. Mother left her bedpans behind, and gladly so, to become Father's *Sprechstundenhilfe* (a combination physician's assistant, nurse, and bookkeeper), and a homemaker. The practice developed quickly. A number of people who knew Father from Frankfurt or had heard of him were waiting to become his patients, and word of his availability day and night, in walk-ups as well as elevator buildings, for the poor and the comfortably placed, spread. Most of the patients were German-Jewish refugees living in the neighborhood. He did have some from up in Washington Heights, and soon acquired some native New Yorkers, mostly recommended by Fritz, the doorman, or elevator men in nearby buildings.

Mother and Father worked together as if they had done so for decades. The only thing that reminded me of Reinheim and Frankfurt days was Mother's occasional rebuke that father was too unconcerned about deadbeats, who didn't really need home visits but were spoiled by my father's automatic response. "If someone wants to pay for an unnecessary consultation or visit, all right," she would say. "But to be a hypochondriac and not pay for it is too much—that's making a fool of you!" As always on such occasions, Father did not argue. His response was merely that pulled-up right eyebrow and the shake of the head toward the right. Father always erred on the side of believing a patient or would-be patient. Even when someone had demanded service that was not needed, Father would respond the next time anyway. The only concession he would make would be to do other things first.

The changes in Grandfather's life were more gradual, less perceptible, but perhaps most significant. At seventy-six, having spent virtually all his life in a Hessian village, Opa made an adjustment to New York and America that my parents and I never would have predicted. Even as he complained about practical and logistical items, he was in the process of becoming an American.

Mother had told him that English classes were being given to foreigners at a nearby public school, and they were free. Both she and I expected him to turn the suggestion aside. But he did not. He went to a class, and it became the center of his life. A notebook from the fall of 1943, a year after he entered the course, contains homework written in the almost perfect German-style handwriting that was

Grandfather's mark of distinction. A letter of September 27 to "Miss Treacy [*sic*]," his teacher, from a student's mother, says: "Henri was absent Friday because he caught a cold. I think he is better today, so I have sent him back to school. I hope he has not missed any of his work. (Respectfully) or Very truly yours. . . ." An American reading it would not have been able to make out the handwriting, and a German would not have understood the contents. Opa's notebook represented the convergence of two cultures.

As one leafs through the pages, it becomes evident that Miss Tracy was teaching not just English, but American history, citizenship, and government. Page 2 notes: "This is registration week. Citizens who are twenty-one years old or over may vote. You must prove you are a citizen. You must be litterate [*sic*]. Some must take a literacy test." After several pages of vocabulary lists, pages 6 and 7 display, in Opa's finest, respectful handwriting, the names of the then forty-eight states, and of the then thirty-two American presidents, with their terms of service in separate columns, in perfect Prussian alignment. Page 15 shows the list of cabinet officers and their departments. There are lengthy compositions on "The Beginnings of America" and "Wall Street." Page 27 lists the growth of the American population, from four million in 1790 to 122 million in 1930. On the penultimate page is the text of "God Bless America," with a German translation, followed by a letter, clearly suggested by the teacher, showing my grandfather as a lobbyist:

> I hear that the continuation of the Evening School is doubtful, because of the small appropriation in the budget. After I attend the Evening School since two years, I made progress as well in the english language as in american education . . . Closing of the school would mean to me a great loss for which I could not find compensation. Therefore, I take the liberty to make the courteous and urgent appeal to you, to keep the Evening School open . . . Thankfully and respectfully yours, Hermann Frohmann, Pupil, Evening School.

Nobody had asked or urged Grandfather to learn English or to study American history. It all came with the school. To be sure, the school became part of the routine of an old man to whom a regular routine was as essential as breathing and eating. But he could have chosen or developed different daily habits. He might have gone on long walks. He might have attended social gatherings of refugee groups, where the conversation or the lectures were in German. He chose to stay with the school for several years, because he enjoyed learning about the new country. And in the process of learning, he became an American enthusiast.

To be sure, he didn't like and never could accept the *Unordnung* (lack of order) on the shelves of fruit and vegetable stores, where he was used to seeing perfect symmetry; or the *Rücksichtslosigkeit* (lack of consideration) of people who nonchalantly littered on the street. But this was now just something unpleasant that he took in stride. Opa was absorbing all he could about America, and America was absorbing Opa. It was a process that happened naturally, without manipulation, almost without trying.

The same thing was happening to us—flawed and accented English, German-style food, and lots of other European habits notwithstanding. We all rushed to get our "first papers" and eagerly looked ahead to naturalization. It wasn't a decision at all. It was as obvious as the hand in front of our eyes that we would want to become Americans. For unlike in Europe, one could speak, eat, keep house, and wear clothes as one wanted to without being stared at with that "hmm, a foreigner" look that we often got in London. Finally, we could feel comfortable! In Germany, it was "Jew," in England "foreigner"; in New York, nobody paid attention.

Father's practice developed nicely, and our bank account was growing. Opa did an increasing amount of work for his daughter, who was busy helping the doctor, by going shopping, often washing dishes, and assisting with other household chores. I stayed at Crystal's, added a course to evening school (philosophy), and began to go out with girls I had met there or at the dances to which I had been invited.

Paulette was my first serious "affair." She was eight years older than I was. I had met her at our house after she had been introduced to my parents by a friend. She sought a kind of home away from home, because she lived alone in an apartment two blocks away. Paulette was German by birth, but had lived in France. More important was that she was beautiful, had infinite charm, and was happy-go-lucky. What attracted me to her was not just physical, but her easygoing way, her ability to have fun without feeling guilty.

Paulette helped me to understand what a complete and intimate relationship could be and mean. We spent many hours together over the next few months, and they were glorious hours. After a while, though, I realized—and Paulette did nothing to change my impression—that our relationship was much more important to me than to her. She had experienced other close and intimate companionships. For me it was a first, a discovery, a full-blown romance. But Paulette also realized that it had to cool off gradually, for my sake, and she was exquisitely considerate about it.

My parents sensed that we were spending a lot of time together. I made no bones about my intentions, and my mother, who was nervous about "losing" me, relaxed: Paulette was too old, and there was no chance that we would be serious about marriage.

I had a full life in 1942: work, Paulette, homework . . . That additional course, philosophy, was beginning to do things to me. Our professor was a disciple of John Dewey and the pragmatic school. I was drinking in Dewey's writings, and it all made such perfect sense. Here was a person who did not ask where you came from, tell you about rituals to observe, duties to perform, ways to think and believe. Political democracy, ethical conduct, liberal education—all the elements that "worked" when one thought about a life built around the individual rather than service to the state, religion, or some other institution or set of beliefs and requirements—these were the things that mattered.

I read hundreds of pages of Dewey, and became more convinced with each book or lecture that he was on the right track—and that it was my track. The strain I had long labored under when it came to religion—especially since 1933, when Father immersed me against my will, now resolved itself: I became a member in good standing of the Ethical Culture Society.

I went to meetings with what E.C. called their "leaders" (instead of priests or rabbis). I thought that a bit strange, since it translates into "Führer" in German, but I was grounded securely enough in my Dewey to know that it was a coincidence rather than a meaningful convergence, so I shook off my initial uneasiness. What I heard fit with Dewey's approach and helped resolve my long-felt discomfort with all-out commitment to a particular religious doctrine. Finally, I had found people who wanted to bring the human family together rather than practice rituals and adhere to beliefs that, albeit unintentionally, divided faiths and nations and supplied or added fuel to conflicts and wars.

I had become a universalist and was proud of it. But even these Ethical Culture folks had a ritual. They said the right things once they were together, but why did we have to come together to do so, like in a synagogue or a church, on Saturday or, as in E.C.'s case, Sunday? My instinct to do things by myself, my preference not to become involved in communities, even individual relationships, gave me trouble on those Sunday mornings at E.C.'s meeting house on Central Park West.

I was alone with both my enthusiasm and my uneasiness about the E.C. ritual. I knew that my father was hurt by my dropping out of Jewish observance. My mother was too taken up with the practical chores and requirements of everyday living to care. Opa, who had always gone to synagogue simply as a matter of habit, was now busy with evening school. And Paulette was disinterested.

There was no one I could talk to. But there was also no one I wanted to talk to. Throughout my life, I have preferred to work out conflicting feelings and pressures within myself rather than risk a deep involvement. In my family, one did not talk about feelings. I did not even know how to identify what a feeling was. And by the time I came to understand something about emotions and how one could share and deal with them, I had learned to do the work myself.

My main response to others, the key element in my relationships, was not to owe anything to anyone (I still pay my bills within an hour of arrival); not to hurt anyone; not to do anything that might produce a "how could you?!" The best way to meet these needs was to avoid involvement with and dependency on others, except for relationships at work, at school, and in other settings that called for performance of duties or getting a degree.

I never had close friends, those one confides in. George Agree has been a friend all my adult life, as has Walter Baum, a school friend from Frankfurt. I enjoy being with them when an occasion arises, but

I don't miss them when I don't see them. Marriage has changed this somewhat, but it has been my wife's doing, not mine.

When I see an acquaintance on the street who has not seen me, I do not make contact. I hope we'll pass each other and I won't have to make small talk, which is a way of saying that I don't want to become involved. I enjoy being alone, being in control of my agenda, and I try not to have it disrupted or upset. When this happens, there is generally no visible evidence of my discomfort, but I am ill at ease. I prefer reading to hearing others speak; a magazine or a book can be perused at my discretion. My time is under my own control. In professional meetings, or as a reporter interviewing a source, I have difficulty hiding my impatience with the required niceties like "How's the family?" "What's doing in New York?" or "Before we get into the subject, let me tell you about a funny experience I had yesterday." Most of the time, the questioner has no genuine interest in my family, or the incident to be related isn't funny. Of course, I respond civilly and with the required smile or laugh, but it's such a waste. "Let's get on with this," I think to myself.

My ambivalence about Ethical Culture continued, but I stayed for quite a few months. I paid my dues for years. It was more a sense of responsibility than wanting to go. In part, I was also concerned about my father's injured feelings. He would go to synagogue during the week whenever the practice permitted, and he had found a small group of German refugees who had joined to worship in a member's apartment in the neighborhood. On the Sabbath he would not work and would often go to the large synagogue, Anshe Chesed, on the corner of West End Avenue and 100th Street. He would lay tefillin in the morning and silently say grace after meals; neither Mother, Grandfather, nor I joined in.

When my move to Ethical Culture was mentioned—and it was always briefly—Father would refer to my new affiliation as "eisical culture." It made the organization sound ridiculous, although Father did not intend to make fun of it. His accent, I took it, made it sound the way he must have felt about it. That was about the extent of our communication on the subject.

Along with my shying away from involvements with people, I interpreted my responsibilities and assignments narrowly. I wanted to

get things done—done well, but done—and to feel the sense of relief
and satisfaction when I had completed a task. Whether it was work
on the job, homework, or later more wide-ranging assignments in
higher-level positions, I was always streaking toward the goal: finishing gave me more contentedness than the work itself, even if such
work was professionally challenging. I probably missed developing
and making use of my potential as a journalist and writer because of
my addictive commitment to finishing an assignment and handing it
in "clean." There were many nights when I worked until weariness
stopped me, even though the deadline was days or weeks away.

It was all a matter of getting and holding on to control, avoiding
risk, and, most of all, avoiding criticism and its worst form: "how
could you?!" The fewer involvements I had, the easier it was to control my time, my routine, and to guard against "entanglements." The
sooner I got an assignment done, the farther I would stay away from
a "how could you?!" by whoever was my boss. My mother and my
grandfather, and the culture that made orderliness and on-time performance high virtues, have left their mark on me. I long ago lost
about 95 percent of my German accent, but not what in America
is considered compulsiveness and in Germany, at least in my youth,
normal, even required, behavior.

Toward the end of 1942, some of the young men of my age from
the refugee community were being drafted into the armed forces. My
mother started to worry about me. I was both concerned and challenged by what I might do there. One of my friends had been assigned
to Camp Ritchie, in Maryland, to attend an intelligence school, where
he could make use of his bilingual competence. This was exciting.
My father had the normal worries of a parent about a son going off
to war, while my grandfather, harking back to his infatuation with
soldiering, was discretely proud that his grandson might become a
soldier.

The war was going better for the Allies. In August Hitler's forces
had been defeated at Stalingrad. It was the first clear and solid defeat
for the Nazi army, and a tremendous morale boost to all Allied forces.
Hitler's advance had been stopped, England had held out under the
German Luftwaffe's unrelenting bombing of its cities, French forces
were rallying under de Gaulle, and resistance movements were mak-

ing an impact in France, Norway, and in the Balkans. The only thing that continued unabated was the persecution of the Jews. We did not get much news about it, but there was a string of deeply disturbing albeit hard-to-confirm reports. Most solid and disturbing was the persistent dropoff in communication with Jews in Germany and the occupied countries, even via neutral countries. We had no idea at the time of what was being planned, and less of what was actually being done to Europe's remaining Jews in the last three years of the war. But there was enough known and feared to make it not merely a civic duty, but a personal responsibility, for an immigrant German Jew to serve to the best of his ability and to use whatever potential he had for the cause of America and the Allies.

Still, when the call came that I was to show up at Fort Dix, New Jersey, on February 11, 1943, it was a mixed blessing. There was still a touch of the old homesickness in me, but my greater concern was my worry about not bringing home a salary, even though my being out of the house would reduce the food bills. My mother, of course, was extremely anxious, but both Father and Opa worked on her and kept her anxiety in bounds.

At Fort Dix, at the first opportunity, I applied for assignment to Camp Ritchie as a German translator and for whatever other training might appropriate for a bilingual GI. It was noted, and I was forthwith assigned to the Infantry Replacement Training Center of Camp Wolters, near Mineral Wells, Texas. I had to get my basic training, after all.

It was a long ride on the railroad to Texas. I was more fascinated by it than my fellow enlistees, who were mostly playing cards (I didn't know how), drinking beer (I didn't), and talking about sex (which I considered personal). I did not realize at first how deep the cultural gulf was between myself and most Americans of my own age. I was too interested in the landscape, in getting a look at what America outside New York looked like, to think about how I would fit in.

When we finally arrived at Wolters, it was warmer than in New York, but not hot. I had never seen such landscape. This was the desert I had read about in the Bible. *Hamidbar,* I remembered. And where were the cowboys? I guessed that the train was going too fast for me to see any of those people I had only read about.

We got off the train, and a tall, gaunt sergeant commanded us in a voice that we had never heard at Dix. It sounded threatening, tough, and reminded me of the tone the Nazis used when commanding or shouting at their victims. After we had been assigned to our barracks, I tried to reapply for Camp Ritchie, but it did not go as quickly as I had hoped. We were too busy getting settled in our bunks, listening to all the rules trumpeted out by Staff Sergeant Mertz, even to think that what I sensed then, and what later was confirmed for me, was true: that in this IRTC, where infantry was king, my ideas of a "fancy desk job," as Mertz called it, were out. He was a sun-browned, sharp-nosed, wide-mouthed giant, and I had the immediate feeling that here was an authority figure I could not afford to rub the wrong way.

The basic training routine began the next day. The M2's were dealt out to us, with myriad instructions about their care that all but overwhelmed me. What made the M2 an even more threatening instrument—to me rather than the enemy—was the punishment Mertz announced in case we failed to keep the rifle in tip-top shape. And to top it all, many of my barrackmates from small towns and rural areas knew a lot about guns, which made me, a foreigner, feel all the more inferior! Here I was, the only soldier in the barracks, and for all I knew in the whole camp, who spoke with an accent—and the accent of the enemy to boot—which made me a weirdo or, in those days, a "ninny Kraut."

We soon went on our first march. I had suspected, but tried to forget, that the boots we had been issued were a bad fit. More important, my arch supports, which had been made to measure and inserted into my footwear ever since I could walk, didn't fit into my new boots. It was my good fortune that the corporal in charge of our squad, Corporal Foley, was a considerate noncom who didn't shout and who understood my problem. I soon began to lag behind the fast-marching group, and Foley had to keep me within hailing distance. He did this with seemingly inexhaustible and to me embarrassing and guilt-arousing patience. Foley agreed with me that, even with supports, the infantry was not the ideal place for a soldier whose feet resembled rectangular pancakes.

I had sworn to myself not to complain. But the evidence—bloodied and blistered feet—did the talking. Foley took my case to Mertz, who suggested that I go to the base dispensary for relief. I did, but the nice doctor there did not have facilities to help me, beyond soothing my sores. No arch supports were available or securable. The doctor said I should not have been assigned to an IRTC when I was examined at Dix, but now it was too late to make a change.

I returned to my unit with instructions to do my best. The fact that I had done so and was willing to continue doing it did not, however, change my misshapen and now misbehaving feet. After a while, I did venture to speak to Staff Sergeant Mertz about my interest in Camp Ritchie. It yielded the expected answer. "What the hell are you talking about, soldier?" he snarled. "No fancy stuff here. This is the infantry, and this is where you are assigned. So get the hell out of here, and stop wasting my time."

I had no bunkmates I felt I could or wanted to talk to, so only Corporal Foley was available. I suggested an alternative—duty that no soldier wanted, although each of us had to perform it once every few weeks: sitting in the guardtower to watch the stockade—the camp prison where soldiers who had violated the rules were kept for whatever short term the military command had given them. It was a twenty-four-hour shift, with four hours on and four off. It was endlessly boring, because no other activity, like reading or radio listening, was allowed. At night, it was especially trying. The only thing to do was to watch the minutes tick by.

I volunteered for guard tower duty as a regular assignment because it was done sitting on a bench; it was the only IRTC job that could keep me off my feet. Anybody who volunteered for guard duty in the tower had to be either crazy or had a problem. Since my bunkmates had seen what marching was doing to my feet, they decided I was not crazy.

Dreary day after dreary day I sat up there, four hours at a time. I dreamed of being a translator, glamorously associated with some colonel or general for whom I would make important documents intelligible, somewhere in England; or interpreting the answers of Nazi prisoners in North Africa and, eventually, in France and Germany, once we had landed and advanced on Hitler's cities. But right now, nostalgia was getting the upper hand again, and I was beginning to call home often, to share my worries and frustrations. Meanwhile, I continued sitting in that dark tower.

What I had to watch out for most was the officer on duty, who would make the rounds at unpredictable times during each guard stint to check that everything was in order, which meant more than anything else that soldiers on guard were awake and alert. One night, I failed the test. I suddenly jumped up, pointed my rifle at the silhouette below, then realized it was the officer on duty, and responded— too late—with the proper reply to his challenge. Seeing my rifle pointed at him, and aware that I had dropped off to sleep, the officer was more concerned about my accidentally shooting him than about my infraction. "This is Lieutenant Cohen, Private Goldmann," he said, after I had identified myself as required by the ritual. "Put the rifle down and stay awake. It's all right."

"Yes sir," I answered with immense relief. I also knew that Lieutenant Cohen was a physician assigned to the dispensary. I thought: hmm, this may be a man I can talk to about my foot problem and my interest in Camp Ritchie.

I finished my stint, and no one ever heard about my violation of duty. If they had, I might have been thrown into the stockade I had been assigned to guard! My dozing off would not have put the camp in danger. Those guys inside had no desire to escape. Many of them actually preferred the stockade to duty! But that was not the point: I had failed.

One day, I was taken off guard duty and given a stint as a military policeman in Mineral Wells. This meant patrolling the street, going into bars, and the Baker Hotel—the big place in this onetime resort town—to round up misbehaving soldiers. Their misbehavior was mostly minor, stemming from an overdose of beer. Still, I had to take them in. And after a couple of times, the unpleasantness of disciplining my peers was not worth the gold braid that an MP wore over his shoulder.

I volunteered to go back to guard duty, but someone on a higher level found that I either had to return to regular basic training and infantry duty, or be discharged. This is where my Camp Ritchie ambitions might finally click, I thought. I was assigned to the hospital for a review and repair of my foot condition.

The doctors listened sympathetically, as I made my case for my potential as an intelligence soldier, but they told me this was not their responsibility. The commanding officer of the medical detachment reviewed my file and ordered me to bed. In the army one does not ask questions that raise doubts about a superior's judgment, be he a noncom or an officer, so I went to bed. When the physician on duty visited me, had read my chart, and looked me over, he suggested that I did not have to have complete bedrest, just normal rest, with permission to go to the toilet and make other necessary short trips. Here I did dare ask a question: "Sir, why was I ordered to bed?" "Because of the condition of your feet, soldier!" was the answer. I did not proceed to the next question, which would have been: "But, Sir, how will bedrest cure my flat feet?" This would have been out of bounds, because it would have raised doubts about a superior's decision.

It was now August, hot and dry and desolate. The hospital ward was like a sauna. There was a lot of foolish conversation among us bored "patients," and there were rumors of a "cleaning-out" order that would make this a leaner, healthier army. One of my wardmates, after looking at my feet, suggested that I should have been classified 4F (not physically meeting enlistee standards) in the first place. I did not mention my Camp Ritchie hopes there, because these young men would not have understood.

On August 18, word came: I was to report to the hospital office. I was being discharged honorably, for medical reasons. I was given cash to get home on the train, went through the discharge process, and, together with a few fellow IRTCers, proceeded to the train station.

I had mixed feelings about my discharge. On the one hand, I was happy to go home: I always was, whether it was from work, from a date with a girl, or from a party. But there were bad feelings, too. I felt I had more reason to be over there and fight or work for America than anyone else. The other fellows didn't even know what Hitler and the Nazis were all about, their army indoctrination notwithstanding. So what was I doing on a train going home, while youngsters from farms in Texas or Ohio, from small towns in the Northwest, were on the firing line? And what a ridiculous reason to find myself on that train—because I have flat feet! I couldn't even tell people about that: it would make me a laughingstock.

My return turned out just about the way I had expected. Mother was overjoyed; her happiness was undiluted. Father's joy was slightly tempered by his feeling that we, as German Jews, had a responsibility to fight. And Opa mainly wanted to know what it was like in the American army.

It did not take long for me to settle back into my routine—work and school and occasional dates, usually with girls I met at dances, which was a popular form of social life for young people in those days. But now that I had been in the army, a dream I had nursed for some years came back more insistently: I wanted to be a radio announcer.

It goes back to my days in Frankfurt, listening to opera. I had often been told that I had a good speaking voice—a bass or low baritone—and when I imitated Count Luna or Leporello singing the "Registerarie" (catalogue aria) from *Don Giovanni,* my critical Frankfurt school friends and self-styled music experts did not laugh. In the last two years before Kristallnacht, my parents permitted me to abandon the violin and to take singing lessons with Herr Würzburger, a retired opera singer. He thought it worthwhile for me to pursue my training, and I was just beginning to try my talent at some Schubert Lieder when preparations for the *Abitur* and my planned emigration made singing lessons capricious.

There was neither time nor money in New York even to think about resuming my lessons, and I had long since decided that if indeed I had some gift for singing, the opportunity had passed. It was probably the most unimportant loss the Nazis had caused us! But, I thought, now that I was home from the army, Father's practice was going well, and I had a chance to make some choices, perhaps my voice in its untrained state was adequate for radio announcing.

I returned to David Crystal's because I could not afford to waste time looking for a job; I needed to earn a salary. But I was determined to increase my pay, now that I was a "veteran." I found a new job at a scale manufacturer's in Broklyn that paid considerably more. Then I began my radio announcing campaign. I wrote to every local station in town, on two assumptions: that I did not have experience and therefore was not ready for a network; and that my accent had disappeared. The first assumption was correct, and then some; the second was wrong.

I received one encouraging response, from WQXR, the classical music station, and was asked to come in for an interview. I was elated, and was confident I would get the job. My hopes were founded on my ability to handle the pronunciation of most of the composers whose music was played on the station, plus what I felt was my considerable musical knowledge. Mother cooled my expectations, as she always did, because one neither had the right nor was it good sense to expect something good to happen. Besides, the whole idea of my becoming a radio announcer was in the realm of fantasy. I seemed to be treading in the footsteps of my "Fantast" father!

My interview was with Al Grobe, the head announcer. He was a kind and gentle person, but he made it clear quickly that whatever my merits as a pronouncer of titles and composers' names, the connecting matter between them—English—was not up to snuff. I had not taken into account the difference between what I sounded like to others and to myself.

Grobe suggested that I apply to the Office of War Information, where he did announcing in his off-hours, because at OWI there was a large contingent of foreign-language announcers and there might be a need for German speakers. My voice, he thought, was more than adequate for radio, but I was still a fair distance away from passing as a professional in what he called "educated American."

Grobe turned out to be the fairy-tale prince who made a dream come true. It wasn't the whole dream, but most of it. When I had my interview with Mae Wale, the casting director of OWI, at 224 West 57th Street, at the corner of Broadway, I opened by requesting an audition, at Al Grobe's suggestion. "What language? she asked, gruffly and without a smile or other gesture to make me feel comfortable. "English," I said, as thought this was understood and required no special mention. "What's your native language?" she asked, in the same tone. "Well, it's German, but I also know and speak Spanish." "I could use a German speaker part time," she said. "What's your experience?" "I haven't had any, but Al Grobe said my voice was right, and I . . ." "I'll schedule an audition for you, and we'll see. Good-bye. We'll call you."

Even though it was German, I was full of hope and joy. I'd be on the air, would be heard by millions of people . . . but, of course, not here in New York, by my parents and our friends, and especially the girls . . . That was disappointing, but not enough to dampen my spirits. I'd be out of the garment center, and other uninteresting work, and on my way to a glamorous career. But why did my American future, which I was fiercely determined to shape, have to be continually tied up with Germany? It was a question asked more out of pride as a new American (the army service had speeded up my naturalization process) than of a desire to dissociate myself from German culture or the German language. It's just that I wanted to be "regular." Yet how German was my motivation! I wanted to be *geborgen* in my new country. And, of course, I wanted to have achieved the feat of losing my accent to the point of becoming an announcer in English.

The call from OWI came within a couple of days. I went for the audition and was accepted! Initially I worked part time, on the graveyard shift; after a couple of months I became a regular. Being a ham and a mimic, I had my newsreading routine up to professional quality very quickly. "Hier spricht die Stimme Amerikas—eine der Vereinten Nationen [This is the Voice of America, one of the United Nations]" became second nature to Richard Harris, the American name with which I signed on and off when I read a commentary.

My colleagues were all German ex-actors or had otherwise had careers in public speaking in Germany. We were all supposedly speaking "neutral" German, which meant we were not to have a recognizable dialect. I had never acquired the ugly Hessian vernacular of Reinheim or the equally thick and crude dialect (so it struck me) of Frankfurt. I had always admired German speakers, like our German teacher Dr. Philipp, who enunciated their words in what I felt was clean yet unaffectedly neutral German, and who imparted color to their comments in well-chosen language rather than by twisting vowels or dropping last letters.

I was proud that my colleagues spoke highly of my pronunciation and often said they were amazed that I could hide my Hessian origin. On the other hand, I could tell that Ernest Rose had a touch of Weimar-Thuringian dialect, even as the others all betrayed no local color, except for a bit of Berlinese, since most of them came from there. The OWI was most meticulous about the pronunciation of its German announcers, lest local or regional animosities be stirred up when our objective was to "win hearts and minds." This is why there was a separate Austrian section, with 100 percent Austrian-born writers and speakers. After all, we wanted to emphasize the separateness of Austria, and by implication tell the listeners that we did not recognize the *Anschluss* (regardless of the fact that the Austrian people had welcomed their Adolf with more fervor than the Germans had).

The announcers became fast friends both in and out of the studio, not just Germans and Austrians, but our French, Belgian, Italian, and English colleagues. Two special relationships developed during my service: an infatuation with Ginette, from the French service; and a professional immersion in American English that was initiated by English announcer and speech specialist John Merlin-Aulicino.

Ginette was the most attractive girl I had ever met, and she responded to my interest with a blend of reserve and coquettishness that fed my desire all the more. We became intimate friends, lovers, but always with that measure of tenuousness and hesitation by Ginette that made the time between meetings trying and our dates all the more intense.

Ginette was on the chubby side, but just short of letting it intefere with her attractiveness. Her brown hair flowed in gentle streams down her back and sides, past the perfect white skin of her round face, which was dominated by the most beautiful large brown eyes. Her body always seemed to invite an embrace, and I had a difficult time controlling myself when we were both in the announcers' lounge. Our dates had to coincide with Ginette mother's absence from the apartment the two women shared following Ginette's father's death. And this was far from often enough!

John Merlin and I became friends over the vowels in words like "but" and "won't" and the r sound in "hard." These were among the well-nigh insuperable difficulties facing a German-born person speaking or trying to speak American English. John and I worked in the quarter-hours between the end of his show, fifteen minutes after the hour, and the beginning of mine, on the half-hour (French was scheduled in between), then again in the quarter-hour after the end of mine, at forty-five minutes after the hour, and his next broadcast (Italian fell between mine and his). These were the four main languages, which were being broadcast twenty-four hours a day. Other languages were transmitted at varying times, though not as frequently as the four "big ones." But even among those others, there were different degrees of coverage, with Russian and other major languages ranking above, say, Albanian, Greek, or Thai.

John and I worked intensively, with my repeating endlessly the correct sounds John was communicating, somewhat like in Dr. Plaut's class in Frankfurt, but with less frenzy, exaggeration, and with personal attention. John's interest was both altruistic and professional. He believed that he could help me, and he felt I was a promising case because I had a discerning ear and lacked inhibition when the work required mimicking. We made good progress, and to this day I say "America" with the "eh" sound, as John taught me, instead of the German "ä" that is one of the characteristics of the German accent.

My lessons with John were responsible for my reaching a point where people who don't listen too carefully do not realize that I am not American-born. Most, however, do, including myself when I hear tapes of my words. What John and I were aiming at was a speech experiment, not a way to hide my origins!

The news I was announcing was getting better. After D-Day, we were able to speak of both Allied and Soviet advances, and the end of the war was coming into sight. This bothered Jens Friedrich, an old-time Viennese actor now doing announcing and character roles in radio plays. Jens was in his sixties at the time, and whenever the Allies had scored a major advance Jens would repeat a phrase coined by bureaucrats who during World War I had been hired in Austria-Hungary's expanded civil service: "Kinder, freut Euch, des Krieges, der Friede wird fuerchterlich sein! [Fellows, enjoy the war, peace will be terrible!]" The response from us younger ones was something to the effect that the Austrians weren't enthusiastic fighters or war heroes in the first place. But for Jens, the perverse saying had meaning: what would he possibly do once this job came to an end? He was in his sixties, spoke virtually no English, and possessed an exaggerated sense of his own importance. Becoming an Avon Products salesman, as many ex-lawyers, artists, and other professionals had done, was out of the question.

There were also the usual incidents of "fluffs," or misspoken words, some of which had new and incongruous meanings, such as the newscast in which I spoke of an advance to Avranches, in Normandy, as the seizure of a key streetcar junction instead of a road and rail hub. On such occasions, it was standard procedure for colleagues in the studio or the control room to snicker or laugh, which raised the speaker's nervous tension to extreme levels and produced a sudden and heavy burst of perspiration, which was the price of not breaking down.

To some extent, the humor was gallows humor for us announcers, and Jens Friedrich's candid and cynical phrase was not entirely inappropriate, especially for my colleagues in their forties or fifties. The job at OWI had spoiled them: they had found work that bore a relationship to what they had been trained for and that they never could have dreamed of doing when they immigrated. But now they had found it, and when it ended it meant climbing down. This was more depressing and more damaging to one's self-image than starting at the bottom, which was expected and normal after one had escaped from persecution.

On April 12, 1945, two deaths occurred in our family: my Oma Julie's and Franklin D. Roosevelt's, who, unbeknownst to him, had become the superfather in refugee families. It was my turn to make the announcement, and I shall never forget the words: "Präsident Franklin Delano Roosevelt starb heute."

All became somber. It was so close to the end of the war. Why did he have to die now, when he was needed to make sure Hitler was really and irrevocably finished? Why could he not be allowed to live long enough to see and take pride in what he, more than any other leader, had accomplished? Yes, Roosevelt was greater, because Churchill and Stalin had no choice: they were attacked on their home turf. America's civilian population was never hurt, and FDR had worked, not to say conspired, long before Pearl Harbor, to bring America's power to bear against the Nazis. And who was this Truman? Nobody knew him. How could Roosevelt make him vice president? That was his one big mistake . . .

No one in the refugee community, and few in the general public, had any idea that the "little man" from Missouri would turn out to be a giant. None of us refugees had understood—and many of the older ones never would understand—the regenerative strength of American society. Democracy was different here, deeper, close to what Americans called the grass roots. We did not grasp that indefinable process of interaction between citizen and "authority" that, through debate and eventual consensus, sustained a mayor, a governor, a president. If a person had the potential for leadership, the job could make him realize it in this society. And if he did not have it, like Calvin Coolidge, the nation would be able to manage. Leadership in America was not rooted in a Führer whose absolute power was what made the state live or die; it was to give expression to policies that rested on or could yield a consensus. The president was necessary, but no one president was indispensable.

When we buried Oma Julie in Beth El cemetery in New Jersey, our thoughts were as much on Roosevelt as on her. Julie was a hard-headed, hard-driving woman, with little interest in the family or in friends, and always ready to criticize people, especially my mother. My father and Julie did not click, although he spent endless hours in her final days trying to make her comfortable as her heart failed. He had inherited his feeling for family and people in general from his self-effacing father, of whom he spoke often and with admiration, almost reverence. But he also recognized that it was Julie who had made the decision that both he and his sister Ida would become physicians. Since he loved his work and was, as some of his Reinheim patients used to say, "a born doctor," Julie had made the right decision.

VE-Day came a month after the funeral, and with it come the discovery of the death camps. Auschwitz and others in the east had been liberated earlier, but the full horror of what the Nazis had done did not become clear until American reporters and cameramen gained access to Dachau and to other death camps. Amid the joy of the end of the war, the pictures and accounts of people like us lying in heaps, like garbage, on top of each other, did not sink in at once. It was too much.

Full realization of what had happened did not develop for some time—and some of the refugees never grasped it. What we did was react emotionally. An indescribable anger took hold of most of us. Many said, "I'll never set foot in Germany again." My parents did not say it, but they never did go, either.

But we could not live our lives by surrendering to the anger, which threatened some people's very stability. Again, in our home, my father was the steadying influence. He continued with his work and his routines, and so did I.

Almost forgotten amid the news of the death camps and other Nazi-committed horrors, especially in the East, was the hunger in much of Europe. Refugees got some consolation from what Allied bombing and ground forces had done to Germany's cities. But what about people who had helped us in our hour of need? My parents felt that it was their responsibility to get in touch with three people who had stood their ground under threat and at great personal risk: Lisbeth, Policeman Roeth, and Toni Scriba, a girlfriend of my mother's from her schooldays in Darmstadt. We were able to find out that Lisbeth still lived in Reinheim, and Mutti initiated correspondence with her. We got word that Roeth had been named to a high position in the post-Nazi Frankfurt police, and Mother immediately began to send food packages to him and his wife. And she got a response from Toni, who had a difficult time as one who refused to join the Nazi Party and on several occasions had spoken out against the regime.

What was it about Germany that did not let go of us? Here I was, earning my living as a German announcer focusing on the war against Nazi Germany. In the garment center, my Eastern European bosses, also Jews, had called me "Yecke." We were burning with anger about the crimes of the Nazis, and yet my parents were sending food packages to Darmstadt and Frankfurt. My father, who was fortunate to survive Buchenwald, was cleaning his instruments or writing a prescription humming *Die Meistersinger*. And Grandfather was writing about the Constitution and making lists of the American presidents in German script and with German precision.

Life went on. The Voice of America stayed in business—not just to the Pacific where the war against Japan had yet to be won, but to Europe. Now that the Nazi Reich had been defeated, a job remained to be done against Nazism, to support the new men and women in charge of hitherto-occupied countries, and so much more. Father had to continue earning a living, to take care of Grandfather's more frequent vascular crises, and Mother had her hands full keeping both practice and household going.

There was an imperceptible change in our lives: the war had given them a provisional quality, a kind of temporariness; now it was over, and we had to learn how to deal with normalcy and permanence. This, for me, meant that I needed to think about making an independent life for myself. Was Ginette the girl in my future as well as my present? Not if my mother could help it. Would she ever accept any woman as my wife? I doubted it, and this in turn made me wonder whether I would ever defy my mother. What would my profession be? I couldn't have and didn't want a career as an announcer, German or otherwise. What had once been so glamorous had become routine, was no longer special. Just reading out loud what others had written was becoming a bore as the sheen of the "public voice" wore off. Why couldn't I write, too, instead of just being a set of vocal cords? If I succeeded, I might carve out a career in journalism. But in German, living in America? Well, one step at a time . . .

✤

VI

The German desk at Voice of America was very German: intense, precise, with high standards for its writing staff. Most of the writers were of the older generation, with careers either in journalism or as authors. They were a tightly knit team, and, it seemed to me, as difficult to penetrate as the editorial staff of, say, WQXR or one of the network affiliates—only with less justification. I did know how to write German; I had learned more about America than they had, and it was America that we had to write about in our feature material; and I was of a younger generation, still attending college at an American university, which none of the senior types on the German desk had done. No matter. These arguments carried no weight where past performance and maintaining the established hierarchy were essential.

I tried the Austrian desk. It was a very different group. The cultural characteristics of the Austrians were as clearly reflected at their desk as ours were at ours: the work got done, but with less huffing and puffing. The jokes of the coffeehouses echoed through the room, as did the laughter. Jens Friedrich bellowed his complaints, and no one snarled at him, "Stop it, I am trying to work!"

Hans Becker, who headed the desk, had not been trained as a journalist, but he had been active in propaganda work in France before the Nazi conquest. He was bright, politically alert, and in the Austrian tradition, flexible, to use a flattering adjective. For me, this was a good trait, because Becker recognized that I might be useful, because I did have contacts and an outlook different from the rest of the staff.

I suggested, even as I continued to announce for the "Piefkes" (the Austrian jocular word for Germans, and most applicable to Prussians), that I might try my hand at a feature program for youth. What

I proposed were interviews with young Americans who had distinguished themselves, or with people who were working with young people or in the field of education, sports, etc. Hans thought that was just fine. To try me out, he did not have to go through the process of a new hire and the attendant bureaucratic hoop-jumping.

I was delighted. I came home and literally shouted out my new work, since I had no doubt I would succeed. "Ich bin jetzt Journalist [I am now a journalist]," I declaimed to my parents. My father was delighted, while Mother could hold her breath, and Opa didn't quite know what to say when a twenty-four-year-old who had no experience from one day to the next acquired a new profession. Mother, realizing that my news might be significant as a beginning of a career, did not want to "jinx" it, of course. And Grandfather had learned, even as he communicated skepticism, not to spell it out with the self-assurance he had displayed in the old days.

My tryouts were fine, requiring little editing. Of course, minor differences between German and Austrian had to be corrected. What was more important was that I succeeded in getting interviews with important people. In cases where they did not speak German, we merely established their voices and then translated their responses. Two of my biggest conquests were Leonard Bernstein, soon after he had made news as a substitute for Bruno Walter as conductor of the New York Philharmonic Orchestra; and the philosopher John Dewey, well advanced in years but vigorous and delighted to answer the questions of a young, inexperienced, but boundlessly admiring interviewer.

Life was a lot more interesting now, and the open, easygoing approach of my new colleagues made work pleasant. For a couple of years, I switched from speaking German to writing Austrian. More important, I began to learn something about journalism, both about getting the story and about writing it. We joked around a good deal, but it wasn't all fun and games. It was often hard work, under deadline pressure. And at times those deadlines interfered with my dates with Ginette. Since I was never sure of her feelings toward me—something she made sure would stay that way—I did not want to be the one to cancel or postpone a date, especially because our opportunities for intimacy were so infrequent.

The longer I went out with Ginette, the more serious I became about the relationship. Somehow, I had difficulty accepting dates with girls that "didn't go anywhere." It was all part of an emotional immaturity that subconsciously substituted my mother's judgment for my own, which was either nonexistent or suppressed. Mother had made it clear for a long time that she was not about to look kindly on "losing me." This was conveyed in gestures that I registered with almost anticipatory sensitivity.

I reported on my dates, just as I had reported on my potentially "dangerous" conversations at school years earlier. Since my mother took every casual date seriously, as holding the potential of marriage, I did as well. My mother thus acted against her own "interests." Since she felt every girl was out to "catch me," she led me to take each date more seriously than it deserved, certainly more seriously than any girl I dated casually ever did. Yet, since she probably knew that I would not risk her disapproval, she may have calculated correctly. I know that I could never have married a girl that my mother had not approved of. Either I would stay single, or my falling in love would have to coincide with my mother's blessing. My father, unfortunately, showed little interest in my relationships. America had not changed the "division of responsibilities" in our home. Mutti decided, Father agreed, and Opa drew straight lines.

Before I became involved with Ginette, I had become enamored of a Brooklyn girl whom I had met at a dance. She was attractive, intelligent, and fun to be with. We dated, but neither her upbringing in a middle-class Jewish family, nor our living situations—we both lived with our parents—made intimacy practicable. So we kissed goodnight in front of her door when I took her home, and went home— she through the door, I on the subway.

I had, of course, reported on Millie to my mother. As the dates continued, and I felt pressure (only within myself) to make a serious decision, my mother began to worry and raise questions about Millie's "being right for me." Millie was working in a department store. One day, my mother decided to go there incognito to "look her over." Not only did I not object, but I felt this was my only chance to get a "blessing." So I provided the relevant details to my mother as she prepared for her detective assignment: the department Millie worked in, her height, and other physical characteristics. Mother came back, disapproving, of course. And Millie had discovered what was going on, from Mother's not terribly competent Sherlock Holmsery. It ended the dates, and I was not bitter. For it resolved doubts and dilemmas that were more worrying than the relationship was rewarding.

Ginette kept me at high tension, as she was relaxed, almost playful about our relationship. Every now and then she talked about her boyfriend in the army, who was due back and might cause a problem. She did not think that she was interested in him—he had come from the same French Jewish community where she had been born and raised—but she was not sure. Everything she did and said seemed calculated, and probably was, to make me more insecure. She realized that I took things seriously, which made her game all the more entertaining—for her, that is. I, of course, squelched any doubts I had about her character, because I was infatuated and the idea of gameplaying and manipulation was utterly foreign to me.

On October 11, 1945, Grandfather observed his eightieth birthday. Mother made a special meal, and he got some new evening school supplies as a present from me. He continued to read his *Staatszeitung;* evening school would not equip him to read an English-language paper with a full understanding of idioms, shadings, and other characteristics meaningful to native-born Americans. He also continued to take his long walks, which were second nature to him: instead of walking across fields and through forests, he walked along Broadway, studying merchandise and prices, and acquiring information that would help him when he went shopping for my mother's household needs.

Father was as busy as he had been in Frankfurt. He fought an almost continuous war against the "machines." American medicine was far advanced over that in Europe in the development and use of sophisticated equipment for diagnosis and treatment. Father had come to rely on his experience and the judgment that he called "Fingerspitzengefübl," literally, what his fingertips told him. It wasn't a palmreader's kind of magic. It was a term that described a finding or an expectation that a person had no doubt about, based on what he saw, heard, or felt, and what his experience and innate gift for good judgment told him.

Still, modern practice demanded that Father send some patients to the hospital for tests. He would have preferred to work in Reinheim-style, relying entirely on himself and sending patients to the hospital only when there were serious complications or when surgery was needed. But adjust he did, and the result was frequent disagreements with the "machinists" in hospital labs, or with the cardiologists who, in Father's view, relied far too much on the cardiogram and not enough on their analysis of the patient's condition. For Father, examination and judgment had to be the lion's share of a diagnosis, with the machine as an added component for checking and completeness, but not a substitute. Father was never happier than when a result by machine had challenged his diagnosis and subsequent rechecking showed him to have been right in the first place.

Mother had more difficulty accommodating herself to normalcy. After ten years of crisis and unsettled existence, in Mother's mind normalcy did not really exist, not for her and not for us. There was always a need to worry.

In the wake of Kristallnacht, Mother had shown miraculous, even excessive courage. She maintained this strong stance throughout the four unsettled years that followed. We took it for granted that the experience of persecution and danger had changed Mutti's feelings toward life. If the Nazis had done one good thing, we felt, it was to put limits on Mother's paralyzing anxiety, and to equip her for a more realistic, successful mastery of life. What we did not realize was that normalcy was bringing back the "Flörsheim syndrome," as Father called it: depressive tendencies. Mother again began to show a negative attitude toward everyone and everything, began worrying excessively about what seemed trifles. Again, a cold was tantamount to pneumonia; a patient's late payment was a terrible loss ("How can we pay our bills if people don't pay you?" she'd say to my father, even in cases where there was little or no doubt of good faith on the debtor's part); my involvements with women were bound to land me and the whole family in trouble; and Opa's slightest complaint was the signal of an oncoming heart attack.

In consultation with psychiatrists, Father administered medication, but with only partial success. Eventually, Mother was given shock treatments—an approach in which specialists had more faith in those days than they do today. They helped for a while, and with the special care Father was able to provide for her, Mother managed pretty well. But we were all concerned that her condition would grow worse. It was a Flörsheim family trait, after all: Oma Hilda's father had it, and Hilda herself had provided the most awful evidence ten years earlier.

By 1946 I was taking at least six credits per semester at Columbia, and in my last two years, 1947 and 1948, I raised it to nine. I could afford it, and I wanted to be finished. The high points of those years of "duplication," as I tended to think of my studies because of the *Abitur* disappointment, were my advanced Spanish classes. We read Rómulo Gallegos's Venezuelan masterpiece *Doña Barbara* with the brilliant Arturo Uslar Pietri, who had left Venezuela as an opponent of the man who had authored the book we were reading! Gallegos had become president of the country under a liberal-left party, and Uslar Pietri was a conservative. But the two shared the rejection of the military junta that had overthrown the Gallegos government because both were committed to democracy. Discussion of these issues, albeit from a participant's and partisan's vantage point, enriched our hours on those after-work evenings on 116th Street.

In contrast to the animated, sometimes fiery Uslar, Federico de Onís paced us austerely, with deep learning and revealing interpretation, through *Don Quixote.* I enjoyed working for teachers like de Onís and Uslar, or for Francisco García Lorca, who made no allowances for errors in the subjunctive, or in the *l/s* substitutions that seemed so unnecessary and burdensome! Why couldn't Spaniards manage two *l* sounds in succession, like *le lo,* but had to convert the *le* into *se?* All García Lorca did was explain what and why. He brooked no silly questions about our notions of Spaniards' retarded tongues.

At home, there was increasing discussion of what was happening in Europe. Father was grateful to the Russians for resisting and eventually routing Hitler's armies, but he was worried about our policy of "letting them come so far west." Most of our friends in the refugee community were perfectly happy with what was going on. The more complete Hitler's defeat, the better! Why worry about what was happening to the Germans, or the Poles, or all the others in the East who had been the worst anti-Semites over the years and decades?

But Father thought differently. He felt the same way, but he did not let feelings govern him. His political and ideological outlook made no allowances for Stalin and totalitarian communism. "This won't end well," he would say, as the Soviets established their satellite regimes in Eastern Europe. He enthusiastically supported President Truman's decisions to stop Stalin in Iran, Greece, and Turkey. "If Truman had been President earlier," he would say, "the Russians wouldn't have come so far west." He had boundless admiration for the "little man," probably because Truman shared many of Papi's own characteristics: both were physically short; both had deep convictions; both acted from instinct as much as from thought; and both had the courage of modest and honest men.

Father's and the refugees' special interest was, of course, Germany. With the Nuremberg trials over and the restitution discussions under way, there was concern about excessive American generosity toward the vanquished country. "The Americans forget quickly" was a widely made comment. And with it would come the inevitable comments about American inexperience and naïveté in international affairs. Here were people who had been rescued by immigration to the United States, who knew that victory over Hitler was possible only through the participation of America—both in the fighting and in supplying all Allied powers—and they acted like super-critics! Not only did they not really know what was going on; they were using the same supercilious European, and especially German-style, arguments about "naive" America that had been the earmarks of misjudgment all along. Those "clever" and "experienced" Europeans in Britain, France, almost everywhere, and most of all we German Jews, had shown themselves to be the naive ones! In such discussions, Father would often say, "Come on, stop it, please. What do you know about America? Would you have expected Truman to act as he's acting? Why don't you wait and once and for all stop thinking we are smarter!"

When Konrad Adenauer came on the scene, Father's view of the future brightened. Other refugees believed no German could possibly do anything right; for Father, Adenauer was a good omen. His high expectations were rooted in part in what was known about the man as a staunchly decent, conservative opponent of Hitler, in part in his Catholic political background. Although by inclination, even by conviction, a Social Democrat, in the last election in Germany Father had voted for the Zentrum, the Catholic party, because he admired

Heinrich Brüning, the last chancellor before Hitler dictated German politics. Father believed Adenauer followed in Brüning's footsteps. He saw in "the old one," as he was later called, a return to a modicum of decency in public conduct.

Many German refugee Jews did not care what was happening in the old country. Just as they had sworn never to visit again, they saw Germany as a lost cause, no matter what was said, done, or who was appointed to leading positions. They had simply "turned off." Father continued to care about what was happening there because he never abandoned the culture and the values that had helped shape his standards and actions in life.

My life with Ginette was headed for closure. When her prewar boyfriend returned from the service, she resumed a relationship with him, presumably only in order to break it up "gently." But it took quite some time, and I was not about to hang around waiting in the wings. Besides, I had come to realize, apart from my mother's this time legitimate objections, that it made no sense to try to build a life on the tenuous base of Ginette's iffy love and loyalty. In the last stage a third man joined her admirers, which clinched my decision one day to say good-bye in a taxi.

At work, my boss, Becker, repeatedly spoke of a lovely "eligible" girl from a distinguished "rich family" whom he wanted me to meet. Since a major part of his waking hours were spent joking, Becker's suggestions did not make much of an impact on me. After all, I didn't need a marriage broker. On one occasion I asked Becker why, if she was attractive, intelligent, as well as wealthy, she was not yet married at age twenty-six or twenty-seven? He said she and her family were choosy, and there were things I would understand only if I met her.

It all sounded a bit mysterious, even weird, but when Becker invited me to a party where this "Eva" was to be one of the guests, I accepted. Why not? I asked myself. He had whetted my appetite to meet this mystery woman.

It happened that night. Eva was beautiful, blending excellent breeding with a naturalness that captivated me. She was from Prague, the daughter of an industrialist's family whose name meant nothing to me, but, as I found out very soon, it meant a lot to a lot of people, especially those from Vienna and Czechoslovakia. They were the

Petschek family, owners of soft coal mines in Czechoslovakia and Germany, and a variety of other enterprises, including a bank.

That was all well and good, but what mattered was this beautiful, natural, and—as I found out quite soon—music-loving young woman. I took her home that evening to her apartment on East 57th Street, where she was living with another girl named, unbelievably, Eva Goldman (with one *n*). She agreed to meet me again, which made me go home a very happy fellow.

Eva had the purest, whitest skin I had ever seen. Dark brown, almost black hair and deep-set, dark brown eyes contrasted stunningly with the white. She was small, with a full figure that was somewhere between petite and roundish. Her hands and feet were small, her walk graceful, and her smile conquering. What was different about her from all other girls I had dated was a style, a bearing that was naturally elegant, almost dignified. Yet it was not at all daunting or condescending. On the contrary, because it was natural and she was not conscious of it, it made Eva all the more attractive.

The winter of 1947–48, when we met, was memorably icy. We were getting to know each other by walking the streets, but the cold did not matter very much to me. We had so much to talk about! From the moment we met, we talked English to each other, even though German was our mother tongue. By the time we met, we had both become more comfortable with English, since we were speaking it at work, with some of our friends, and in our day-to-day life around the city. When we talked to our families, though, it was German, even as with time the German became more and more laced with English and American expressions.

After a few dates with Eva, I reported at home. But I had a different feeling about it. I was more reluctant, less ready to speak about someone about whom I felt differently than I had felt before. For the first time, I glimpsed the difference between an infatuation and something deeper.

But report I did, and favorably, though with fewer details than about earlier involvements. I mentioned that Eva was from Prague. This yielded a reaction from Mother that I had never thought about. "*Ostjuden?*" asked Mother, with Father looking up to hear the answer. "What is her last name?" Mother asked next.

"Petschek," I answered.

This rang a bell. "That's the big family who had a divorce that was reported in all the newspapers," Mutti said. "Don't you remember?" she asked Father.

I had no idea what mother was talking about, but Eva explained to me that there was indeed a famous Petschek-Karo divorce case that had made headlines in Europe, because of the large sums of money involved. It involved an uncle—one of Eva's father's three brothers.

The name, and the class of Jews it implied, alleviated Mutti's concern that I might become involved with a girl from an *ostjüdische* family. It seemed that the experience of the previous fifteen years had done little to mellow the antipathy and prejudice of German Jews toward their less assimilated fellow Jews from farther east. We hadn't touched on the subject in many a year in our home, but there it was: those roots of prejudice and class distinction go deep and, as I've come to believe in all my experience since, can never be torn out, at best weakened.

A Petschek, of course, was likely to be different. As Mother would find out, a lot more different than what she had expected: this time it would be the *Ostjuden* who would judge us, instead of vice versa! For the Petscheks of the older generation, and even some of Eva's age group, were ultra-assimilated. Some were even baptized. They were Jews whose loyalty to the Austrian brand of German culture, which they considered more refined than that of the Reich, equaled and probably exceeded that of the German Jews. And if my mother had qualms about *Ostjuden,* the Petscheks would have downright contempt for our sort.

All this and more would emerge later, as my relationship with Eva deepened. And deepen it did. What we had in common above our caring for each other were mutual interests: a deep commitment to our respective families, even as we recognized and were amused by the foibles they took so seriously; and, above all, music. Eva played the piano and knew and loved all music, but particularly chamber music. I was weak in this area, but had a wider knowledge of opera, where Eva's range was limited to German works and a few Verdi operas. She did not know *Otello,* which was one of my favorites, about which I could go on endlessly. The wonder was that she did not stop me!

Our first opera together was *Die Zauberflöte* at the Metropolitan, then located two blocks from where I used to work in the garment center. To this day, we reminisce about our disillusionment with the orchestra, whose members walked in and out from the back rows when there were extensive musical rests. But the evening was memorable, because it was the first of a lifetime of shared musical experience.

Eva's home life in Prague had not been comfortable, what with living in a mansion that since the end of World War II has been the residence of the American ambassador, meals served by gloved personnel, and other features that closed her off from relationships with others her age. A link that tied the family together, in which parents and children came close to being equals, was music. Under the spell of Mozart, Beethoven, Brahms, and Wagner, father, mother, and children—as Eva, her brother, and twin sisters were called into their teens—became a community of participants in what they heard.

Eva's schooling also separated her from her peers. Her first language after German was English, taught by governesses brought to Prague from England. The high school she was eventually permitted to attend, when private lessons no longer could do the job, was the Lycée Français. Eva learned Czech, the language of the country, virtually as a foreign language.

She thirsted for what she likes to call the "normal" life she did not have at home. When the family emigrated—in the spring before the Munich pact that spelled the end of Czechoslovakia and a warning of Hitler's impending extension of his persecution of the Jews—Eva and her sisters came to Canada with her mother, who died soon after they had settled in Toronto. Her father had died from a heart attack in 1934. The sisters eventually came to New York to settle, where the uncles and aunts had made their headquarters.

We had two radically different upbringings, and in Europe we never would have met, much less fallen in love! But America was the big leveler. Eva felt liberated from the constraints, the unnaturalness, and the loneliness she had felt in Prague. She did not rebel ostentatiously; it was not her style. She just lived as she wanted to, setting her own standards.

As our relationship became sustained and serious, Becker, the "matchmaker," began to behave strangely in the office. He insisted on making tasteless jokes about us, and I told him to drop it. He did not, and the relationship became strained. But I needed and liked the work, and saw no reason to give in to Becker's crudeness. So for a while I ignored it.

By spring of 1948, we were talking about marriage. This is when matters became complicated, both in the office and in the process of family "approval." Yes, we were in America, all citizens and democrats with a small *d,* but a lot of Prague and Reinheim still stuck to us, most of all to our older generation.

Eva's one surviving uncle, her father's youngest brother, Hans, played the role of *pater familiae* for the daughters (brother Victor was older and had long since been married and divorced). My parents wanted to meet Eva, of course, but there was less scrutiny than when I met Hans and his wife, also named Eva. My parents wanted to know my Eva as a person, without concern for "class," which was well established. But Hans and Eva had to make sure I was able to handle myself appropriately in larger family and company settings in Scarsdale and Rye, where most of the older Petscheks had settled. Since we were determined to get married, the process of inspection and approval was more amusing than bothersome.

In that process I came to know a Jewish family who had been important not only in Czechoslovakian or even Central European economic and financial life, but on the cultural scene of Prague. Eva's father had been a major supporter of the German Theater of Prague. His favorite operas were the works of Wagner, and he was instrumental in helping to get them produced. The family felt much more German than Jewish, as did most German Jews, but in the class of the Petscheks it was more pronounced. It was one of the ironies of Nazism that the main pillar of German culture in a "protectorate," as the Nazis viewed Bohemia, had to flee the country.

Dinner at Uncle Hans's was awesome. Fortunately, his wife was more informal. There was some small talk, then discussion of my family and my work. Eva—the "little one," as she was distinguished from Hans's wife—seemed tense and had to work hard to hide it. "So you work at the Voice of America," Hans said in well-pronounced, only slightly accented English. "Do you plan a career there?" I spoke of my plans to be a journalist in the broader American context, and there was little other substantive discussion.

Dinner was served by a butler, just as it had been in Prague. The

Scarsdale house was a smaller replica of one of the Petscheks' Prague mansions. It was a sprawling, white-painted home, with a seemingly endless garden, to me a park, spread out in back. Toward the far end was a large swimming pool. Flowers graced the edges of the garden in profusion and a thousand colors. Eva clearly was running a tight ship, and was in command of an experienced staff of household, kitchen, and gardening aides.

Dinner went well, although it was more austere than I had expected. I came prepared for a good looking-over, but hoped that we would eventually warm up a bit to lively conversation. It did not happen that time, but it did eventually, to a degree of animation on the subject of politics that reflected sharply the different class origins of the Petscheks and Goldmanns.

Next Hans and Eva came to our home on West 98th Street. Hans took his responsibilities seriously: he wanted to make sure that little Eva's future husband came from a nice home. That meeting went very well. My parents made no special preparations for the afternoon tea, and were as natural as they always were. Hans and Eva were kind, with what seemed to me the noblesse oblige friendliness one always showed strangers, even though one had no intention of crossing class lines by developing sustained relationships.

To my Eva and myself, all this was a ritual we had to go through, with no danger that our own intentions would be derailed. Still, both of us much preferred to have our families' blessing. If anything, Eva was more independent than I. Her father, who had been the unquestioned source of authority in the family, had died fourteen years ago, and her mother, who accepted her husband's and later his brother's judgment, had died eight years earlier. Though still very much looking to Hans for guidance, especially in handling her money, Eva had to make decisions on her own: to train as a nursery school teacher in England and Canada, to take a job with friends who ran a school in Detroit and to move there, and to move back to New York and take a job in an institution for difficult children, where I once got my thumb bitten while I was waiting for Eva.

The most serious problem for us was Eva's money. I was determined to make sure that we would live on my income. This would entail Eva's giving up her East 57th Street apartment, moving into a far more modest home, and shrinking her expenses to a point where she would have to change her lifestyle. If things went well, I would earn more with time, and we could move up accordingly, as other families were doing.

Eva argued that it was foolish to let her income go unused. What clinched her case was that it was unfair of me to ask her to deprive herself of things she had become accustomed to, just to affirm my "manhood." Neither she nor I had any fears that I would let Eva's money influence my career ambitions. On the contrary, I was determined to reduce Eva's share of our budget as much and as soon as possible. Still, it just didn't seem right . . .

I consulted my parents. My mother had no problem. Of course not! Her "Robertche" would be taken care of! She did not say so, because she knew both Father and I would have violently objected, but her nonchalance in the face of my dilemma told it all.

Father understood. He was not comfortable with my being what I perceived to be a consort, but over the past several months he had come to know and like Eva. The two shared an unblemished honesty, bordering on naïveté. Papi thought Eva had a strong argument when she said that it was unfair of me to force her into giving up things she had become used to just to make me feel better. What Father made clear to me was that I was showing my insecurity if I had to demonstrate that I was a decent person. "You don't have to demonstrate it to yourself or anybody else. It's fine that Eva has her own money, but you are neither marrying her for it nor do you have to show the world that you aren't. So let people think what they want. What matters is what you and Eva think and know about each other," he said.

The discussions about money showed me a great deal about myself that I had not realized. I was thinking too much about my inadequacies and had to show that I was not weak; I was worrying too much about what other people thought of me, even as I was sure of my own intentions. In part, this "other people may think" problem was integrated into my upbringing, and currently it was being reinforced by Becker's growing intimation that I was a golddigger. I wondered whether marriage to Eva might lead to my having to quit my job, or at least to my trying to find one in another department. Given my specialization in German, that was unlikely to happen.

The straw that broke the camel's back was Becker's demand for a car as a "matchmaker's fee." When he mentioned it the first time, and given his normal pattern of capricious conversation, I did not take it seriously. He also said it in the half-serious tone that was habitual with Becker. What I found, once we had decided to marry, was that he *was* serious. The problem was aggravated by Eva's friendship with Becker's wife, a friendship dating back to school in Prague. The families of the two women also were close friends. But now this Viennese husband was making things sticky. Of course, Becker's wife backed him up, making me the culprit.

"Where are we?" I said to Eva. "In New York or in Vienna or in some small Eastern European shtetl?" What made the story all the more bizarre was that Becker was not Jewish, yet he had assumed the customs of *shadchens* and *yentes* when it came to that car! Eva was both sad and angry—sad because she did not want to lose a lifelong friend, angry because Becker, whom she did not care for, was forcing the issue.

The problem was also aggravating my concerns about using Eva's money. If I lost my job and could not find another one soon, could we get married? Then Eva would be providing the only source of income!

This led to a very different discussion of finances, taking into account my career plans. I was determined to become a journalist—an American reporter rather than a German-language specialist with little chance for advancement in the American job market. My plan was to get a job as a junior reporter, perhaps even as a copy boy, and work my way up. It would mean a temporary reduction of income, but was a necessary investment in the future. This plan was one of the reasons why I had had doubts about meeting my responsibilities as a married man.

Discussion in the light of the situation brought about by Becker turned on this issue of "investment." Eva argued for my trying my hand at writing in English and attending journalism school, which would give me a better chance to start at a higher level of work. With positive advice from both our families, we decided to move in that direction once I left the Voice's Austrian desk. It made me feel uneasy, but I decided to accept such unanimous advice. I knew, though, that I would not be able to rid myself of the bad feeling that went with it.

Was I sure that I didn't marry Eva for her money? Would I have married her if we had to live on my income? Would I be able to or dare take a year off to attend journalism school if we didn't use Eva's money? Of course not. But we loved each other, and by going ahead as planned, we might speed up my career, let Eva live as she was used to and wanted to live, and still not use more than her income plus whatever I would bring in.

We worked out a compromise that was a long way from my original stand. We were planning on a two-way, possibly two-year, career-building plan: developing my Spanish and some Latin American expertise by doing freelance work from the scene, then attending Columbia's Graduate School of Journalism for master's degree (if I were accepted!). It turned out that both investments would pay off handsomely over the next ten years and indeed would shape my professional future.

But first some immediate decisions lay ahead: graduation from the School of General Studies, and a wedding. All this time I was still working for Becker in an increasingly tense, raw atmosphere.

I was heading for an exciting life, but also for a life that would be far more complicated, less predictable, less controllable. Life with Eva was beckoning insistently. The wedding date was set for June 30, 1948, after my graduation. But where would I, would we, go from there? Plans were all well and good, but how well would they work out? And what about my parents? They had come to love Eva, and there was no tension in our family about the big event. Mother gave no sign that she was "losing" me. Even Grandfather had good things to say about the marriage. Father, of course, left things to me. He was the only one at home who had treated me as an adult since we went to England. And yet, wasn't Mother saying to Father, or perhaps only to herself, "how could you?!" when she thought about my moving out? Was I hurting her even though she had decided to hide her feelings?

Then there was my continuing universalism, which to my parents, and especially to my father, meant estrangement from Judaism, our roots, and his deepest commitment. In the Petschek family, I would find myself at home. There was little if any Judaism there. One thing was decided quickly about our wedding, though: even though neither Eva nor I had any synagogue affiliation, a rabbi would have to officiate.

The only thing solid, honest, and unencumbered by doubt and

worry was our love for each other. All the rest seemed strained: the class difference between our families; my father's strict observance of Jewish ritual and faith, and the Petscheks' Jewishness in name only (with quite a few of them not even that—they had converted to one or another Christian denomination); the perception, among some relatives and friends, that I was "marrying into money," which I had no desire or way to deal with; the gnawing feeling, even after our interminable and brutally open discussion and the "compromise" over money, that I was a mini–Prince Albert, as Becker had trumpeted so often in front of everyone in the office . . .

Could we really cut through all this, or could I manage my feelings of guilt, inadequacy, unease. Eva was the key. It wasn't what she said; it's what she demonstrated that made the difference: she cared not one bit about class or cultural difference. She even had admiration, perhaps envy, for the simpler lifestyle on West 98th. How often had she said, and still says, that she hated the formality and stuffiness in the Prague mansion. It was not understanding or noblesse oblige that made Eva feel good about us; for her this was a home with the warmth and informality she had missed in her youth. She wanted to be part of us, the Goldmanns.

As the wedding day approached, we made plans for me to move in with Eva on East 57th Street. This meant that her friend Eva Goldman had to find new quarters. We felt bad, but there was no way around it.

As the wedding drew closer, I met more of Eva's family. It seemed to be an endless succession of cousins, aunts, and uncles—and, as in so many other ways, a sharp contrast to our small one-child tribe.

It seemed that the Petscheks were trying to re-create their life in Prague, move it lock, stock, and barrel to Westchester Country. Each uncle or aunt had a mansion like Hans's. They all had live-in servants, gardeners or chauffeurs, or both. It was not an attempt to play nouveau-riche; on the contrary: they were "ancien-riche," and their money made it possible to continue their life from the old country, with only minor modifications. This, however, seemed to cut them off from the life around them. Unlike Eva and others of our generation, the older folks seemed to look on America as a place where old habits and traditions could be practiced in security rather than as a new country with new challenges to be understood and lived.

How different this was from our life on 98th Street! We had left Germany with no resources of our own. We never got that carefully and riskily packed liftvan with our furniture. After it got stuck in Antwerp, it returned to Germany, for the use of some Aryan family! And while we had never had the luxurious life and homes of the Petscheks, we did have a comfortably upper-middle-class existence in Germany, way above what awaited us in London and New York. Yet we were never happier, never understood each other better, than in that one room on 100th Street. And just as naturally as the Petscheks lived on their islands of luxury, taking their large homes and staff for granted, we lived in close contact with the larger urban community. We learned more about America as a result, not by study but by experience.

Money made the difference. Eva and others in our generation of Petscheks did not let it dictate their lifestyle, merely influence it. And with marriages to spouses like myself, the old Prague effect was further diluted. In Eva's case, she welcomed marriage as a part of the process that left Prague behind.

I, of course, did not need to be liberated from the effects of too much money. I had to find a way to live with Eva's "liberation" without becoming its prisoner. Once I could settle our relationship in this respect, I was sure the rest would fall into place: the class difference, which meant something only to some of the older Petschek generation; my family's and, without realizing it, my own deeper commitment to Jewishness; the questions that would be asked by some in the refugee community, and the eyebrows that would be raised by others when the name Petschek was mentioned—all this was either unimportant or amusing. Eva and I had to make sure that what we had agreed upon would be manageable in practice and that I would develop a career where things would eventually balance out in the income bracket.

Next up for discussion were the wedding arrangements. In loco parentis, the bride's Uncle Hans and Aunt Eva would host the event. They decided to have it in their Scarsdale home. It certainly had the space. The date, June 30, offered a chance of a beautiful spring day, and some of the activities might take place in the garden. The Scarsdale rabbi, Mr. Schwartz, officiated.

The list of invitations was long. Our family was a small group, our friends somewhat more numerous, but the Petschek family was a tree with so many branches that it could hardly be perceived with one glance. I had met quite a few of them during the spring, but the list was so long, with so many new names of aunts, uncles, a great aunt, and countless "children" of our generation that I was sure I would never learn who was who. And these were only two of three "branches." What we were dealing with were the offspring of the two "Prague" groups—those of Grandfathers Isidor and Julius. The third brother, Ignatz, and his children had lived in Aussig (in Czech, Usti) in the German-populated northern range of the mountains that form the western border of Czechoslovakia. Ignatz and the two Prague brothers had had a falling out that was perpetuated in succeeding generations.

I had years of learning to do before I knew who was who in that huge family—and who was Jewish and who was not. One aunt, who had become an Episcopalian, and even active in the local church, did not eat dessert on Yom Kippur, just in case . . . One uncle's family had emigrated to Argentina and converted to Catholicism . . . It was all most complicated. Although I had for my own reasons become a universalist, the story of Eva's family made me wonder about my own "conversion," and created a renewed awareness of my Jewishness, and some twinges of conscience, especially toward my father. But I made no basic changes at the time, adhering to my Ethical Culture beliefs in the oneness of humanity . . . including some unease, especially on the Jewish High Holy days.

All of us—the large, multireligious Petschek clan and our small family—gathered at Hans and Eva's mansion in Scarsdale on a perfect sunny June 30 for the wedding. Rabbi Schwartz, a Reform clergyman, handled the ceremony with Jewish ritual and Scarsdale-style tact. The party was magnificent, as only hostess Eva, with ineffable taste, knew how to make it. And it was Jewish for all concerned in one important respect: the quantity and quality of the food.

By mid-afternoon, it had become quite warm, and some of us decided to jump in the pool. Eva did not join us, but preferred to stay dressed in her wedding gown. The inevitable photos include some with Eva thus dressed at the edge of the pool and me looking up at her from the water.

In spite of the infinite variety of religious, class, and style differences, it was a glorious occasion. It seemed to me equally clear that, like so many things, it could happen this way "only in America." Yes, we or two people of our respective backgrounds might have met in Europe . . . unlikely, but possible. Yes, we might have fallen in love . . . perfectly possible. But get married? Possible, but unlikely. And if so, get married in the warm and informal atmosphere of that day in Scarsdale? Impossible.

We would probably not have married for several reasons: Eva's parents or elders would have discouraged further contact between us because they had someone from a different background in mind for her. In the face of this, my parents would have dissuaded me from persisting, because it would have been a forced thing. And I probably would have continued in my Orthodox Jewish ways, even though I felt I was doing it only because my father had demanded it. Neither Eva nor I was cut out to defy our elders.

But this was America. Without realizing it, we had changed. America had changed all of us: the Petscheks limited their influence to making sure to know and have respect for my family; and my parents did not worry about whether it's right and wise in the long run, and about the children of our marriage crossing the social and religion-related barriers. Eva and I did not have to defy our families, because in America most families did not find it appropriate to raise obstacles that would have posed the issue.

After the marriage, we got into Eva's Plymouth convertible—souped up with a Pontiac motor because the old one had gone bad and no Plymouth motors were available—and drove off for the honeymoon on Cape Ann. We both had some doubts and questions in those first days, but our love washed them out. After a week, we came back to New York as happy and excited as, I suppose, newly married couples should be. We had no doubts. We were sure of everything. Even too sure, I felt. I resigned from the Austrian desk, and the pressure and tension that Becker had kept up for so long was lifted.

From one moment to the next, I was completely free—free to make my own choices. I didn't have to be at work at a certain hour, as I had for almost ten years, since the Frohwein job in London. But it did not feel good. I had never been on my own. Once I had a job, I was given orders or assignments, or, if I suggested an interview to

Becker, had to have the boss's approval. I was glad to be out from under Becker, but I felt lost with my freedom of choice.

Eva had no question about our decisions, which made it easy for her to encourage me to release myself from "having to be told what to do." Eva's independence gave her a more balanced view, a less approval-craving perspective. But still . . . who was going to tell me "how could you?!" I decided I had to tell myself, not realizing that I had long done this anyway!

I moved my things into Eva's apartment, as Eva Goldman with one *n* moved hers out. It was one of the first "how could yous" after our marriage. But Eva-One-N made it easy, and the two Evas remained good friends.

Another worry was moving out of 98th Street. I was abandoning my parents and Opa. I was stepping out and "up," leaving them to their own devices. They were getting older, and Opa had more frequent bouts of weakness. At eighty-three, he could not even make it to the wedding.

But there were also real and meaningful feelings of regret: except for two months in London, I had always lived with my family. We had been both too tightly knit, with all the problems this entailed, especially for my mother and me. "Home" had a powerful, even overpowering, meaning for me. And here I was leaving it?

For once, Mother was convincingly positive. There was not a trace of "how could you?!" in her voice. "Don't talk nonsense," she would say when I indicated my bad feeling about "abandoning" them. As for Father, there wasn't even any question. He'd just laugh it off.

The years that followed demonstrated the "love at first sight" between Eva and my parents amply and wonderfully for all of us. Was it the money, the security? I asked myself. But then, when I saw how much Mother and Eva cared for each other, and knowing that this was purely, absolutely, superbly real, I began to permit myself to feel good. And so my parents, especially my mother, helped me to understand: I knew that I had a new address; Mother convinced me that I had a new home, perhaps two homes . . .

❖

VII

I t was all wonderful, different, exciting: East 57th Street. A different world. Different from West 57th, where I had been working, and very different from West 98th: nicely dressed people walking their tiny dogs, the Gripsholm Scandinavian restaurant almost next door. Across the street was Mario's, an Italian restaurant, much better and more expensive than Schiavis around the corner from David Crystal's, where we used to eat a four-course meal for a dollar on special occasions. We ate out a lot in those early days, before Eva got into the habit of cooking. She learned a great deal from my mother, and we'd often go to my parents' home for dinner . . . always on Friday nights.

The apartment was modern, furnished nicely by Eva, for whom good taste without ostentation has been an important guideline all her life. The big red couch in the living room began to feel like home after a while. Calling my mother—more often than was either necessary or sensible, but making me feel good—became routine.

On weekends we would often drive to Scarsdale or Rye for lunch or dinner with one of the Petscheks or Gellerts, who were two brothers married to two of Eva's aunts. That first summer we'd also take advantage of the warm weather to invite ourselves to Aunt Eva's to swim. First, we'd have lunch. And for the first time, one Sunday in August, Hans criticized me: I had come "undressed"—without a tie!

By fall we were making plans for an extended trip to South America. I had some nonbinding expressions of interest from magazines for stories, but we did not count on a significant harvest. What the trip was primarily designed to do was to improve and come close to perfecting my Spanish, and to collect background through interviews and research on the spot that would help on my résumé.

At the same time, I applied to the Columbia Graduate School of

Journalism for the 1949–50 class. I had serious doubts about my admission, since in those days this top-rated graduate school admitted only sixty to seventy applicants a year. After all, I had little to recommend me: English as a foreign language; experience only in foreign broadcasting, and only in German; and graduation from evening classes—at Columbia, yes, but still, evening classes. To Eva's, my parents' (including my pessimistic mother's), and my own surprise, I was admitted! Not only was I happy about what it might do for my career, but because I was accepted despite the missing elements in my qualifications compared to the other, U.S.-educated applicants. Perhaps Columbia, unbeknownst to itself, had wanted to make up for my disappointment back in 1941!

It was fun to speculate, but I let that sleeping dog lie. With that admissions document in hand, the decision to make career investments looked more realistic. I still wasn't earning money, so my conscience was still far from relieved, but this was something I had to work out with myself.

The trip to South America had been planned with care. Although it was not yet the jet age as we came to know it some years later, flying by propeller-driven planes had become routine. Not for us, though. Eva hated flying and felt panicky just thinking about it. And since we had time, making as much of our trip as possible overland would be more instructive than capital-hopping by air. To get to the overland part, however, we went by ship from New York to La Guaira, the closest harbor to Caracas, Venezuela, where we started our nine-month journey.

We began to learn things about each other that it has taken a lifetime to adapt to, and even after more than forty years of marriage we still both must exercise tolerance. We started from a common denominator: Central European Jewish ultra-caution. But I had never known, even after much experience with my mother's packing of the steamer trunk, the various weights of coats and sweaters for different temperature ranges, and the pharmaceutical products, sterile gauze, and other medical paraphernalia that had accompanied us in Germany, how much more one could think of and take along. Whether it was Prague, or the family, or both, the Petscheks traveled heavy. It was also imperative to arrive at the train or the ship or, as was eventually the case, the airport in time: for Eva this meant at least one hour at a station or a pier, and a half-hour earlier than required by an airline.

Why? To make sure. And since there was no guaranteed way to make sure—one could have a problem getting a taxi, or the traffic might be heavy, or the taxi might have a flat, or the luggage might not fit and we would need two taxis, or any other contingency that only a Petschek imagination could conjure up—one just made sure as far as humanly possible.

As we prepared for our trip, my parents' correspondence with Germany had developed into regular exchanges. They began to tell us about what Lisbeth and Toni Scriba were doing and thinking, and to give us an inkling of what had happened to Police Officer Roeth of Kristallnacht. It was the beginning of a process of trying to get reacquainted over the deep divide of the late 1930s and the war years. My parents shared the hurt and disillusionment that all surviving German Jews felt. Yet, on the personal level, other feelings emerged: Mother was concerned about Lisbeth and her family, and said so, both in words and packages. And Lisbeth responded with the story of their experience: Fritz had been on the eastern front; they had trouble getting basic necessities; and everyone in town "still speaks about the doctor." "When is he coming back?" they asked. "We need him." Even though Lisbeth knew and felt strongly about what had happened to us, the letters were one-way messages: my mother trying to be helpful and Lisbeth pouring out her heart.

It was not selfishness or lack of consideration on Lisbeth's part; it was the limited experience and the pressure of personal needs that made our and the Jews' suffering a low-priority item on the Meyers' agenda. Lisbeth was not callous. She had proved that. She was a simple woman who for four years had lived in fear of losing her husband in the snows of Russia, and with a sickly and dependent daughter. Mother was sure she would always be there for us, as she was in Reinheim. What the correspondence and the resumed relationship after the war pointed up was that all people think of themselves first—and to ascribe it to ethnic disregard for human values is unjust and unrealistic.

Toni Scriba was a different story. She was a widow, with wide-ranging interests and with much room in her universalist attitude for the fate of German Jewry, both in fundamental human terms and as yet another stain on Germany's record. She said so, even as she demonstrated her special concern for Mother and our family. A steady theme in her letters, and later in conversation when Eva and I visited her, was: "The crimes committed by Germans against Jews must never be forgotten. We can survive them only if we always think about them."

As we got ready to leave for LaGuaira, Germany and Europe were stored away, but not permitted to wither, in my mind. First place had to go to Spanish and whatever I had learned about the nine countries we were planning to visit. I took along reams of paper and loose-leaf covers for a diary I would keep, in addition to whatever writing I might do for publication. How would we get contacts for my work? How could we learn how people live and what they think? German refugees were most readily available, of course. We and many of our acquaintances had relatives or friends in one South American country or another. Eva's sister lived in Brazil, as did a cousin of my mother's and her family. Eva had other relatives in Buenos Aires, with a farm a couple of hours away in the pampas. Then there were the Kahns in Caracas, the Langers in Bogotá, the Goldsteins in Quito, and the Hellers in Santiago. And each of them would have other contacts for us, I hoped: some called Diaz, Posada, or Errazuriz . . . and not changed from Darmstädter, Posner, or Ehrlich.

Before we departed my father gave us instructions about possible diseases. He warned against snakebite, typhoid, and cholera, and suggested that even with inoculations we could not be careful enough about what we ate. The conversation became downright scary, especially for Eva. With the lecture came a sizable container of pills, capsules, and ointments. Father was especially concerned about malaria, and equipped us with the most up-to-date products to deal with its manifestations. He was frustrated that he could not find a way to give us injections, because he feared we would have trouble finding reliable physicians there. Mother listened to all this with great respect, but also with an occasional smile. My parents complemented each other when it came to anxiety: my mother worried about the psyche, my father about the body. And in South America, there was ample cause for both: there were dictatorships and old Nazis around there, and there were all these malaria, typhoid, and cholera carriers.

We went aboard that cruise ship inoculated not only as required by the U.S. authorities, but against every imaginable and imaginary assault upon our health. We didn't really consider ourselves defenseless, but my parents wanted us to feel as though we were. Though we realized that we might catch malaria and would be able ward it off if we did, the "how could you?!" remorse would probably be worse than the discomfort from the disease.

We set off for La Guaira in December, planning to return in September for the 1949–50 year at Columbia. Caracas was a small town then, and what was in those days the center, Plaza Bolívar, has long since become a virtual relic of history amid the skyscrapers and freeways that make the Venezuelan capital look like Los Angeles. I was pleasantly surprised by how serviceable my Spanish was, and made full use of my inclination to adapt to the local vernacular and pronunciation. This turned out to be an almost country-by-country habit until we arrived in Brazil some seven months later. I couldn't fake knowing or speaking Portuguese!

Through the Kahns and Hellers I got to know Venezuelans in business and the professions, and Uslar Pietri had given me some references in the political and public worlds that came in handy. Running the country in those days was a three-man junta headed by Delgado-Chalbaud, but whose strongman and eventually real ruler of the country was Perez Jiménez. What I learned quickly, from my own experience and that of the German refugees in Caracas, was that a military junta in Latin America was nothing like a European totalitarian regime—a distinction that the U.S. media, public, and many politicians found it hard to make in those days. Juntas, decidely nondemocratic and capable of cruelty, are effective chiefly in enriching themselves. It's a far cry from the massive efficiency of totalitarians.

When we began to make plans for an overland trip to Bogotá, Colombia, our Caracas acquaintances looked incredulous. Even in those days one went there by plane! But not we, with our dual motivation of plane fright plus education-by-driving. So we found a car and a driver willing to drive us as far as Cucutá, on the Venezuela-Colombia border, where we would have to make new arrangements. A price was agreed on, and two stops had to be planned: in Barquisimeto, in the foothills of the Andes, and in Mérida, on the mountain road along which we would be driving toward Colombia. We were warned that hotel accommodations and rest stops would not be what we, and especially Eva, were accustomed to. But again, Eva's and my interests coincided: Eva was willing to risk bedbugs rather than fly; and I didn't mind "roughing" it, and in the process getting to know people and pastures, which served as restrooms.

As for food, we followed our instincts and kept my father's explicit cautions in mind, eating bread, potatoes, and thoroughly cooked or roasted meat. Coca-Cola, which was not an item in our icebox at home, replaced water. All this had a significant effect on our weight, but the watchword was "better fat than dead."

Something we could not do anything about was the road. As we drove higher into the Andes, it seemed to become narrower, and the abyss below more menacing. Things reached the point where Eva's fear of driving began to rival her fear of flying. When the mountain mists reduced visibility to zero, the driver opened his door to check how many inches he was from slipping into the valley far below. When he told us that the road from Cucutá was even higher and narrower, Eva made her decision: we fly. We did, for the short hop to Bogotá. While it was traumatic for Eva, it was an intense scare for an hour instead of the endless anxiety on the road.

My diary grew by leaps and bounds, my first article was in process, and interviews in the Colombian capital, with a politically democratic structure, were easy to come by. Our social contact were the Langers from Vienna. He had been an attorney and was now in business. More interesting was Frau Langer's career.

Soon after getting settled in Bogotá, she had an opportunity to invite some local people to dinner. This was a discovery for the guests: Viennese cuisine, right under their noses. Although they had traveled in Europe, eaten at fine Parisian restaurants, and enjoyed Swiss and Austrian pastries, when they returned home, it would be back to those nice but oh-so-boring dishes. Could Madame Langer teach them how to cook? It wasn't what this attorney's wife had in mind when she left Vienna, but she was an enterprising woman, and so— why not? Out of the suggestion grew a busy and prosperous Colombian version of the *cordon bleu*, or perhaps better named the Blaue Donau-Band. Madame Langer became the Escoffier of the Andes, the Queen of the "Esnitsels," as the Colombians referred to the famous breaded veal slices that are so universally served, and so rarely, except in Austria and at Mrs. Langer's, as they should be: thin, dry, and with squeezed lemon the only liquid component.

Madame Langer's close contact with the local crème de la crème also spurred her on to become more acculturated to her new environment than we had found to be the case for those in Caracas. For example, she had become an ardent fan of the bullfight—so ardent that, despite Eva's gentle and polite plea to be excused from what she feared would be a bloody and unhappy scene, we felt we would have insulted this Viennese fanatic of the corrida had we persisted in making excuses. Together with her quiet, bald, and distinguished-looking husband and her grown-up son, we proceeded toward that perennial Sunday afternoon pastime of Spaniards.

Madame Langer was middle-aged, solidly built, with the broad, heavy features that are common in Central Europe. With graying blond hair, and dressed as she would have in Vienna, she did not look like her disciples. When the matador made a bold dash toward the bull, only to avoid the deadly horn by inches as he slipped away gracefully, Madame Langer jumped up, her voice firm as she exclaimed, "Olé, wunderbar!" Nobody but Eva and I noticed amid the roar of the aficionados.

It was the triumph of a new wave of assimilation, the resolution of the oh-so-aweseome cultural differences that are the stuff of so many tomes and the livelihood of almost as many social scientists! Madame Langer had done it! Neither Queen Isabella, nor Torquemada, nor Adolf Hitler would have imagined it, and none of them were there to stop it. It was yet another triumph of Jewish survival.

Another flight took us from Bogotá to Medellín, in those days known as the commercial capital of Colombia. In Bogotá Jews had told us that Medellín was really a Jewish city, which, they said, was the secret of its faster pace, its industriousness, and its commercial activity. "Come now," I told Mr. Weil, a German refugee who had done well and lived in Bogotá some fifteen years, "not everybody can be Jewish!" The tendency of Jews to see Jews wherever they go was a subject to which I had long since been sensitized. Jews like to see more of us around, especially when they are a small minority in a country with a very different culture that is difficult to penetrate, much less become assimilated to. The South American countries we visited fit this description. No wonder, then, that Mr. Weil and others, who echoed him when I checked his assertion, were satisfied that Medellín had been settled by *marranos,* Jews who during the Inquisition had feigned conversion to Catholicism and over the course of generations had become genuine Catholics. The fact that the Medellín newspaper was called *El Católico,* and that the Antioqueños—Antioquia was the province—were among the staunchest and most conservative of Colombians did not weaken the Jewish claim. On the contrary, we were assured, it helped prove it: those folk with Jewish roots had to prove their Catholicism by deed, not by birth as others could.

We arrived in Medellín still disbelieving Mr. Weil's story, but it was worth checking out. During an interview with one of the city's leading businessmen and most prominent civic leaders, I gingerly posed a question about the different pace and purposefulness of people on the streets, who seemed to rush everywhere they were going. What was it about Medellín that made it so different from Bogotá, I asked as innocently as I could manage. The answer was simple: "Pues somos judios, no sabe? [After all, we are Jewish, don't you know?]," said Julio Pinero, as if I had not done my research or otherwise been made aware of one of the best-known facts about Medellín. I later was told that many of these distinguished Catholics continue to adhere to candle-lighting and other Jewish rituals that the generations had kept up over the centuries. Early on it was secret and deliberate; by the twentieth century it had become routine as a custom without religious significance.

I still was not convinced, but it certainly had a more solid ring of truth than when I first heard it from Weil in Bogotá. "In Medellín, too?" I said to Eva. "Are we really only a few million in the whole world?" She did not have an answer, and neither of us was sufficiently concerned with Jewish history and Jewish lore in those days to keep exploring it further. Twenty years later, I would have dug a lot deeper, but that is another story.

As we went on to Peru and Chile, we began to realize that I was speaking two languages, Spanish and German, and Eva mostly one, German. The refugees in South America took longer to adapt themselves to their surroundings than those in the United States did. Foreigners remained foreigners much longer than they did in North

America, which was much more heterogeneous. And though we in New York and other U.S. cities retained our German accent, we spoke English sooner and with greater ease than I found our peers in the southern hemisphere speaking Spanish. When they did, it often sounded like German, with the North German guttural *r* and the occasional insertion of a Spanish word designating something less familiar in German: "Hier gibts ja herrliche mariscos! [There's marvelous seafood around here!]" would be typical.

By the time we reached Santiago, flying had become routine for us—or rather routine for me and inevitable for Eva. We managed to travel overland from Medellín to Cali, via Cartago, where I caught an infection at the Hotel Mariscal Robledo. We flew from Cali to Quito, Ecuador, where a refugee physician diagnosed malaria and caused me to hear my father's warnings loud and clear. But it turned out to be a false alarm. I could now hear the voices on 98th Street say, "But it *could* have been real! So be careful!"

Quito to Lima and Lima to Santiago were negotiable only by plane, as was Santiago to Buenos Aires. This was an especially trying leg for Eva, since the propeller plane had to virtually wind itself up to the height that would allow it to clear the highest peaks of the Andes. Eva abandoned herself to her anxiety and the imagined danger, but I was fascinated, particularly when we crossed the Andes, with their snow-covered peaks seemingly within reach.

While Eva enjoyed visiting with her aunt and cousins in Buenos Aires, I dove into the Peronist world, soaking up this attempt to imitate the "corporate state" of the fascists and Nazis. I also got an interview with the then quite lonely and unpublicized opposition leader Arturo Frondizi, who later became president. It was good article material, and did find its way into print in New York.

A brief visit to Montevideo was followed by two weeks in Brazil, where again Eva felt at home with her sister and I with relatives of my mother's. Partly because we were exhausted, partly because I did not speak the language, and mainly because we enjoyed our family reunions, I did not do much business in this vast country. It was also dauntingly big and complex, worth a few months all by itself. So my memory of a cool and rainy July-August period in Rio and São Paulo is of a good deal of reminiscing and updating each other on family matters. I tried feijoada, the Brazilian national dish, once or twice.

Most of the time it was *Tafelspitz,* or *Kalbsbraten,* and, since my grand-mother's sister was living with her daughter in São Paulo, that same mean *Apfelschalet* Oma Hilda used to make.

My diary had swollen to seven loose-leaf volumes, four articles had been published in U.S. magazines, and I had learned a lot of Spanish, to the point where I conversed easily, but I was still making mistakes. Thus, in Chile, I became red-faced when, responding to an insistent request to talk to a group, I was apologizing for my flawed Spanish, saying that I was "embarazado," forgetting in the heat of the moment what I had been taught: that in Spanish this word means pregnant. My gracious listeners did not bat an eyelash. Only later did one cor-rect me most privately—with apologies, and only to guard me against a repetition.

We returned to New York by Moore McCormack liner. I spent the ten-day voyage relaxing and writing. Once back, I got ready for Columbia Journalism. I had no idea what would await me there, but I believed there was not much that could be learned, since the heart of journalism is writing, and writing is more of an art than a craft. The more daunting question was whether I could match or come close to the quality of English that indigenous Americans, most with expe-rience on a paper or at a radio station, were naturally and effortlessly using.

We had stayed in close touch with home and had gathered that Opa was aging fast. We found, when we returned, that the still quite sturdy and enterprising old man had thinned out and slowed down. His circulatory problems had increased, his spells of weakness become more frequent. It was my father's close proximity and the immediate availability of the right dose of the right drug that kept him going.

Opa was glad to see us again, but he seemed removed. He kept to himself and his cushioned chair by the window looking out on 98th Street even more than before. He no longer went to evening school, but still enjoyed using the English he had learned. Germany seemed a thing of the past. He did not talk about his onetime favorite sub-jects, and I did not bring them up. I doubt that he had forgotten anything, but he seemed preoccupied with his life, literally, and with his condition. When I tried to tell him about our trip, especially about his relatives in Brazil, he barely showed interest. It all seemed too much for him to handle.

As I sat there, trying to talk to him but primarily watching him, it became evident that the world had passed him by. Here was a man whose life had spanned almost a century in which Germany had been at the center of events: intoxicating in the latter part of the nineteenth century, followed by three decades of dashed hopes and economic ruin, and then by the twelve years no word in the dictionary could describe—which was later named the Holocaust, or the more awesome Hebrew Shoah. Now here he sat, shriveled and quiet, the Jew called Hermann, the enlisted man in the army of Kaiser Wilhelm I, the proud citizen whose wife had given away her jewelry so it could be turned from gold to iron, the same woman who later smashed her frail body on the pavement in Frankfurt. Under the new rulers, "Hermann" had to become "Hertz," which was the Jewish original at birth. His farmer-customers shunned him now, and he perforce became an early retiree, but still hanging on in a Germany that had shown him so many different faces—until he was literally dragged out and ended up on this cushioned chair in a land whose presidents he had neatly listed, to which he had warmed as he had not expected, but which he never really understood. It was too late. He also never understood Germany and the Jews' place and fate. It was too much. So he thought about his meals, his personal needs, his rest—and, as he often said, about trying not to burden Martha and Jacob. His was never a full life. Now it had been all but drained of what little there had been.

At Columbia, we all were one class. The master's degree would come after one year, after courses in reporting, typography, headline writing . . . Most of my fellow students had experience as reporters or writers. All I had was a couple of years of practice in interviewing and then producing a script in German. I did not bother to count the few English-language articles I had produced in South America.

As Professor Roscoe Ellard, a former reporter, strode up and down the aisles, hectoring us as a city editor would his reporters (my friends in class were sure this was precisely what he was doing and enjoying), I got the drift: in America newspapers wanted articles to tell it all in the first paragraph. Ellard went into ecstasy over the five Ws (What, Who, Where, When, and Why) that needed to be answered in the lead. He smoked constantly and let the ashes drop down on his dark gray jacket or vest. Some of the students seemed awed. Others smiled occasionally, indicating they did not take him too seriously, but not daring to let him know. I just took it all in, wondering how the "learning" process would shape up.

One of the first things was a spelling test. A spelling test? I asked myself. For sixty-five students chosen for their excellence in English writing? And when it was given, I was among the top performers! I, the foreigner!

I realized that this was not a great feat, but rather the result of very different styles of early education. In America, even professional writers were not sure of their spelling. It was no shame to misspell. Nobody cared very much, and few even noticed it. In Europe, to spell correctly was not only a requirement for anyone who went beyond minimum schooling, but a mark of social standing, of class. To misspell was to be *ungebildet*—uncultured comes closest. It was intolerable not just as a lapse in learning, but as a flaw in class.

So my spelling achievement was "no big deal," as Ben Franklin, my neighbor in class, said. Professor Richard Baker gave some disciplined lectures, and Mr. Gerstenzang of the *New York Times* taught us all about copyreading. This, I decided, was a skill, almost an art when performed imaginatively. Also instructive, both in content and in presentation, was Theodor Bernstein's class on typography. But when we were sent out on assignments, which turned out to be pseudo-assignments, the weakness of the curriculum showed: we were not too gently or considerately smiled at by the real professionals at city hall or in the court building. It was not at all the same as really doing the job! So much so, I felt, that it bordered on the depressing, and I was glad when the ordeal was over. Uncle Roscoe, as we called him, meant well, but I was just not able to play the game of reporter as well as he was playing editor in that classroom on 116th Street.

I learned things that were useful later on, but I doubted then and still doubt that the one year was worth a master's degree. I received it gladly, even though I wasn't sure I deserved it. It was signed by Dwight D. Eisenhower, who spent a few years as president of Columbia University before running for and becoming president of the United States. Nice interim if you can get it, some of us students thought.

Now I would test whether my investment of time and money had been worth it. Master's degree and résumé in hand, I began my campaign for a regular news job—in the English I could spell so well. It turned out that I had a problem I had not focused on: I was twenty-nine years old, and was told several times, most clearly by the *New York Times,* that I was too inexperienced to be hired as a reporter and too old and overqualified to be a copy boy, which is the normal way for an aspiring newsman to start.

Eva was more upset than I was. The people at the *Times* and the news magazines where I had applied had a point. Eva did not accept the "overqualified" argument. She said, "If you are so well qualified, why don't they give you a chance as a reporter?" The trouble was that it was a discussion among ourselves. It had been discussed only briefly at interviews, because I did not want to wear out my welcome. The galling thing to Eva and me was something that no managing editor hiring reporters would consider: that my "advanced" age was due to the rude interruption Adolf Hitler had caused in my career, and compounded by an undergraduate admissions office that had taken no account of this interruption. Papers like the *Times* wrote analyses and features about such career problems, with pictures of ex-lawyers who had to flee the Nazis peddling Avon products on Park Avenue. It seemed not to have occurred to them to do something about it in their own practices.

Again my past was impinging on my present life. I resented it, because I had not realized, as I did later and do most clearly now as I write this story, that there was no way and no point trying to escape it, that it would forever be part of my life, and that I would enhance my opportunities by making the most of it. At the time I felt that only my trip to South America was "international experience" worthy of being included on my résumé. In fact, the unintended experience of life and schooling of the previous twenty years was deeper and fuller. It was an invaluable resource, intellectually and emotionally, that cried out to be brought into play in a career that would benefit from it. I brought to my work a dimension of thought and observation shaped by my life that could routinely add to and round out my reporting or analysis. When I wrote about Czechoslovakia, I did not just know how to spell it, but I knew where it was located without looking at a map; I knew why its recent history made it a special case in the developing postwar climate without reading up on it in some encyclopedia.

"Let's stop being frustrated," I said to Eva one evening after yet another disappointing interview. "Let's stop worrying about my advanced age and make use of it." What I was thinking about was going back to VOA—not to my old German-language haunts, but the central news and English-language operation. There, perhaps, I could make my combination of earlier work at VOA, journalism degree, and international experience count!

I felt I had an additional asset: I was not emotional about Germany. My father had been the key influence in shaping my feelings and thinking: he had always separated the Nazis from what was valuable, positive, and creative in German life and culture. Germany and American policy toward Germany or concerning Germany in relation to other countries would be a key subject at VOA. If I had an irrepressible grudge that would cramp my style or lead me into skirting policy or, worse, veracity for personal emotional reasons, I should not even apply for the job. This turned out to be a major issue later on, when I found myself in a decision-making job for the entire VOA operation, and encountered in others unrestrained personal feelings that governed work on the job.

In mid-1950, I did land at VOA, but in a very different and more promising job than I had been in before: I was hired to prepare news scripts for the worldwide English broadcasts, which set the pattern for foreign-language transmissions. Even though I would have much preferred to work for a "real" American news organization, such as the *Times* or *Time* or *Newsweek,* I had crossed the threshold into English. All my colleagues as well as my boss, Barry Zorthian, had been born and educated in America. I was the only foreigner. What was satisfying was that it turned out just as I had hoped: I was able to hold my own, in style and speed, with my fellow writers, and I was able to add that little extra that came with my history. We were a congenial group. No one was too proud to ask the other fellow a question, and I soon found myself on the receiving end of many questions. Not only did I not mind, I found myself doing just what I had projected. And when Jim Fletcher said, "It's easier to ask Goldmann than to waste time leafing through the encyclopedia," when it came to the spelling of Fürstenfeldbruck or Przemyśl, I was happy on two counts: that I felt confident of being able to answer correctly and that Barry had confidence in my doing so.

I was earning a respectable salary, a good deal higher than I had received at the Austrian service. More important, the Voice was here to stay, and there was a wide range of opportunities, not only within VOA, but in other foreign policy offices of the government. There were chances in the State Department, Central Intelligence, and even the possibility of entering the foreign service. Many of my colleagues had that ambition and waxed romantic about it. I saw it as a possibility, but did not feel like "seeing the world," some of which I had seen under unfavorable circumstances. Eva felt even less disposed to lead a life of moving around the globe, especially when it came to germ-risky places like Africa and Southeast Asia. Latin America, with its malaria scare and the imaginary menace of deadly plagues my father and Eva had felt the need to guard against, was enough for a while.

One place I did want to see was Paris. My teachers in Frankfurt and some of my lecturers in Spanish literature at Columbia had brought up Paris time and again. It had to be seen. I'd had that ambition in Frankfurt, when the sheer romance of Paris had seized hold of me. But France was one of the first countries Hitler had barred to Jews, and I never did get to see it. I decided that, even if I did not join the foreign service, which probably would land me in Timbuktu, Karachi, or Pago Pago before I could ever dream of being assigned to Paris, I would bide my time. Maybe, Eva and I decided, if things went well, we'd visit it at a time of our choosing, when it would be much more satisfying.

As I settled down in the job and the newswriting focused on Europe, the old days exerted a pull on me. I remembered the one vacation my parents and I spent in Wengen, in the Bernese Oberland, and developed a strong desire to revisit it. And gradually, but perhaps inevitably, Frankfurt came back into range, and then Reinheim. The houses we had lived in, the streets, the road from Darmstadt to Reinheim, Darmstadt itself . . . Lisbeth, Roeth. What was happening to me? Was I becoming nostalgic again? I had lived in America for ten years, married here, spoke English at work and at home with Eva, and with my parents. What was going on?

In those first months of newswriting I learned more than I had learned about writing in all my schooling, including my journalism courses at Columbia. We had to produce twelve minutes worth of copy, about 1,500 words at the rate our slow and precisely elocuting announcers were reading, within two and a half hours. That meant about eight to ten triple-spaced, wide-margined pages. The process involved planning the news roundup, or sequence, picking up part of the previous full newscast and its updates, selecting new material from four wire services, writing up the new material, recasting what we had picked up or were updating, writing the headlines, and marking optional copy. It meant either producing what was needed or not staying on the job. It was one of the most exciting challenges of my life, because meeting it meant something: that I could write acceptably and professionally in English, and that I could produce at a rate that was expected from professionals with a respectable record.

In addition, I brought an asset to the section that had not been there: I managed French, and Agence France Presse was one of our wire-service sources. As a rule, it had only been used as a backup source where no other second source was available—and two sources was the strict rule for any story we were using. In those cases, the AFP copy was taken to a French-speaking person in another department—usually the French section—for translation or checking of what my colleagues believed it said. Now there was no need to take it, and, more important, we could treat AFP as a first source against which we could request checks from our English-language wire services. I had never been a good French student, just passable in Darmstadt and Frankfurt, but it was serviceable for West 57th Street's news operation—yet another piece of evidence that one never knows what even a little knowledge may be good for.

By 1950 Stalin had fastened his rule on all of Eastern Europe, most hurtfully to us on Czechoslovakia—not merely because it was Eva's family's home, but because it was the one democratic country in Eastern Europe. From the euphoria of victory and the immediate postwar friendship of the Allies, we found ourselves once again in the familiar mood of tension and danger. This time it was the unprecedented danger of nuclear war, which had not registered with many of us when President Truman dropped the bombs on Hiroshima and Nagasaki.

"If the Allies hadn't finished the war when they did, Hitler may well have had this bomb," Father said. "It's a blessing that he was dead before he had it. But now Stalin has it, and this is not much better for the world." Again, Papi was ahead of the crowd. Our relatives and friends did not agree with Father when he worried about the agreed-upon, and to Father dangerously generous, line that had become the Iron Curtain. Nor did they agree about the danger of the bomb in Stalin's hands. "Didn't he sacrifice more than any other country, certainly more than America, to defeat Hitler?" was the argument of the Nussbaums and Neus and Steins. Father would get angry at them, saying they were sentimental when the issue might be life and death for America and Europe, and for the surviving Jews!

This argument had no impact on them, but it did on me, and has been an increasingly significant principle, even guideline, for me personally and professionally ever since. At the office, too, the argument recurred as we discussed the increasingly strong resistance by the Truman administration to Stalin's expansionist activities in Iran, Greece, and Turkey. Here, it was less the gratitude that German Jews felt toward the Soviet Union than an inchoate, ideologically unshaped, yet intense feeling that "left" was progressive and "right" reactionary.

Thirty-five years later, a leader of the French-Jewish community was still making this argument. We were discussing Israel, and voting patterns on Arab-Israeli issues in the European Parliament in Strasbourg. My conversation partner was arguing against helping a strongly pro-Israel conservative, "because he sometimes votes the same way as Le Pen [of the extreme right National Front]." "But," I suggested, "when you object to helping a decent person who is supporting what we believe in, how can you make excuses for a socialist government that relies on communists for its parliamentary majority, and that is cool, and sometimes downright hostile, to our Israel-related concerns?" "It's not the same," answered my French friend. "The communists were on our side in the war."

From the Slansky trial to the doctors' plot to East Germany portraying itself as a "victim of fascism" as it blithely declined any responsibility for what had been done to Jews, Gypsies, Poles, Russians, communist cynicism was there for all to see. Yet it did not sink in emotionally among my fellow Jews who had escaped Hitler's hell.

One fear that did sink in as the Cold War became more intense was the Bomb. New York City would be a prime target. And we were thinking of raising a family. In New York City? I was opposed to moving, both because I did not feel that even Stalin would explode a bomb, and because I loved the asphalt. I never could figure out why the latter was true. After all, I was born in a village; the intervening stops—Frankfurt and London—were brief. The explanation that makes sense is that New York became my real, lasting new home. It had offered us not just refuge, but the first new chance after almost ten years of persecution, insecurity, and movement to sink roots again. I came to feel fond of our streets, streetcars, trees, scraggly as they were. But I warmed up especially to those buildings that looked like those in Darmstadt and Frankfurt—with thick iron fences protecting thin and thirsty patches of green in front of the stone walls. Whenever we went visiting in Westchester, I felt out of place. These feelings have not changed through the decades. I became the perverse character in both families, enjoying all seasons, and especially the empty city on hot summer weekends, and feeling impatient and uncomfortable amid the lawns of the suburbs.

Yet it was to the suburbs that we moved. The practical arguments for the move won out easily over the implausibility of my sentiments. With a decent salary contributing respectably to our budget, it was not unreasonable to make a down payment on a house whose mortgage, maintenance, and tax burden would barely exceed what we were paying for rent in the city. We found a French colonial in the Fort Hill section of Scarsdale. The die was cast. I became a commuter.

Eva and I became directly and emotionally involved in the 1952 election. We were among those who became unquestioning fans of Adlai Stevenson. And, fortified by the self-proclaimed "scientific" calculations based on polls and mainly on the wishfulness of a colleague at the Voice, we felt confident of his victory over a nice general who was not very smart.

Father had instructed me well on ideological and world affairs, but I had not learned the first thing about American politics. Ignorance combined with wishful thinking, but also began to sober me up. At any rate, Dwight Eisenhower continued to pursue me, from one presidency to another.

Eisenhower's presidency became an almost fateful event for my career. The new president had not intended to promote a senator named Joseph McCarthy to the chairmanship of a committee from which this Wisconsin demagogue could besmirch American democracy and ruin the lives of individuals. Yet the election produced this consequence. And the president either was insensitive to McCarthy's activities or for tactical political reasons permitted them to go on until, as those who gave Eisenhower the benefit of the doubt thought, McCarthy would self-destruct. It was an unrealistic and callous interpretation, since in the meantime dozens of people and institutions, not to mention the good name of America, were suffering considerable damage.

As a minority senator, McCarthy had made a name for himself. He had made the most and the worst out of the public's legitimate concerns about Stalin's aggressiveness by posing as the discoverer of pro-communist rottenness within the country. It was not Stalin and his war machine that was the threat; it was the subversives at home who were doing his work, and the most damaging of those operated right within the government, in its most sensitive departments and agencies.

McCarthy had done plenty of damage before the ascension of Dwight Eisenhower to the presidency, carrying a Republican-controlled Congress with him. In that Congress, ranking minority members became chairmen—and Joseph McCarthy of Wisconsin was one of them. His aides, Roy Cohn and David Schine, were two young men on the make whose relentless ambition matched the senator's need for unscrupulous assistance. Once in the Congressional saddle, they decided to ride roughshod over any individual, no matter how innocent and unsuspecting, who could serve their purposes, creating an atmosphere in which fear of the communist around the corner would enhance their and their boss's chance to run the country.

The McCarthy reality hit me directly. And it coincided with Eva's fifth pregnancy, after a succession of miscarriages. Now she was in her fifth month, well on the way to hoped-for success, and duly pampered by all as she tolerated both her confinement to bed (on doctor's orders, as a precaution) and the oversolicitousness of family and friends when a man we thought was a colleague brought me and two others under the klieg lights of the McCarthy committee.

I had by this time moved a notch higher into the Voice's operation as an editor in the central newsroom, where the material for all languages was prepared. The Wisconsin senator's committee had made the Voice its first object or victim, using it as an easy target on which to hone the smear-and-publicize technique he later used on weightier institutions, culminating in his attempt to besmirch the U.S. Army.

It seems normal for people to feel that what happens near them is not going to affect them personally. So it was on February 20, 1953, when, sitting around the central desk where final editing was done, as we were listening to the hearings on a direct line into the McCarthy committee's room, we heard the name "Virgil Fulling." A massive double take occurred among us listeners. "Hey, Fulling, did you hear it, too?" Eric Halling asked. And before we could answer, Fulling's voice came out of the speaker, mumbling, as was his wont, about people who were changing copy in favor of the communist cause.

I looked over to Fulling's desk, a few feet down the aisle of writers' places in the newsroom. "Hey," I said, "he isn't around."

"Of course not," Halling responded to my indeed foolish "discovery," adding: "How can he be? He's in Washington testifying."

My comment could be explained only by the incredulity that this self-effacing and not very bright writer of Latin American news items was a central figure in one of Washington's most publicized hearings. Also, because his inconspicuousness, both personally and professionally, caused no ripples, and one had to look to see whether he was indeed at work.

Before I could register it all, Fulling droned out my name, along with that of Donald Taylor, who was sitting a few feet away from me in the slot—the name for the editor in charge of the central desk during one of the three daily shifts. Then he blurted out the name of Harold Berman, who headed the newsroom and was listening in his office.

One must have lived at the time, perhaps even gone through the experience of a McCarthy hearing, to grasp that six senators and four staff members were engaged in discussing the professional editing of four lines in one wire story out of scores that passed the central newsdesk every day, a process that covers eleven pages of single-spaced committee transcript! At the end of Fulling's testimony, the three of us were tarred. "Do you think they [my two colleagues and I] were communists?" asked the late Senator Henry M. (Scoop) Jackson.

Duly coached by staff, Fulling responded, "I would not like to state my opinion on that, Senator. I would be very glad for the Committee to determine."

"Are you convinced it is friendly to the communist cause?" asked Chairman McCarthy.

"I do believe that," answered Fulling, ever so reasonably.

But Senator Karl Mundt, well before Fulling's testimony was complete, had already pronounced the sentence: "Are Mr. Goldmann and Mr. Taylor and Mr. Berman still employed by the Voice of America, where they can exercise this skillful manner of helping communism to the detriment of America?"

Case closed. But no. We immediately demanded a hearing to clear our names. The facts posed no problem; they rarely did in a McCarthy hearing. Our crime was that I had changed Fulling's repeated use of the word "anti-communist," as it had indeed appeared in an International News Service wire story. The story reported on demonstrations by anti-communists in front of the U.S. embassy in Guatemela—at that time governed by an extreme left and anti-American regime—applauding the election of General Eisenhower to the presidency. They shouted anti-communist slogans, and they were members of anti-communist organizations. I made it read that "citizens" were demonstrating, that they shouted anti-communist slogans, and that they were members of democratic organizations. Using the term "anti-communist" three times in as many lines was just bad and heavy-handed writing. "Citizens" was truthful, did not presume to know whether the demonstrators were anti-communist or just pro–United States; and "democratic" in place of the third "anti-communist" served to nail down that adjective as pro-American at a time when the Communists were trying to appropriate it to describe themselves in Latin America. Don Taylor was guilty because he permitted the editing changes to go through, and Berman because he was in charge of the office. These small changes had become a mountainous "pattern" of pro-communism. No other "evidence" was introduced.

Some American liberals saw or wanted to see a rebirth of Nazism in the person and activities of the Wisconsin senator. We who had lived in Germany through the 1930s knew better: America, even at the high point of McCarthy's power, was nothing like Nazi Germany; but McCarthy's techniques had borrowed a good deal from the Führer and Joseph Goebbels, and we saw too many Americans either take the senator seriously or remain indifferent. We wanted a more vigorous defense of individual rights, particularly from the president, whose silence we could not understand.

When I became a target, it was ironical. My father could not believe that, fifteen years after Buchenwald, he had to worry about me all over again. To be sure, things had not gone nearly as far as on Kristallnacht, but the source of the threat was similar. It was fueled by ideology and ruthless ambition. The big difference was that in America we could fight.

In the twelve years we had lived and worked in the United States, we had ceased to cower and regained the urge to defend ourselves. It was heartening that my mother had lost much of her high anxiety, which she had demonstrated to the point of recklessness on the morning of November 10, 1938, but which had since settled down to normal proportions for a Jewish wife and mother. Grandfather, now eighty-eight and becoming weaker, could not quite grasp what was happening, which was just as well. It was Eva we were worried about. It seemed she had finally overcome whatever had prevented her from carrying a pregnancy to full term. Now, we asked ourselves, would the anxiety and tension of my "trial" by Joe McCarthy jeopardize her chances? She was bearing up well, the doctor's prognosis remained encouraging, and I decided I had no choice but to concentrate on the two tasks I could do something about: doing my job, and preparing myself for a hearing Don Taylor and I had requested on the day Fulling testified against us. Berman did not join us, because he did not want to face having his personal affairs examined in public. He later resigned.

I was more determined to fight Fulling's nonsensical charges than Don, who was a "leave things alone they'll go away" type. But he agreed to take part if I took the initiative. At the time, under the Damocles sword of a McCarthy "guilty" pronouncement, the Voice experienced a rapid succession of directors. It was a revolving door: some thought they could stem the tide and gave up once they were in the hot seat; others, assigned by the State Department, then the supervisory agency, requested transfer as soon as it could be arranged. Consequently, it was idle to look to our "leaders" for support. On February 20 I did go to see the director in charge to request permission to address ourselves to the committee and to make the demand for a public hearing in the media, where we had good connections. "Go right ahead" was the answer from the director-for-the-day, whose name has escaped me, and that was it.

We assumed that, should McCarthy grant us the requested hearing of response to Fulling, it would probably be with minimum notice. We got busy immediately, gathering material with the help of virtually the entire newsroom staff. I wrote a prepared statement and had it cleared by an attorney, to be sure I was on safe ground in anything I volunteered.

When Fulling returned from Washington the day after his testimony, he faced a solid boycott. As we all worked on the Taylor-Goldmann defense, Fulling was cut off from any contact in the office. He had never been popular. Now he was a pariah. Several years later, I learned that he had committed suicide.

For a couple of weeks, I carried the briefcase with the material for my defense with me wherever I went—just in case the call came. I left word at all times where I could be reached. The call came in the late afternoon of March 5, 1953, requesting that Don and I appear in Washington the next morning at 10 A.M.

Don and I took the night train. George Agree, my friend going back to garment-center days, accompanied us. He was working in the Washington political arena, and both his presence and his counsel were helpful to me. George told me after the hearing, "When you went up there, I thought, here walks a solid hunk of man, and he'll come out flattened and limp." It did not turn out this way. As I listened to Don Taylor, who was by nature low-key and soft-spoken, I felt eager to go up there and make the points that needed to get across. By the time I was called, I had forgotten about career, reputation, and the other risks and dangers that had weighed us down since Fulling had smeared us. I was impatiently anxious to tell the story of what really happened. I had to succeed.

Practically the entire hearing turned into a debate on the meaning and use of the word "democratic" in the then Latin American political context. In the course of my prepared statement, I was dealing with this central, intellectually obvious, but in the McCarthy setting dead-serious issue. I said, "Mr. Fulling clearly implied that the word 'democratic' should not be used in our copy, because of possible confusion in Latin America. I think that is wrong. I think we should never let the communists steal that word from us and use it for their own big-lie campaigns, which is exactly what they do."

McCarthy interrupted to ask, "Do you not think they have already stolen that word in South America?"

Here is where that study trip came in handy. I had learned something important in Santiago. "I don't think so, Mr. Chairman," I said. "For instance, the Chilean law, which forbids and outlaws the Communist Party, is called and referred to commonly as the Law of the Defense of Democracy. . . . I have spent almost a year in Latin America, and it is not general usage among people there to identify the word 'democratic' with communism."

Mc Carthy then seemed to have got the point. "In other words, you think that part of your function is to keep the communists in South America from taking over the word 'democratic'?"

Eureka! I said to myself, but it was not the end. The chairman persisted in rehashing this dialogue for some ten or fifteen minutes, when suddenly he asked, "What is your name, incidentally?" This led to my becoming Mr. Goldmann in the next exchange, but brought no change in the theme.

McCarthy finally said that in changing the words in the dispatch at issue, "you were telling the people of Guatemala that the Communist Party was parading, showing their approval of Eisenhower's election." Logically, the next witness should have been President Eisenhower, to answer what he had done to merit the applause of Guatemala's communists!

Soon afterward, the chairman lost interest. I was permitted to read some more of my VOA writing into the record. The other senators were of no help and seemed uninterested from the outset, which surprised me, because men like Scoop Jackson and Stuart Symington must have known what was at stake, yet they were only perfunctorily involved.

When I was dismissed, I ran to a phone to call Eva, who was fine and delighted at the outcome. I told her that the hearing took only five or ten minutes. George Agree overheard and corrected me. "It was more like forty!" he said. My concentration had been so complete that I lost track of time.

I went back to work the next day, eventually got the galleys of the transcripts for correction, and never heard again about my "skillful manner of aiding communism."

Peter Daniel Goldmann was born three months later, weighing nine and a half pounds.

We had settled into our Scarsdale house with Peter, happy about the almost simultaneous outcome of two high-stake risks, when another decision had to be made. Eisenhower had decided to establish the United States Information Agency (USIA), gather under its umbrella all governmental foreign public affairs activities, establish a foreign service career system for USIA staffpeople, and—here was the rub—locate the entire apparatus in Washington, D.C.

Those who argued—some for reasons of effectiveness, others like ourselves for self-serving purposes—that our kind of work required creativity, and that the pool of people whose talent was useful, even essential, was largest in New York, got nowhere. It was Washington or look for another job. So it became Washington—for me, anyway. Others with experience in private journalism and not yet too old had other options. Mine were even more reduced than they had been when I returned to VOA in 1950. I had moved up both in position and salary, but I still did not have newspaper experience; plus, I was four years older. More important, I liked my job, and though we had no interest in becoming permanent nomads assigned by bureaucratic decision, the creation of USIA had given our work a higher level of respectability and permanence than when we were a mere appendage of the State Department, which looked upon us as just that.

So, with a live-in baby sitter taking care of Peter, off we went to Washington to hunt for yet another house that we hoped would become a home for four of us. We found it in Chevy Chase, Maryland, just across the district line, at the edge of Rock Creek Park. Our New York friends envied us: Washington, the White House, Congress, and a house off the park! I moved for the job—nothing else. Scarsdale was far enough from the New York asphalt for me. But a one-industry town like Washington? The one advantage Washington had in my eyes was that it mattered little where one lived: it was either slum or suburb. One can't make a metropolis out of a bureaucrats' settlement. Without the mix of activities, professions, and people, without Wall Street and the Upper East Side, without Madison Avenue and 57th

Street, you've got, yes, Washington. Call me perverse, but I still prefer New York vastly, despite the mess on the streets and the nastiness of the people. One thing for which I blame those men who made decisions in the early days of the country's history is that they decided against making New York the capital. Then we'd have it all together as the British, French, Italians, and other sensible people do.

We moved to Chevy Chase in the fall of 1954. A few weeks later, Grandfather Hermann died. He was almost ninety years old. The two most eventful years since we had arrived in America were ending. There was every sign and reason that the family could now settle down. But I had two itches: New York and Europe, more precisely, Reinheim.

VIII

When we buried Opa Hermann in New Jersey, far from the place he had reserved next to Oma Hilda in Frankfurt, new life was beginning again in the family: Eva was again pregnant. This time the doctors allowed her more freedom of movement. Eva became large fast. Might it be twins? There was a history of twins in the Petschek family. Eva had twin sisters. But, then, "it always skips a generation" was the endlessly heard refrain in those days.

Theorizing and guessing ceased as the pregnancy progressed, and it was twins. Andrea and Judith were born on May 21, 1955. Andrea was first and larger; Judy, as we came to call her, had to spend a couple of days in the incubator to develop more strength. When we moved to Scarsdale in 1951, we often wondered what we were doing in that big empty house. On Daniel Road in Chevy Chase in the spring and summer of 1955, I sometimes wondered whether the house was big enough, or whether we should have bought a series of soundproof studios like we had in the office.

It was about this time that an assignment was offered to me by newsroom director Barry Zorthian: to cover the Big Four meeting in Geneva for VOA. It was to bring together the "twins" of the Soviet Union—head of government Nikolai Bulganin and Communist Party chief Nikita Khrushchev—with President Eisenhower and Prime Ministers Anthony Eden of Britain and Edgar Faure of France. The Big Four meeting was to begin July 18.

It was a professional godsend. It also further stimulated that pull back to Europe. But I did not feel like going alone. I wanted Eva to share my first trip back—especially if I visited Frankfurt, Darmstadt, and Reinheim, Reinheim most of all. But why? I had left it twenty years before, as a thirteen-year-old. What was going on? I talked to my parents about it. They felt no pull back. In fact, they would have resisted going back, they said, if someone had suggested it.

"What do you want back there?" my mother asked. "Look what they did to us. Nobody there cares about us. Why should you care about them?"

Father was less emphatic. His questions were less argumentative. "Do you just want to see again where you were born? I could understand that. But make sure not to give any of those *Verbrecher* [criminals, meaning the local Nazis] the satisfaction of talking to them. Now that they've lost the war, they probably would like nothing better than to crawl back into our good graces . . . "

Father was thoughtful or sensitive enough not to probe more deeply about what was going on inside me. Perhaps he guessed that I did not know myself. I didn't. But the thought of going back, especially since it had become a real possibility, made the pull almost irresistible. Was it sheer nostalgia, a regression to childhood and a longing for the pampered past? Was it something about Germany, made up inchoately of the so radically different influences of Opa and my father, but both focused on Germany? And why did I want Eva to come along so badly, not merely because she was my wife, but because I craved sharing the experience, perhaps because I was afraid of it?

First we had to settle the question of leaving so soon after the birth of the twins. Eva felt that, as long as we considered going, we ought to do it quickly, before the girls were older, while they still were hardly aware of our absence. Peter had fallen in love with our housekeeper-nurse, and we talked to him about our plans. Of course, he did not grasp it, but he seemed to have an idea of us being away when he woke up in the morning. "And Mae-Mae," he mumbled about his beloved. "She'll be here, all the time." Mae-Mae nodded, adding, "I'm here, with you." A huge smile came over Peter's face. He helped settle the matter.

And it *was* settled, for then. But a price was paid—not by our three-week absence, but by my nearly complete absence from home even when I was in Washington. I was more than a workaholic; I was obsessed with that "how could you?!" if something should be wrong in a piece of copy that would be read over the air and heard by thousands, perhaps millions of people if one counted both English and the translated newscasts prepared on the basis of our output. The professional responsibility, which was considerable by rational standards, was, of course, overlaid, undergirded, and enveloped by my lifelong emotional response. This response paled gradually in later years, but never disappeared, even as retirement radically reduced my workload and day-to-day job requirements.

Eva did her best to understand me and to provide the extra parental support that I failed to give. I realized much, much later that I had bugged out, had felt far too little "how could you?!" about the vacuum I had blithely left at home as I responded to it slavishly in the office. I did feel concerned about leaving that summer after the birth of the girls, but it was more of a sense that what we were doing might look irresponsible to others than a personal need or feeling. It never occurred to me that what I was doing day by day, which was not noted or which I thought was not noted by others, was far more insensitive and irresponsible than our temporary absence in Europe.

Even though air travel had developed rapidly by 1955, Eva still preferred the ocean liner. It was the first of several times over the next few years that we crossed the Atlantic separately. Eva went by ship, I by air, allowing me to continue working in Washington for a few days and then meeting Eva in Paris, where she'd go by train after arrival in Cherbourg.

Paris! I would finally get to see the magic place: the city and the country that Hitler had early on barred us from visiting; the symbol of urban beauty, political openness, with a language that sounded more beautiful than any other I knew, and the cuisine everybody was always talking and writing about. I fell into step wholeheartedly with the romance Americans had with Paris.

Paris was indeed glorious. It is the one city I know that in no respect has been oversold. In 1955, when Eva and I stayed in the Hotel Lotti, just a few steps from the Tuileries, in lovely weather, I was overwhelmed. "You must say this is incredible," I would shout to Eva as we came upon the Place de la Concorde or some other awe-inspiring spot, giving vent to an irresistible enthusiasm. There was one thing in Paris that reminded me of Reinheim and Frankfurt: house numbers on a blue background with white numbering. "Blaue

Hausnummern," I would shout, as Eva looked on a bit puzzled. She, too, drank in the beauty of the city, but she kept her wits about her.

Blue house numbers became a symbol, and remain so even to this day. As we went on from Paris to Geneva, they popped up again on the older buildings in that city. They symbolized the same sense of *Geborgenheit,* the warmth that I reached out for, when I passed the old fenced buildings with mini-gardens in front in Manhattan. But in Paris and Geneva, these buildings seemed to pull me toward them, almost physically.

"Come on," Eva would say. "If you're getting so excited here in Geneva, where you've never been, what's going to happen in Germany, and especially in Reinheim?"

"I don't know, but I have to go, now more than ever," I said. "I have to go to Reinheim as I never felt pressed to go to any other place."

"What about after Kristallnacht?" she would reply. "Don't be ridiculous. You can't tell me that you and your parents didn't feel pressured then."

"That was different. That was risk, danger. That was a matter of saving our lives. Now no necessity, no danger, no risk is telling me to go. Now there's something else telling me. I haven't figured out what it is. Maybe if I try too hard to figure it out, I won't like what I find, I mean about myself. Maybe I'd have to face that I'm not grown up . . . "

"Come on," calm and collected Eva said. "It's okay to go, but don't overdo it."

Geneva was lovely. A small furnished apartment in a U.S. compound was available during the two weeks we would stay there. I had colleagues there who were stationed in Europe and had been called in to beef up the coverage of the most important postwar meeting. We worked hard, treading a difficult path between the official briefings and the wealth of background material that was coming in from a variety of sources. We could confirm some of it, as did our commercial colleagues, but could not use it with the same professional freedom, because we were an official agency. We VOA people had to contend with two problems: the customary adversarial relationship between source and media, in which the sources try to hold back news or shape it to their advantage; and the explicit or self-censorship that our special official status imposed on us. It was especially trying for those of

us who understood one or more foreign languages, and either overheard tips about things going on behind closed doors, or sat in on
informal briefings in French or German by lower-level delegation
members.

Finally, after six days of conferring, the five summiteers gave their
wrap-up news conference. Its tone was optimistic, its content meager.
Afterward there was another story to cover: a news conference by Konrad Adenauer. The old man came out, ramrod straight, the lines in
his narrow face sharply drawn. I was prejudiced in his favor by Father's view of him and what he represented. Adenauer said nothing
spectacular, but he did show time and again that his and his government's commitment to the West—both to the Western European and
Atlantic communities and to free and democratic political institutions—was an article of faith, not just the thing to say.

What struck me even more than the personality and the substance
of Adenauer's comments was the language. This was the first time
since I left Germany in 1939 that I heard the voice of a German leader
who was not Hitler. I heard German spoken not by an exile, not by a
visitor, not by a refugee, but by someone who had stayed there, who
lives there now, and who, above all, reflects public feeling or must
defend what he says should there be disagreement at home. If one
could boil down the difference between prewar and postwar Germany
to personalities, the contrast could neither be sharper nor more
hopeful.

What was still in my ears was the voice that came at us like an
artillery shell, gaining decibels as it approached the crest of the sentence, and then ending with a blast of hysterical shrillness. This was
the Hitler pattern. In both content and delivery, it had the quality of
a menacing wave from which there is no escape, to which there is no
appeal, a wave that buries everything in its way under its relent-
lessness. And here was this old gentleman in his stiff collar and dark
suit, speaking in a barely audible voice, articulating his sentences
slowly, deliberately, in that lilting cadence and those wide-open vowels characteristic of the Rhineland. Yes, it was the same language, but
the meanings were utterly different. The two cultures could not even
be compared.

With the job in Geneva done, we could now move on to our vacation, which was my return to Germany. We rented a car and headed

for Frankfurt. It was virtually all Autobahn driving: I had chosen the quickest way. My feelings were racing so far ahead that I had to restrain myself from engaging those high-powered Mercedeses, always seemingly on the verge of becoming airborne, in speed tournaments.

My first impression of Frankfurt disappointed me. It wasn't the city I had known. There were skyscrapers, just as in New York; there were one-way streets where there used to be expansive boulevards. Empty spaces, where bombed-out buildings had stood, had still not been filled in. The famous Frankfurter Hof hotel was still there, the same yellowish-brown stone I remembered from when I used to pass it. We stayed in a more modest hotel, and immediately went out walking: out of the central city up toward the Anlagen—the ring of parklike strips that borders the inner city. Up Peterstrasse we went, and there it was: the house we had moved to from Reinheim, untouched, with the protruding rounded window on the corner of every floor. I looked up at our window for a long time. It had been my favorite spot in the apartment, because I could look down toward the inner city and over the green of Eschenheimer Anlage, watching the traffic seemingly headed right for me, and then turning either into the Anlage or into Unterweg, which merged into the Anlage at the western side of our building.

There were two other spots I needed to look at, against my will but determined to do it: up on the top floor, in the center of the slate wall that was an integral part of the roof structure, was the cursed mansard window to which Oma had climbed twenty years ago; and there was also the spot on the sidewalk where her body was found. Eva and I stood there for what seemed a long time. She did not say a word, as thoughts raced across my mind in a jumble, colliding with each other, interrupting each other: Oma's terrible silence and unchanging look; her smile and laughter for so many years in Reinheim, as she gave me *Kuchenteig* (cake dough) to taste off her finger; serving *Gerstensuppe* to us all on Friday night, followed by a roast and then *Apfelschalet;* that morning after Father's birthday when we raced downstairs and saw the ungraspable sight; Reinheim again: my grandparents' living room, where I spent more time than upstairs in my own home, and Oma telling me not to pull on the *Deckchen* (small crocheted decorations) on the sides of the sofa. I stood there, reliving scenes or just glimpses of memory. After a while—I don't remember how long—Eva gently tugged at me. I knew. It was time to go.

We needed to get to the cemetery before closing time, so we took the streetcar, but not until we had walked a bit farther, to the Scheffeleck and into Scheffelstrasse, where number 13 was also undamaged and unchanged. Here was the gate through which I had passed innumerable times. And our apartment. I could almost look into Opa's room on the corner, with the little porch in front. Inside the court, at the entrance, was the glass awning over the door, where Roeth and the SS man came the morning after Kristallnacht, where Roeth came two more times that morning after we had watched Father pass under the awning. It was quiet in the street, but number 13 was not: it was pouring out memories—the terror of Papi's arrest, the joy of his return, the noise from the Philanthropin across the fence of the backyard . . .

Then, around the corner, to the Philanthropin. It was unchanged, but smaller than the vast, majestic structure I had remembered. I realized now that I had built into my memory the importance and augustness of that institution from which it was so vital to graduate, making its physical dimensions reflect awe and possible unattainability.

The name was still gracing the light gray stone, wrought in iron according to German print style. A plaque near the entrance said that it housed the office of the Frankfurt Jewish community. Toward the other end was a theater. We went in, and there was the stone staircase I had run up and down, and the dark wooden guardrails we were always told to hold onto and never did. Again, I stood silently, trying Eva's patience, of which she fortunately had the full measure. Here was Mathilde going up the stairs, her golden hair skipping up and down. Dr. Driessen, at the top of the stairs, beckoning us to get to class . . . it was time. Up there, ridiculous Dr. Plaut, sounding out "Mr. Goshen has no notion . . . ," and finally, the *Abitur.* The grayness had become grayer after Kristallnacht. Dr. Marbach with his face wound . . . Dr. Philipp looking so frail . . . and then a big swastika popped up, as large as the wheel of a car, hanging down from the Schulrat's lapel, almost pulling him down to his knees. Philanthropin means "a place loving people." It never was this for me. It taught me a lot, it probably meant well, but after November, 1938, it became a mix of danger and promise or, as it turned out, false promise.

I tore myself away once more, walking down Hebelstrasse to Eckenheimer Landstrasse, where we took the streetcar up to the Jewish cemetery. It was the same old streetcar line, even though the cars were now larger and more modern. Now we passed the streets I knew so well and where Father had patients: Grüneburgweg, all the way up to Glauburgstrasse. We'd pass the Main Cemetery, and the next stop was where we got off. Here was our cemetery, Hebrew letters again over the main gate. I went to the office. All I knew was Oma's name. A clerk with a *kippah* opened an old-fashioned file drawer. There it was: Hilda Frohmann, 3B, number 64. The clerk explained to me how to get there. Thanks to the garment center, I had an easy time making out what he said. No doubt he was one of the displaced persons who survived the camps and formed the new Jewish community of Frankfurt. Neither Oma, Opa, nor my parents would have understood him. He spoke Yiddish.

We started our walk. It led us past the center aisle; on both sides were the graves of people who died within a period of two to three months in the spring and summer of 1942. Many of them came from the same family and had died on the same day. They were the suicides who made their decision after they had received incontrovertible information about the death camps: Rosenthal . . . Freund . . . Hamburger . . . Singer . . . Frank . . . Wertheimer . . . Bloch . . . They were my parents' and my peers. They lived in apartments like ours, they were our extended family . . . with the same background, aspirations, worries, vacations, reading the same papers, going to Kulturbund performances. The only thing that was different was that they did not have or seize the chance to leave in time. "This might have been me," I said to Eva, pointing to the grave of a twenty-year-old. "Opa left Frankfurt just a few months before all this happened!"

Eva and I moved a little closer together. Here was the turnoff to the left that we had to take. But on the central path, the small whitish stones continued, it seemed, infinitely. We turned, looked for the well-marked block, and found what I was looking for: *Hilda Frohmann, geb. 26.9.1871, verschieden 24.2.1935.* Next to this inscription, in black on a greenish-grey background, was a black square that would never carry any writing. The grave was tended, but much of the green cover had thinned out. I would need to do something about that. I said Kaddish, slowly and full of thoughts. I had heard Kaddish said innumerable times in Reinheim and Frankfurt, and had joined my parents and Opa in saying it after Oma's death. Now I hadn't said it in fifteen years. I had taken my pocket prayer book along, just for this occasion. Father had given it to me in New York, with a dedication in English: "Think of our God and our past, and have confidence in our future with God. Love. Your parents."

I opened the prayer book, but I found I didn't need it. I was happy that I remembered the prayer. That afternoon at the end of July 1955, in Frankfurt's Jewish cemetery, I "dropped in" again, as naturally and necessarily as I would come home to the family from work, or go to my parents for a visit, or as I would eat breakfast. But I didn't realize that it was happening. Another dozen years would pass before I would understand.

Again, I stood there letting the memories come in from all sides, crossing each other, cutting each other off: the terrible funeral; Rabbi Hoffmann's deeply felt and beautifully worded eulogy; Mutti inconsolable; Opa standing there, white and motionless; and my father, who so valued Oma Hilda and her unarticulated but unmistakable sympathy and support, shedding tears! I had never seen Papi cry! And again, as earlier in the day, Oma came to mind so clearly: there she was in her gray dotted dress, apron around her waist, asking me to look at the *Apfelschalet* she was making.

As I stood there, I kept wondering, asking: What was Oma thinking during those two years when she did not speak? Perhaps she sensed what would happen? Perhaps she wondered why we were staying and worrying about her? She never wanted anyone to worry about her—worrying was her job, her responsibility.

We placed stones on the grave, in accordance with Jewish custom: five for our family; two for my parents; one for Siegfried, Oma's nephew in New York; and one, of course, for Opa. Nine in all. As we left, I kept looking back. We had to pass those 1942 markers again. I looked up at the sky. Did it really look the same in 1942, 1943, 1944?

I stopped by the office and ordered the grave replanted. Then we took the Elektrische back down Eckenheimer Landstrasse, with another look at the Philanthropin as we passed Hebelstrasse. It all looked the same. How could it?

The next stop was Roeth, the policeman of Kristallnacht distinction. We visited him in his police station office. He received us warmly, but not excessively so. He thanked us for the packages my mother had sent in the immediate postwar period; they had helped him and his wife a good deal.

It was an awkward meeting. How can one express gratitude to someone who does not find what he has done worth this much attention? There was a wide gap between my parents' and my feeling for Roeth's actions in 1938 and his own assessment. I could not show how we felt with a simple "thank you," and he would have found a more elaborate—and to us more satisfying—expression embarrassing.

I felt it best to recall the morning of November 10, and he joined in reminiscing. He said he felt close to resigning then and there, and had he known what would happen later, he would have quit. But at the time he believed that this was only a temporary, though abhorrent and unwarranted, action. Later on, he had to find various ways to absent himself from work in order to avoid having to perform duties he could not bring himself to do.

Roeth never mentioned politics or ideology. Here was a person who instinctively, without weighing merit, risk, or other consequence, followed the direction of an inner compass. As we said goodbye, I said to myself: *ecce homo!*

One more stop was obligatory: the site of the Börneplatz synagogue, which we had attended and my father had treasured. We had trouble finding it. It was in the old city, which had been destroyed and was in the process of being reconstructed. The old streets down which we had walked were gone. We literally had to grope our way. I looked ahead, to the back, to the sides, even up. We finally ended up in an open space, at the edge of which was a gas station. We asked the attendant whether he knew about a synagogue that used to be there. "Yes it was here, exactly here," he said. "That's what people have told me."

It was time to go back to our room. I felt heavy, stuffy. I needed to sit down. I needed time for all that traffic in my head to clear a little. And Reinheim was yet to come.

We left Frankfurt for Reinheim the next morning, traveling the old road via Langen to Darmstadt, where we stopped. I wanted to see and show Eva my old Gymnasium, known as the Humanistic, which in light of the experience in Frankfurt the day before had a strange ring. I noticed it the moment I said it. It was, of course, merely a designation of the classical nature of the curriculum. But in our minds, because of our experience, and because it was the place where I had my first personal encounter with anti-Semitism, it was an odd name for the school. What was more ironic was that it was no longer there. The Kapellplatz itself, of which it formed one side, was gone.

I had greater difficulty finding my way in Darmstadt than in Frankfurt. The bombing had had a more devastating effect on this smaller city. We had heard and read, and I had on several occasion broadcast reports, about the bombing of Darmstadt. We never could find out why this city, with no apparent military objectives in or near the center, was such a favored Allied target. There were two chemical plants, many of whose workers commuted from the Reinheim area and whom Father had treated. But these—Merck & Co. and Roehm & Haas—were located far from the city itself. I still wonder, why Darmstadt?

I did find the Catholic church, with its round roof, and tried to orient myself around it, with little success. The store where Mother had shopped for clothes—Schuermann—catty-corner from the church, was gone. The column with Grand Duke Ernst Ludwig was still there, or restored, but around it little was left. The Landestheater, where I had attended that memorable *Trovatore* performance some twenty-five years earlier, was badly damaged. Mutti loved this building and the great music and drama she had experienced there, but I was not sure whether it would touch her now. Too much had happened, I was almost sure, to give her little more than a twinge. Perhaps not even that.

We did not go straight to Reinheim, but stayed overnight at the Hotel Traube, which had been repaired and was functioning where it always had been. I had passed it innumerable times, and was always impressed with the resplendent scalloped curtains and its grand entrance, into which as a young man I had never ventured. I had always wondered what it would be like to sit in that dark hall, where Jews were not welcome. It was as exciting for me to go in as it was natural for Eva. It was hard to explain why such an ostensibly ordinary thing as entering a run-of-the-mill hotel was so fraught with emotion for me. It wasn't just memories coming alive; there were conflicting feelings: the *Goborgenheit* conveyed by those thick curtains . . . the fear of what plans against the Jews might be made behind that awesome entrance . . . how my parents would feel if they were here . . .

We approached the desk. A courteous receptionist welcomed us. Routine. She had been born about the time Hitler came to power. She must have been about twelve when the war ended. Maybe she had experienced a few years of hard times; perhaps she had been evacuated to the country during the bombing raids. By the time she could have fully meaningful experiences, it was all over and things were getting better again. How easy it was for her to do this job routinely. She and I were worlds away from each other, standing across the desk of the Traube that afternoon. We spoke the same language, but only in the operational sense. We came from such vastly different emotional places: she from a brand-new shiny building with just a few minor scratches on it; I from an older structure that had suffered a good deal of damage, been lovingly repaired, added to, with fresh paint on the upper floors, but the chipped and banged-in spots on the lower wall were still clearly visible. And I did not want them repaired. I wanted to keep looking at them and find out more about how it happened.

We went to Reinheim the next morning. We drove via Ober-Ramstadt, the better known and slightly longer road, coming into Reinheim through Hahn, up on the hill. I remembered the turns in the road, and, so it seemed, even some of the large trees. This was a road on which Opa and I had started out many times on many summer mornings, only to branch off through woods and fields a little later.

We passed Herr Scriba's *Apotheke* (pharmacy), and would visit his daughter Toni on our way back through Darmstadt. Now we were approaching the center of town. I felt giddy, almost ready to give up the wheel to Eva, but I knew she did not like to drive rented cars, particularly in other countries. We crossed the brook, saw the Wolffs' old reddish-brown house on the corner of Heinrichstrasse. They had the leading dry-goods store in town. But I drove on toward Darmstädterstrasse. There, on the right, was the big linden tree in front of Nelius's house. And here, across the street, number 16, white resplendent on blue. The original!

The shingle that once said "Dr. Jacob Goldmann" still read "Dr.

G. Jansen"—the *Auslandsdeutsche* to whom Father had sold both house and practice. Across the street, an old man was coming out of Nelius's house. What generation Nelius was he? He looked at us, at the Swiss license plate on the car. Why were we standing there, staring at that house? I was sure he suspected it was me, but I did not pay attention to him.

Down the street, at the bend, was Appel's house. He was the butcher who my father was sure had thrown that firecracker into our yard in 1933—the act that triggered Oma Hilda's break with the world and her eventual suicide. Now, I looked at our house again. The window on the ground floor, looking into the room where my grandparents ate and where I spent so much time and had so much delicious food. Upstairs, where we lived, was both physically and emotionally more distant. Strange, I thought, but I did not say it. I communicated only facts to Eva, not feelings. I wanted these all to myself. But I wanted Eva to know where everything was, who lived where, which was the living room and which the dining room. I felt like grabbing the stone, clutching at it, but I resisted. Silly, my mother would have said.

I did press my face against the door to try to glimpse the yard and the steps to the garden. I managed, and then asked Eva to look through the thin opening between boards. Those were the same stones, the same window shutters on hinges that were pulled closed at night. Only the paint was not the same. And there was number 16. That was the same. White on blue enamel, reflecting its blueness in the sun. Home. Not just the house, but the people, the furniture, my mother at the top of the stairs, waiting for me. Father zipping out on the bicycle. Oma up in the garden, tending her flowers, Opa straightening out his file folders. Lisbeth calling me back from playing with the Steiermanns. "Come home, we are eating," I heard her shout out of the corner window upstairs. Nothing brought it back more than number 16.

Then I looked next door. The Stuckert yard. One son had been a gang member in 1933, when the Reinheim Nazis harassed us—the one, Mother told me, whom Oma Hilda's family had helped keep out of the First World War, alleging an illness. After the war, when Mother resumed correspondence with Lisbeth, we found out that the whole family was a bunch of "super-Nazis." This is the yard I used to watch when they slaughtered their pig, and where the blood flowed over the cobblestones. Ever since I had seen that, I identified the Stuckerts' house with blood. The blood that flowed then now assumed another meaning. Number 18 was blue, with red running down its enamel, wiping out the number . . .

We looked up the street toward the station. There was still a gas pump in front of the Steiermann house. Who knows what happened to the Steiermanns? But you could still buy gas there! People are born, live happily or are persecuted, die one way or another, but the things and habits they created stay the same. Are things worthier than people that they have a virtually endless life?

We got back into the car and drove slowly up Darmstädterstrasse, with a glance at the Lieschen tracks that we would cross later. We turned right on Jahnstrasse. Every German town and city had a street named after Turnvater Jahn, the man who had made gymnastics a requirement and a civic virtue in Germany. I let the car roll down the street, which meets Kirchstrasse at the bottom of the hill. The Meyer furniture store was on the corner. We were headed to Lisbeth and Fritz's home, a few houses up on Jahnstrasse. Before we parked, out came Lisbeth and her daughter. They ran toward us, embracing us and welcoming Eva as though they had known her for years. It was Lisbeth's way . . . that spontaneous love of people. "Robert," she cried out, "you really got fat, but you have a beautiful wife!" On the way into the house, she said, with her disarming candor, that she was so glad I got married, that sometimes she worried that I would never find a wife, because none would be good enough for Frau Doktor.

Inside was Fritz, much older-looking and with a frailer bearing than Lisbeth, who, except for some extra girth, looked just as we left her twenty years before. The beautiful *Kachelofen,* the tall stove covered with painted tiles in the corner of the dining room, was the pride of every middle-class home. On the table were five cakes and *Torten* Lisbeth had made for us: cheesecake, strawberry tart, *Bienenstich* (a caramel pastry filled with a tangy custard), the indispensable *Zwetschenkuchen* (plum cake), and a *Streuselkuchen* (coffeecake). Cozies covered the two pots, coffee and tea, and everything was set for making me still fatter. Fortunately, we had skipped lunch. We had dawdled on the way from Darmstadt, and then spent more time than I had realized exploring and reminiscing, before we got to Lisbeth.

We talked about my parents, of course, and our children, and Opa's last years, and what I was doing professionally, which seemed to impress them although they seemed not to understand fully. Fritz immediately launched into a tale of his war experience on the Russian front. He seemed only mildly interested in what we were reporting, not because he did not care, but because for him the world seemed to have ended with his return from the grisly war in the East.

But not Lisbeth. "You know," she said, "I don't think a day has gone by since you left Reinheim that the doctor's name hasn't come up. 'Ach if we only still had de Goldmann,' Rückert would say, or 'Such a one we'll never get again.' 'Ja, if Dr. Goldmann had been here, she would still be alive,' Herr Kopp said of his late wife."

Eva listened incredulously, but I understood, because I had been old enough when we left to get a sense of my father's role in town, even though I did not grasp it fully.

Then they started coming in: Schmidts' Kätt and Friseur Daum and the old Gerstenbauer. "Ja, Du bist de Robert?" "Robert, do you remember, I used to cut your hair?" And then, raising her voice above the others, was Kätt, saying, "Well, is he coming back? Tell him we need him! I still take the pills he prescribed. Without them I would long be dead, tell him that . . . "

There was a groundswell not of nostalgia but of demand—demand for my father's return. It was not sentimental; it was serious, pragmatic, self-interested. I listened to it all, surprised not by the feeling but by the insistence that almost put me on the defensive on Father's behalf. They seemed to feel he had left them in the lurch . . . run out on them. Eva seemed to be watching a play with strange and implausible people in the cast. And Lisbeth, at whom I glanced often throughout the importunings of the uninvited guests who knew no etiquette when it came to "de Dokter," just smiled, seeming to say something like "You see what they think of your father?" and "I told you!"

None of them asked what had happened to us. There were just a few cursory inquiries about my mother and grandfather. I did not resent it. None of these people acted differently from how people anywhere in the world act: they were concerned with themselves, and with the most important part of themselves—their health. For them, Dr. Goldmann was a once-in-a-lifetime person. They had been lucky enough to have him, he was still alive, and they wanted him back—to give them the care, the instant response, the understanding and concern that they had not had in the last twenty years.

Did they blame the Nazis for robbing them of "de Dokter"? Some did, perhaps. But that era was over. There was no reason for him not to come back. Were some of them anti-Semites? Probably, in the primitive, pre-Nazi sense in which many country folk were. When one stumbled in Reinheim, one would say "Jud' begrabe" (A Jew is buried here—underneath the stone one had stumbled over). Those Nazi race theories meant little to most people in Reinheim. In the course of the afternoon, I raised the issue of what the Nazis had done. Kätt again took the floor: "Dieter and those others, they were *Lumpe* [bums]. They made themselves big shots and never did an honest day's work. Who were they to bother de Dokter? I told that to Dieter once. He said I should shut up or I'd be arrested. I told him to go to hell, that I could be his mother, but was damn glad I wasn't . . . "

Kätt was not afraid, but not because she was anti-Nazi. She, like most if not all the people in that room except Lisbeth, was apolitical. They had had a bad time, but this was life. There wasn't too much to expect from it. Just have enough to live and be healthy. Healthy! And that's where Dr. Goldmann came in. If Kätt had been there when Appel and Dieter got ready to throw that firecracker in our yard, she probably would have asked them what they were doing . . . not have taken any excuses or pushing aside for an answer, and, if she had discovered the object, she would have tried and probably succeeded in tearing it out of their hands. Kätt was no Klaus von Stauffenberg; she wanted her doctor unharmed. This wasn't a matter of Nazis harming Jews. It was more like a vandal putting graffiti on the church wall. Kätt needed her Goldmann, and Kätt needed her church on Sunday. Anyone harming either was a *Lump*.

Some started to leave, but others came in. Kätt stayed a long time, and when she was ready to leave, she held my hand for a long time, looked me in the eye, and said, in a quiet voice, "I know he won't come back. But tell him not a day goes by that I don't think of him. I need him so . . . "

Finally, everybody was gone. Eva seemed exhausted. "You didn't even have a chance to taste the pastry," said Lisbeth, as Fritz looked on with the same distant expression he had worn all afternoon.

I was stunned, tugged at by Kätt and others, but mostly Kätt. I was thinking of my parents on 98th Street. Would they take this more calmly? Is what happened today one reason they won't consider a visit? But here was number 16, and Darmstädterstrasse, and Lisbeth, and *Geborgenheit.* But mostly it was home: the streets, the house . . .

Eva gently suggested it was time to go. We said good-bye. We'd be back with the children. "Send me pictures in the meantime," Lisbeth said. "And tell Mutti and the Dokter what I said, what the good people here said."

We went out to the car. Barber Daum was looking out from his window across the street. We got into the car. I drove down and turned right on Kirchstrasse. I stopped, we got out, and we walked down the alley where the synagogue used to be. There was a barn there. Only the dirt road was the same.

Eva and I looked at the magnificent *Fachwerkhaus* on the corner, where the Meyers had part of their store. Kirchstrasse was the street with the oldest houses. It was tree-lined, and the church with its tall (as I remembered it) steeple was on the left. More *Fachwerkhäuser* were along the way. We had passed Butcher Strauss's house. What might have happened to them? We turned back into Darmstädterstrasse, drove past our house, past Café Hanemann, where my parents never went because they did not like the people who frequented it. Anti-Semites, they said, and especially Dr. Möllmann, who spent much time there. But the pastries looked just as delicious as they did when I passed by in the old days.

We drove past the train station. A few cars stood on the side track. They were the same, too! Or were they? I wanted to believe they were the same. I wanted to wait for a Lieschen to come, to look at the engine, feel the doorknob on a third-class car . . . but there was no more third class, only second.

We came to the tracks, to the road back to Darmstadt through Spachbrücken and Rossdorf. I stopped. I did not want to go back. "Come, let's go," said Eva. But I couldn't. I stayed in the car, just sitting there, across from Café Hanemann, paralyzed.

I could not bring myself to put my hand on the wheel. I turned off the ignition. We sat. My thoughts were spinning around as they never had before. This was home. I belonged here. How could I leave?

Yes, my parents were in New York, and my children were in Washington. Yet number 16 was here, right here. And all these people who wanted Papi back. But he wouldn't come back. And the Stuckerts' house. The blood. Dieter and the Nazis. Where were they? I had to get at them. That's why I had to stay. Nonsense. Nostalgia was getting the best of me. But was it just that? Childish sentimentality? No, it was more. Home. Number 16. Oma at the stove. Opa coming home with the *Würstchen*. Blanka, our old dog, limping around the yard. Going up to the Lieschen for the trip to Darmstadt. Right here, where we were parked. No, I could not go back to Darmstadt.

"Let's go," Eva said, "it's getting late." I had to respond. I did not want to say what was tearing me up. Eva tugged at me. Kätt and number 16 tugged at me. I knew I had to go. But I wanted to wait. "Wait? What for?" Eva said.

"I don't know, but I want to stay for a while."

"You know we can't stay here on the street. Let's go back, and we'll talk about it."

"Okay, but then let's come back tomorrow for a while."

"Let's see how you feel," Eva said.

I was sure how I would feel: I would want to come back the next day. I realized we had to go back to Darmstadt for the night, but then we'd come back after breakfast, we'd change the schedule. Suddenly, the sacrosanct schedule meant nothing.

Shaking myself out of my daze, I turned on the ignition, and we started moving—slowly, unwillingly, the jerking of the car reflecting my feelings. "Come on, don't stall, and don't be silly now," Eva said, and I resented it, even though I knew she was right. We passed Opa's old storage building, where he had grain stored pending shipment. Kätt lived somewhere up here, but I did not know where. Papi would have found it in his sleep. We were on the open road. "Spachbrücken—2 km." Same old sign. Same old road. Same grass on the sides. Spachbrücken, a tiny village, a kind of suburb of Reinheim. Now we were on the road to Rossdorf. How I recognized each turn. When Mutti drove to Darmstadt to go shopping, on days when Father spent the day in Reinheim but always had the motorcycle for emergencies, she'd take this road. I would never go with her in the morning. She left too late, but I'd come back with her after a *Schokolade* and *Torte* in the Café Jolasse in Darmstadt.

We went on to Rossdorf. We drove in silence. I paid just a minimum of attention to the driving; the rest was engulfed by Reinheim. People flashed by: Kätt time and again, Lisbeth, Friseur Daum, Fritz sitting there listlessly . . . I wanted Father to be here, to hear it. What would he say? What would he feel? I was just a proxy. Why did I have to hear it all? But I wanted to hear it. I wanted to hear more of it, in fact. I had to go back . . . but what was the point? It didn't matter. I wanted to be home again . . . yes, with Mutti at the top of the stairs and myself fearing what "how could you?!" she'd come up with next. I was happy to pay that price for the *Geborgenheit*. Hadn't I outgrown all this? Here was Eva sitting next to me, we were parents, and all I could think about, yearn for, was the punishment and *Geborgenheit* of a child. Stop it, I told myself. But I didn't, and didn't want to.

We had passed Rossdorf and were approaching Darmstadt. It was only sixteen kilometers. It went by so fast, so much faster than in the days I was here last.

We went to our room. I was exhausted, as though from a day's hard physical labor. I flopped onto the bed. Eva sat next to me. "I want to go back tomorrow, I have to go back," I told her.

"No, you won't," Eva said firmly, almost menacingly. She knew what she was saying and doing. I sensed it, but I had to fight her.

"What's wrong?" I said, "I just need to spend some more time there. Another morning, perhaps . . . "

"No, we won't go. You have to sleep on it. Reinheim is not your home, not *our* home. I think I understand what you feel, because I was there with you, even though *I* can't feel it. But I was astounded hearing these people talk about Papi. I know what kind of person he is. But Papi and your mother would not want you to go back either. They don't even want to come here, perhaps because they don't want to risk this kind of experience. But even more so, because they have moved away, broken off, finished with Reinheim, with Germany. Perhaps it's because they were adults when all of you left Reinheim, and you were only thirteen. Anyway, relax and let's take a walk, and you'll feel clearer about things in the morning. We still have to visit Toni Scriba, don't forget!"

Normally, I am a gourmet plus gourmand. That night I nibbled at my food in the Traube dining room. We took an after-dinner walk.

I was heading for the school again, but Eva steered me away from it. She knew why, and she was right. We walked over to the Ernst Ludwig column, looked again at the theater, and came back to the hotel. I was calmer now. We called Toni Scriba and made a date for the next morning.

By the time we were ready to turn off the light, I was so tired that I fell asleep instantaneously. Eva had to wake me in the morning. It was a beautiful day, and I was relaxed. It was a new day. Going back to Reinheim was still a thought, but not a compulsion, not a must anymore. Then it was up to Toni Scriba-Ritsert on Mozartweg—an apt address for her and for us!

Toni was in excellent condition—too fat, but very agile, and intellectually in top form. She was Mutti's closest friend, but Toni's interests, concerns, and sensitivity to public issues and needs far exceeded my mother's. Toni was an anti-Nazi by conviction as well as by instinct. She hated bombast, was horrified by terror, but above all had a merciless contempt for people who compromised with terrorists and bullies. This included her father, who was one of those conservatives who thought Hitler had some good ideas but wouldn't qualify to be invited to dinner at the Scribas.

Toni got to these issues after we had responded in detail to questions about the family, especially about my parents and Opa Hermann. She had learned a lot from her correspondence with my mother, but she wanted to know much more. How long did it take Father to get admitted to practice again? Were there any aftereffects of his Buchenwald stay? Was I able to leave without having to run risks? And how did Opa Hermann get out? Mutti had not been specific about that. Toni knew everything about Oma Hilda, of course. That had happened early. I told her I had visited Oma's grave, and ordered new planting. Could she handle this for me? Had we heard anything of the Wolffs, Metzger Strauss? Nothing was said solicitously. Toni was like a sponge, soaking up all the information I was able to give, out of pure, unadulterated interest and concern.

We knew from the correspondence with my mother that Toni had been very ill during the war, and that her husband had died from pneumonia, due to exposure, when the roof of their house was blown off in a bomb raid. She did not say a word about their own suffering, their problems, or those of her sister, who lived in the Rhineland and also was a friend of my mother's. When I asked, she responded, but briefly, as if to say, "I have no right to complain or seek your compassion." She did, of course, but she felt she didn't.

More questions about us, our children, Eva's family. Eva and Toni took an immediate liking to each other. She knew from Mother that Eva had come from Prague. Then came the next set of questions—about New York and the United States. She knew that New York was not just skyscrapers, and she wanted to know about life in the city. What were the house and the neighborhood like where Martha and Herr Doktor lived? How did practice and living quarters fit into one apartment? Was it that big?

Toni did not share the customary German prejudices and stereotypes about "uncultured" America. As a music lover, she knew intimately about America's burgeoning musical life. "I am so happy that people like Bruno Walter and Wilhelm Steinberg weren't just saved physically but got an opportunity to resume their work, to give of their creativity," she said. "That we Germans did not realize what we were losing, and what we had yet to lose, when these men, and so many others who were our cultural backbone, were driven out . . . that was our basic sin. I have not one bit of regard for all the academics and artists and editorial writers who kept their mouths shut in the early days, in 1933, 1934, even 1935! I think if Furtwängler and people like him in the arts, and scientists and academic people, had spoken up loud and en masse, we might have had a chance!"

Toni did not make much of her own attitude, but I knew from Mother that she did not stay silent. "Yes, one of the poobahs threatened me," she said. "But what did they want of me? I wasn't a great prize. And if they wanted to take me . . . well, then it wasn't worth too much living in this kind of a state anyway. As things turned out with the war, and all the bombing and suffering that Hitler caused us, we were in one big countrywide concentration camp anyway!"

"But weren't you worried that you'd be denounced, and then it could really have been bad for you?" I asked.

"I'm sure I was denounced, but they had too much else to do, with Jews and more 'dangerous' people. And so what? Here I found myself rooting for the people who were bombing us, because the only way we and our country could be saved was if your armies and air forces won!"

What I was hearing from Toni made me regain control of my emotions. I still felt twinges about Reinheim; I still looked with a special feeling on the blue-and-white house numbers in Darmstadt—and still do, whether in Switzerland, France, or wherever they are used. But Toni Scriba had jerked me back to reality: the America of Bruno Walter was my home, my family's home, the home of my parents.

Toni also clarified my hitherto somewhat cloudy, even romantic feelings about Germany. It was all right for me to reminisce about those blue numbers and all they represent, but what was important was to go beyond that—to the reality of Germany's history of crime and destruction, and then beyond that by seeking out the Roeths and Tonis and Lisbeths and developing ties with them. I came away from Toni Scriba relaxed, refreshed, as if I had grown a good deal since the night before.

I was in the right kind of work at VOA, I decided. But perhaps there was a better way to focus what this experience had given me. There remained one major unresolved tension in my life. I did not realize it at the time. But it was there, and it would force me to face it a dozen years later. It had to do with my father, but I would not realize it until after he was gone.

Twelve Years Later

We were sitting in our living room one Sunday morning reading the paper. We were then back in the New York area, living in Englewood, New Jersey. The bell rang. Strange time, Eva said. But in those days one was not yet as guarded as today. Two gentlemen stood there on the porch, introducing themselves as Arthur Fisher and Jim Grossman. Could they come in? Of course. The two men represented the United Jewish Appeal (UJA). This visit became another turning point in my life: I dropped back into Judaism, even though I did not realize that Sunday that it would happen.

Much had happened personally and professionally in the twelve years since 1955, but nothing that changed my outlook, my professional interest, and the link to Europe—and especially Germany— that I had developed in the wake of our first trip back.

I moved up to heading the VOA news operation in 1958, steeping myself even more in my work and absenting myself, if not physically then in every other way, from the family. When I was home, I read news copy I had taken with me, kept up with newspapers and magazines, was on the phone to the office . . .

In 1961 Father became critically ill for the first time in his life. He was seventy-four, and the attack of intense fever and shivers came in April, a couple of months after his birthday. Various specialists with whom he had worked over the past nineteen years were consulted. He was taken to the hospital, given every conceivably helpful kind of medicine. His fever went up to 104, then 105 degrees. He temporarily lost consciousness. There was no diagnosis. His body did not respond. He died five days after he was admitted to hospital. The specialists stood around after he was pronounced dead. The postmortem showed a bacillus that at that time was not treatable with any medication. It tore up my father relentlessly. He, the diagnostician by *Fingerspitzengefühl,* died undiagnosed.

I only glimpsed at that time how much I owed him. I knew I could never equal him or even come close to him in personal courage, in the matter-of-fact way in which he had endured terror, stress, unfair criticism, and the way in which he responded to never-ending demands. I did feel more acutely than before that I had caused him anguish by dropping out of Jewish life, in ethnic-cultural as well as religious terms. If I changed my mind, I could no longer let him know, which probably is one reason I did change it a few years later.

Mother had occasional attacks of dizziness, and was helpless without Father. It was the helplessness of the assertive woman who is unaware of her dependency. Now she became aware of it. Only I was left. She had hypertension and depressive episodes. It did not take much to persuade her to move to Washington, to be close to us. She was under constant medical care, even as she enjoyed a new life in her own apartment, but with frequent visits to us or vice versa. She became deeply involved with the children, who were by now in elementary school. It was a last and good new start for her.

In 1962, buoyed as we were by the Camelot atmosphere of Washington, I left VOA to join the State Department as spokesman for the newly established aid program for Latin America that became known as the Alliance for Progress. The 1949 trip was paying off! The investment was good! But it lasted less than two years, until John F. Kennedy's assassination. His successor and the people Lyndon Johnson appointed were "practical." They snuffed out the tender shoot of a new and hopeful policy toward Central and South America. The policy had flaws, and was wide open to attack once its young champion was no longer there to protect it with the shield of his popularity.

When the policy was dropped, I dropped out. It was the end of government service for me. And it was all to the good. I was over forty, and it was high time I tested myself in the private sector. I was offered a job in New York, as senior editor of the Latin American news magazine *Vision.* For almost a year I commuted. I had taken a room on the East Side, near the *Vision* office, while we were working out the orderly transition from Washington back to the New York area. Not only did we have to worry about the kids changing schools;

it also meant moving my mother again, who by that time had developed recurring fainting spells, and her blood pressure was barely responding to heavy doses of medication.

In early 1965 we found a house in Englewood, a community in the midst of racial integration efforts and tensions, which made it attractive to us as a place where large national issues centered on civil rights were played out. I took my mother up within days of our own move, and installed her in a garden apartment a stone's throw from our new house. She died days later from a stroke.

Mother's death hit me hard. A new life, a new career, children moving into their teens, and Mutti gone. Emptiness. For many years, I had not needed my mother as I needed her in Germany. I needed her then to make sure I had done right, to endure her censure, or to receive the delicious balm of her approval. Now that she was gone, I needed just her presence. Eva was there, yes, but I was in love with her. Mother was in reserve in my loneliness. I never wanted to belong. I did not need people. I had friends, none close. I wanted to be alone, but not quite. The risks of commitment, obligation, and giving that I could avoid by being alone were not present when it came to Mutti. I could be alone and still have Mutti, and in that way avoid loneliness. Now I was lonely. I was paying the price for wanting to be alone.

Eva understood how empty I felt. The time for Peter's bar mitzvah was approaching, but there would be no bar mitzvah. I stuck to my universalism, albeit without the activist, proselytizing enthusiasm of my early Ethical Culture days. I went to my job, which was not demanding, giving me more time to cater to my feelings. What was I doing working on Latin American subjects, anyway? After Kennedy's death, they had little attraction for me. Europe was on my mind— Germany in particular. That's what I wanted to work on.

I started visiting a psychiatrist. This turned into a lengthy process. I did not feel I was making headway. Eva counseled patience. She knew more about the process than I did. The High Holy Days approached. We were not affiliated with a synagogue. Of course we weren't: I was a universalist. Unlike in Washington, Rosh Hashanah and Yom Kippur were real in New York. My Jewish colleagues at *Vision* would not think of working, so I did not, either. But what should I do? If I don't go to work or to synagogue, then where do I go? For several years, the uneasiness, the unhappiness, the feeling of lostness, emptiness was hard to bear. I took walks along the Hudson River with Eva. For the first time, we talked about synagogue, Jewish things. That my parents were gone made things more difficult. Father never made me feel bad or guilty about having dropped out. Now his generosity made me feel worse. I felt something here in New York, now, that I had not felt before, and he would have been the person I could have talked to about it, without fearing the response. Even Mutti might have helped. Eva tried, but she couldn't really help, because Jewishness never was made to mean much to her. I could not wait for Yom Kippur to be over so I could get relief from the extra burden of guilt, or whatever it was, that these ten days piled on me.

The new accent in public life was on urban affairs. I was offered a chance to work on a new program of providing social services for New York City's poor. What was more natural, it was suggested, after the work I had done in economic and social development in Latin America, than joining people with similar experience in tackling the same kinds of problems right here in our city? But no, I was a foreign affairs man. Europe was still my desired focus. But Europe is a stalemate was the response. There's nothing to do there but resist the Russians when they try to expand. Germany? Who cares? Let it be split forever! Wasn't it de Gaulle who said that he loved Germany so much he was all in favor of having two of them? Nonsense I replied. There was work to do there.

But there was no offer. And there was an offer, an insistent one, here at home. Civil rights was on our minds. We had marched with Bayard Rustin in Washington. Eva had been active in the Democratic Party there. It seemed natural to join in, and as Jews we could understand better than most. As Jews? Again it came up. What was it about New York that kept bringing it up?

The year 1967 was the year of riots in Newark, Plainfield, and, yes, even Englewood. I received a call from a friend with whom I had worked in Washington who was now active in New Jersey public and political affairs. "I'd like to see you write the report for the governor's commission on the riots," he said.

"Me? What do I know about that?" I responded.

"As much, or rather as little, as anyone else," he came back, "but you know how to write."

This call came within days of another visit by Arthur Fisher. This time, in addition to repeating his appeal for a contribution for the UJA and Israel, Arthur suggested that our part of New Jersey should have a chapter of the American Jewish Committee, of which he was a member, and that I should be involved in organizing it. Again, that Jewish knock on the door! "The Committee is very active in urban affairs," Arthur said, "and we could use someone with experience like yours. So if you don't want to do it for one reason, do it for another, and help me get AJC off the ground here!"

I agreed, and it was the end of a twenty-seven-year pause.

We started a chapter in our area and had speakers on urban topics, and soon after also on Jewish ones. Only a few months later I was attending meetings of the national organization in New York City, and I was an active Jew again—minus the synagogue component. What had speeded the process of my reinvolvement was the Six-Day War, which sparked an interest in Israel that ever since has been the focus of my life as a Jew.

Now I found myself in a new kind of debate: Germany and Jews, second half of the century. My interest in Europe and Germany, my strong feeling that we must build on what was good in postwar Germany, remained unchanged. And this led to sustained, often heated arguments in my new activist Jewish environment. It has been a stimulating, creative discussion that continues today.

Even as this intra-Jewish debate developed, another ideological front began to shape up: American establishment liberals versus Zionists and, when the slip was allowed to show, versus Jews.

Before these new challenges opened up, an important family event occurred: In early 1968, just as we were putting the last touches on the New Jersey riot report, I received a call from a former colleague in Washington to discuss joining the Ford Foundation. It was one of America's most prestigious institutions, and the offer I received was most attractive: to develop a simple and timely system of evaluating projects that Ford's domestic affairs division was supporting. On both professional and personal grounds, I found myself fortunate to get the offer and accepted. But before starting, I wanted some time to spend with the family. Peter was fifteen, Andrea and Judy thirteen, and I still had not had or taken time to get to know them, to really become part of the family. It was close to the beginning of summer. Ford agreed to have me start in late summer so I could take a long trip with the family. It would be a trip to Europe, and the highlight was to be a visit to Reinheim.

About two weeks before our scheduled departure, Eva broke her foot. With the orthopedist's agreement, she decided not to cancel or postpone the big event, and we set out, leg in cast, crutches in hand, wheelchair in baggage. The accident had a fortunate consequence: the four of us had to work together closely and smoothly to ease Eva's progress and meet our schedule. It would have been a magnificent immersion in family life even with all bones intact. But there was that extra incentive, and it proved to be the best thing to happen to our family relationships.

For transportation I had rented a Mercedes with a huge body, large enough for eight people, and a small motor, known as a "Pullman." The trunk accommodated all our luggage plus the wheelchair Eva was using to get around.

For four weeks we traveled together, helped each other to make it work, laughed, saw the sights, and ate too well and too much. My son, daughters, and I opened ourselves up to each other. We started in Paris, went on by train to Germany, where we rented the car, and ended up in Naples, where we left the car and went aboard an Italian liner to go home.

The highlight was Reinheim. This time it was all lovely—no trauma, no confusion about past and present. Lisbeth had, of course, prepared even more cakes and pastries than thirteen years earlier: after all, those hungry children had to be taken care of! But the house is what mattered to them. They, too, wanted to touch the stones, and they did. Peter said to me, "But, Pop, I thought you were born in a log cabin!" That's what being born in the countryside meant to our young Lincoln scholar!

The children also wanted to see their mother's house, but 1968 was not the time for a Petschek to return to Prague, after the Soviets had crushed the revolt. The time would come seventeen years later when we'd make another family trip, complete with spouses.

History was coming alive as we stood by the house. Reinheimers walking by wondered what this strange-looking family with the huge Mercedes was doing there. This time the rumors of our visit had not spread. Only a few people stopped in at Lisbeth's. How different this visit was for me! With Eva and the children around me, my mind was clear about Reinheim and Germany, and about the roots we had sunk in America. It was exciting to bring the children close to my beginnings, and the blessing of the experience was unmixed.

We went on the rest of our trip through Germany, Switzerland, and Italy serenely, drinking in sights and sounds. We were never the same after this hegira. We had become a family. My eyes, my mind, and my feelings were opened to my children. And my intention to play a role in future relations between Jews and Germany was firmed up. The experience was also in part responsible for Peter's becoming interested in Germany and the German language. He developed this interest into a career opportunity a few years later.

After our return, I started work at the Ford Foundation. The work was focused on urban issues, and required me to spend much time in minority communities. It taught me a great deal that I could not have understood had I continued to follow black-white relations and social and economic inequalities merely by reading the papers or participating in living-room discussions.

I began to feel tension between the way in which my colleagues— including some who were Jewish, albeit inactively so—viewed Israel's situation and the way they looked at minority issues and jeopardy to minority rights in this country. Even as the black power movement was changing both the objectives and tactics of the civil rights drive in which Eva and I had been involved, I found that the Jewish and black situations, especially the hostility that surrounded both Israel and American blacks, had much in common. Not so my colleagues. "Anti-Semitism is dead," said one of the higher-ups at Ford, and with this fiat ended the need to concern oneself with the Jews. "Jews are fortunate enough to take care of themselves," this same philanthropist leader told me. And this included Israel.

The strict separation of divisions at Ford did not favor contact with our international colleagues. But both my interest in Europe and my increasing involvement with Israel through the American Jewish Committee prompted me to find out more. The first thing I found was that, unlike our division, which under McGeorge Bundy had been reshaped and expanded and was headed by a Jew, the international folks pretty much followed the WASP pattern of most foundations. And while the mix of backgrounds on the staff of the National Affairs Division made it possible, even inviting, to discuss issues not immediately within our professional purview, the international professionals seemed to feel that "outsiders" had little if any standing to talk with them about world affairs.

This did not deter me. On Europe, where I felt we had some things to learn in terms of immigrants and correctional reform, I was able to get some work done within the division. But on the Middle East, Vice President David Bell and his Ivy League experts ruled supreme. With Bundy's encouragement, I did enter the pristine precincts of the Bell preserve, and found out that something that was natural and obvious to my colleagues was just as unnatural and obscure to me: to them the Arabs were the oppressed minority and the Jews the quasi-colonialists; to me the Arabs were over one hundred million fiercely declaring their undying hostility to the Jewish state and trying to wipe it out, and the Israelis the minuscule minority.

The International Division's view was, of course, not original or isolated. Rather, it reflected a widespread feeling and policy among Near Eastern specialists both in and outside the government, and among the academic and philanthropic elites whose staffs and officers shuttled between Foggy Bottom, the Ivy League institutions, and the think tanks and foundations of New York and Washington.

What was new was that, for the first time, I was spending my working hours among these people, and I could learn firsthand rather than from cocktail talk or the *New York Times* what made them tick. More important, I could see the concrete results of their thinking: grant-making by Ford in the area of the former mandate of Palestine went primarily to Palestinian colleges and institutions, and for area-wide research and development in such fields as water supply and professional training for Arab applicants. I could see that "the Jews can take care of themselves" were not just words but policy.

Meanwhile, I had launched a comparative piece of research in Europe on "guest workers." It demonstrated that an assumption I had made was correct: that a self-generated, self-interested concern of the wider community for the preservation of its city's physical and social health was more effective in integrating immigrants into housing in widely scattered sections of the city than policy directives from governmental agencies. This was the result of comparative studies in Frankfurt and Zurich. In the Swiss city, where decisions flow from the community level up and require the participation of local businessmen, residents, and communal institutions, there was little love for the Italians, Spaniards, Yugoslavs, and North Africans who were badly needed to do work the Swiss no longer wanted to do themselves. But there were no ghettos comparable in size and level of misery to those in German cities. In Germany, where the federal and state governments provided both directives and considerable funding, large ghettos spread like wildfire. The difference did not stem from concern or goodwill or resources. The difference was the decentralization, the resultant assumption of community and neighborhood responsibility, and the manageability of decisions flowing from this pattern that was characteristic of Switzerland's political culture.

I thought the results of this study ought to make us rethink our positions. What seemed important to me was the community participation that had developed in Switzerland, in enormous contrast to the dependency on government funding we were constantly talking, writing, and politicking about regarding our schools, housing, and other communal institutions. The study made no impact: it didn't fit. It would have required policies based on centering more real responsibility at the community level than was deemed "fair" or "realistic." I learned then that I was being "conservative" in my approach. I did not think of myself in liberal-versus-conservative terms in those days. I wondered, had that cussed European habit of ideologizing everything contaminated America?

I was learning so much about our cities, but even more about how people in a major American institution think, and I was getting paid handsomely to boot! I was recharging both my Jewish and European batteries in the process. Some of that learning was hard on me: we Jews had it against us that we were successful. The same thing had been true in Germany. Wasn't that one big reason for what had happened?

Some Jews at Ford yielded the hardest-to-take lessons: they out-WASPed the WASPs when it came to Jewish and Israeli concerns. To start with, they were Jewish only on Chanukkah, when equal opportunity called for a menorah and Chanukkah songs to parallel the Christmas tree and carols. As to the Middle East, and the developing animus against Jews as special white targets among black activists, the Jews at Ford tended to agree with prevailing Foundation thinking. They seemed determined to assimilate in a country that did not press them to do so, even as they applauded black, Hispanic, and Native American celebrations of distinctiveness! I decided that, to them, it made sense. By assimilating when it was not required, they imperceptibly became part of the WASP culture—so they thought. As long as one was distinguishable within America's pluralistic society, one hadn't really made it. One's insecurity was so acute that the only way to assuage it was to meld, at least in attitude and thinking, into the unspoken but still perceived WASP aristocracy.

My interest in Israel had become sufficiently known by 1973. I was asked to accompany a member of the Foundation's board on a visit to Israel, where he had been invited to attend a conference on cooperative banks. It was my first trip. I preceded my guest by a few days, to supplement book knowledge with direct experience. Shortly after checking into my Tel Aviv hotel, I rented a car, got a map, studied it as I looked out over the blue water, and got ready for a drive around as much of the country as I could manage in a day. It was the single most exciting day I had spent in many a year: from Tel Aviv I drove south to Beersheba, on toward the Dead Sea, on the way drifting off into what looked strange and turned out to be Gaza!

On I went, picking up two Dutch tourists on the way—on to Arad in the Negev and to the Dead Sea and Masada. I dropped my hitchhikers in Jerusalem in the early evening, could just glance at the city, and was back in Tel Aviv at about 9:30 P.M., exhausted but not tired. This was created by Jews? All this? And I hadn't even seen half, even a third of it! This was "ours"? Not mine, I had done nothing to build anything, but they—the Zionists—said it was. I had to think about that . . .

The next morning I met another group of early arrivals: the German contingent to the bank conference. They were reluctant to make contact. When I spoke German, the ice began to break. A tour north was being offered: three buses were going, each led by a guide speaking a different language: English, French, or German—the three largest delegations' languages. I chose German. I wanted to get to know these fellows. I wanted to experience Israel with them. We talked much; they thawed up all the way. Israel was so exciting that it smoothed out any potential rough edges. But there were few, if any. I found myself more comfortable talking about Jews and Israel with these fellows than with my colleaques at Ford!

It was another of those extra-full days that Israeli tour guides invariably stuff into the visitor. Finally, after a stop in Acre, we were on our way back, riding along that seductively blue-gray Mediterranean. And what do I hear? "Das Wandern ist des Muellers Lust"—the marching song I used to sing on excursions with my class in Reinheim! Reinheim, "Das Wandern," here, between Haifa and Tel Aviv? As my daughter Andrea would say, "it blew my mind." In those days, I said to myself: how will I put all this together?

Another escalation of my Jewish reinvolvement came in 1977, when Menachem Begin was elected prime minister of Israel. It was a shock to many in the American Jewish Committee, that old-line organization of German-Jewish origin that was converted to a reluctant Zionism only after the State of Israel had been created. Needless to say, Begin's blunt nationalism and his Polish-accented English did not go over well with the folks at the Foundation, either. There, and at AJC, one was comfortable with Golda Meir, that Jewish mother with the Midwestern accent. And, of course, with Abba Eban, who sounded like Churchill instead of like a delicatessen waiter.

I had not known anything about Begin. My reimmersion was too recent to make me conversant with Zionist history. (I caught up later, but never enough to become genuinely knowledgeable.) But both AJC and Ford had made me alert to the reactions I was observing. And Begin himself did the rest.

Soon after he had been installed, Begin came to the United States. By that time, I had attended several mass meetings of Jewish "leaders" with visiting prime ministers, such as Golda Meir and Yitzhak Rabin. But Begin was a new kind of experience. He talked to me as a Jew, not an Israeli. He made me feel equal, not different and guilty for not living there. Neither his accent, nor his policy of a "Greater Israel," with which I did not agree, were what mattered to me then. His honesty did.

In an article in the *Jerusalem Post* in 1978, I wrote:

> Menachem Begin has made a lasting contribution to Jewish life when he says . . . that Jews need not be perfect, cautious, inconspicuous, or whatever else centuries of anti-Semitism have called for, to be granted acceptance.
>
> I am convinced that . . . this is at the root of the difficulties that many

Americans, including assimilated American Jews, have with Begin. The [West Bank] settlements and [U.N. Resolution] 242 are merely handy symbols to which they peg their anger and frustration. It is Begin himself they have trouble with. . . .

It's uncomfortable to see this quintessential, short, bald Polish Jew as the leader of Israel. He is too Jewish, too easy to feel anti-Semitic about, too easy to become embarrassed about. . . . It was all so easy with Golda Meir, the wonderful Jewish mother . . . and Yitzhak Rabin, with a slightly different accent, could have been prime minister of Norway or Holland.

When one visited Israel, one admired its Hebrew University, its Weizmann Institute . . . the marvels of science and technology . . . all wonderful things one could associate with as a Westerner and an American. And rightly so. But who came back from Israel and said how wonderful a place it is for Jews, how good, or perhaps not good, is the quality of its Jewish life. . . .

But that *is* what Israel needs to be all about. That is the point that Menachem Begin is making. And he is the first prime minister of Israel who is making it, at least for me. . . .

Working at the Ford Foundation and active in the American Jewish Committee? one might well ask about me. Yes, I was, and in the view of those two organizations I had become "radical." Yet at the same time I was working on programs at Ford and supporting urban dialogues in which black or Hispanic spokesmen and leaders held equivalent views about their groups and were applauded for it. But then, they were "minority," and we Jews had graduated to "other," which meant WASPs and other whites. The tension between my developing Jewish assertiveness and the institutions I was associated with rose, and it was not "creative," a term that foundation folk and urbanists bandied about a lot.

In the second half of the 1970s, my two major interests—Jewish security and a new relationship of Jews with Germany—were reflected in decisions made by two of my children: Peter decided to spend a semester abroad in Germany, after making German foreign policy his major at the University of Michigan. He later pursued the subject in graduate work at the London School of Economics. Andrea, who together with her sister Judy attended Duke University, was ignited as a Jew at this southern institution. After taking one course in comparative religion and meeting a charismatic young rabbi-teacher, she transferred to Brandeis University to major in Near East–Jewish studies, went on to graduate school in Jewish community service studies, and decided to emigrate to Israel. By then she was fluent in Hebrew. I knew that Andrea was a romantic and idealist, not unlike her grandfather, and, playing a modified version of my mother's role as the "practical" one, I asked her to discuss her reasons for moving to Israel with me. I had anticipated a lengthy exploration of the pros and cons of *aliyah* (literally "going up," as Zionists call moving to Israel, in the sense of qualitative upward movement), but Andrea had an answer that brooked no debate: "I can't split myself up anymore," she said.

What she was saying, and what she had alluded to on occasion for some time, was that she was bothered by the ambivalence of American Jews in relation to Israel. In part, her conversion to Zionism was due to the influence of a group of Israeli graduate students at Brandeis. But in part it was also what she had experienced at school in Englewood: other Jewish students had gone through a Jewish Sunday school experience, yet, she felt, with the hindsight of Duke and Brandeis, seemed woefully "inadequate" as Jews. And, most important, she had observed my development, from complete nonidentification all the way to militancy, after a youth that had been steeped in religious observance and forced study. In recent years, too, she had heard me unburden myself at night about the frustrations and sterile debates I had gone through at meetings of the Committee and about my experience at Ford. She had decided to live a "completely Jewish life," as she put it, in a country that might well lack many of the comforts she had come to take for granted, but where one was a Jew among Jews, not at the margins, a place where the quality of Judaism was not strained.

Andrea made good on her plan: she went to live in Israel in 1983, now has her own twins (also girls—third generation in succession!), lives in the countryside, and has shed many of her pre-*aliyah* expectations. She complains like a native Israeli, is dissatisfied with the quality of Jewish life, and has even planned to come back to America with her family, but then . . . she stayed.

As American relations with Israel became strained after Begin became prime minister, my involvement with Jewish and Israeli affairs became interesting to McGeorge Bundy—interesting in a personal and programmatic sense. This prompted me to propose, and Bundy to agree, to a conference at Ford to be attended by a group of representative and knowledgeable Jews and non-Jews. They were to explore together what could be done about feelings expressed in the bumper stickers "Oil, not Jews" that appeared quite widely during the gas shortage following the 1973 war. The participants would also talk about the Middle East: Was that oil crisis likely to change the U.S.–Israeli relationship? Could new approaches be developed toward a resolution of the Arab-Israeli conflict?

In terms of my personal experience, the years from 1974 to 1979, when Bundy resigned, yielded new insights, especially into the responses of my Jewish colleagues at the Foundation. Bundy and I had developed our dialogue on the Middle East, which became both more spirited and sustained after Begin took office. Begin, Likud, and Herut were virtually unknown, except to some experts in the State Department and in Middle East study centers. Bundy wanted to meet some people who knew about that strange new breed that had so unceremoniously dispatched the Labor Party, which had run the government for close to thirty years.

Bundy, whose incisive mind and political sensitivity were of the highest order, had grasped that something important had happened in Israel and wanted to know more. Most American Jews who had been involved with Israel—as contributors, frequent visitors, or members of boards of Israeli academic or health institutions—did not understand it. What had happened was that the Labor Party, in boilerplate terms associated with the left, had become the establishment of the Jewish state. Marx was still on the party's bookshelves, and the prime ministers and heads of the party—Ben Gurion, Levi Eshkol, Golda Meir—were regular attendees in good standing at meetings of the Socialist International. The party and its functionaries in Israel controlled the economy and social policy: Histadrut, the labor federation, was theirs; Koor Industries, the largest industrial concern, was theirs; politics and jobs and the shape of society were under their control. The left had become the aristocracy, even in the sense that the prime ministership was inherited. The right, ideologically committed to the free market and to a militantly Jewish state, including the retention of the occupied territories, had for thirty years been as insignificant as advocates of a republic under Louis XIV.

But here they were. They'd come, seemingly, out of nowhere. And most surprised were the safely ensconced—or so everybody thought—leaders of the Labor Party. The sea change that had occurred developed precisely out of Labor's "establishment" character: large numbers of immigrants from Near Eastern countries, who had been dubbed "the second Israel" under Labor, had voted for Begin and his party. They did not care to be a second Israel, whose members would, as Labor's policies though not its rhetoric said, gradually graduate into first-class citizenship. When? Once they became assimilated to the prevailing European Jewish culture. But they neither were nor cared to be European. They had come from Morocco, Tunisia, Algeria, Iraq, Iran, Yemen. They had their own customs; they had probably never heard of Marx or experienced socialism or what went under that name. What they did know and care about was that they were Jews. And just as Menachem Begin reached out to me in New York as one Jew to another, so the Sephardim of Israel had grasped his Jewish hand.

Begin's opponents and other doubters saw his appeal to the Sephardim as a smart political ploy. I believed and still believe that political success coincided with conviction and commitment—which I also believe is the mark of a leader. If it was only a political tactic, then why was it Begin who broke the stalemate over bringing in the Ethiopian Jews? There were not terribly many votes there. Whatever Begin's faults may have been—and he had many—the depth of his Jewish commitment is beyond doubt. To him Jews were what mattered, and Israel was the vehicle for their "coming home." It was not a Western-style or socialist or capitalist Israel; that was secondary for Begin. It was Israel as a land for Jews, and to him a Jew was a Jew—Moroccan, Polish, or Ethiopian.

This was some of the stuff of my and some guests' conversations with Bundy. He was avidly interested in the subject, and showed it. As he did, some of my Jewish colleagues came out of Ford's teak woodwork. At a staff meeting, Bundy referred to "the goyim" in a discussion of a Middle Eastern issue. Then came responses in Yiddish, when the subject lent itself to it. My friends had not become more Jewish, only more assimilated to the "new" Bundy.

The experience and learning I had absorbed on the urban scene in America and Europe, and the increasing toll that internecine struggles took in the developing world—as in Nigeria, the Indian subcontinent, Malaysia, and a host of other countries in what had become known as the third world—led to another initiative. In 1976, responding to an invitation to propose new projects, I suggested that the Foundation was remiss in dealing only with economic and educational needs, and providing only technical and related "development assistance" to projects in the developing countries. I suggested that, from Europe to North America (Canada-Quebec) to Africa and Asia, ethnic conflicts were tearing at the very existence of countries and regions as organized societies, making the kind of technical and economic assistance we were providing questionable, if not wasted. In Europe, where Ford was not active, I cited Northern Ireland, Yugoslavia, Spain (the Basques and Catalonia); in Africa one could start in Morocco (Polisario), go on to Nigeria, Rwanda and Burundi, the Sudan, and barely scratch the surface of conflicts that had brought tribes into deadly combat. In Asia, the perennial dispute about Kashmir, the tensions and recurrent outbreaks of violence of Malays against Chinese and Indonesian Muslims against Chinese in that country, as well as the civil war in the southern Philippines, were symptomatic of the worldwide problem.

Yet the only two ethnic conflicts—and ethnic in this context is meant to cover all group differences, from race to language and religion—in which the United States as a country and institutions like ours seemed interested were those pitting whites against nonwhites: South Africa and the Middle East, where the Jews were seen as whites and the Arabs, particularly the Palestinians, as nonwhites. I had become convinced that only where we could identify with the issue did we find it "exciting" to become involved. ("Exciting," incidentally, was a heavily overworked adjective at Ford, and had come to mean what "excited" us as grantmakers, that is, as missionaries, or, more precisely, as supporters of the "downtrodden" against the "oppressors.") In situations where whites were pitted aginat nonwhites, our role was clearly marked out. Yet where the conflict was among nonwhites, the grantmakers' "excitement" waned.

As one who had experienced Nazi rule and now was a strong supporter of the State of Israel, and as a Jew for whom the missionary spirit has no appeal, I felt that the Foundation's policy and my colleagues' attitude was more apt to meet the grantmakers' personal need for excitement and psychic satisfaction than to deal with substantive priorities: how could an institution devoted to "human welfare" and actively engaged in the developing world ignore the tragic bloodletting in Rwanda and Burundi, the religious and tribal warfare in parts of India demanding hundreds, even thousands of deaths, as it sent study missions to South Africa, supported legal action on behalf of South African blacks, and West Bank Palestinians? These were worthy endeavors, but thousands were dying elsewhere!

It took me five years to get approval for funding an Institute for Ethnic Studies (ICES) in Sri Lanka. Its scope was much more limited than what I had hoped for—which was to set up training for mediators, to provide expert counsel to governments and ethnic group leadership. But all ICES was able to do was study the issues. The reasons given were that "there is little an outsider could do," or we were risking involvement in domestic politics. Yet we did risk such involvement in South Africa and Israel. Why were we spear carriers for justice in these situations, but left it to the Red Cross to put Band-Aids on the gaping wounds of massive fighting all over Africa and Asia?

I concluded that my experience and my reawakened Jewish identity and involvement did not mesh with established thinking, and, more important, with the prevailing attitudes at Ford. When I say "Jewish," I refer to what my colleagues might call "militant," and what I call the normal and expected sense and assertion of identity of minorities.

The shift in my priorities and my departure from Ford, in a massive fire-the-old, hire-the-new-and-young action by the new president, Franklin Thomas, coincided. Before I left, I had a call from a Jewish philanthropist. He wanted me to set up a professional service for Jewish foundations that did not operate on a large enough scale to warrant having their own staffs. I accepted readily and happily. Even though the client foundations made grants to a wide variety of institutions, work in Israel was part of the agenda, and it required me to become knowledgeable about agricultural and immigration issues in Israel. In taking this position, my professional experience in philanthropy, in writing and editing, and my interest in Jewish life and Israeli needs had now merged.

Everything came together in 1986 when I moved to Paris to direct the European office of the Anti-Defamation League (ADL). I had joined ADL in 1980, after I had become increasingly uncomfortable at the American Jewish Committee, mainly over Israel-related issues. My views were now considered too militant. I felt that my contributions were no longer being taken seriously. I decided that my distance from the majority had widened too much, so I explored alternatives and joined ADL as a volunteer. ADL's more militant, less assimilationist atmosphere was a relief. I felt good about not having to fight anymore. At ADL I was, if anything, a voice of moderation.

Ideologically I felt comfortable; socially I did not. But then I never did. I always preferred to be alone, private, uninvolved. Ever since I was a child, it was my preference. It was the best way to avoid a "how could you?!" It was also the best way to control how I spent my time. Being alone was the most important part of being free. I paid tribute to the niceties of being social, but stayed aloof in my own mind. It was a preference, an obeisance to a lifelong compulsion to be "safe" that made it possible to avoid commitments, but this approach limited my opportunities to be integrated into a group or community, and to be effective as only such involvement makes possible.

Whatever I undertook had to be done well, fully, and before the deadline. It had to be done fast, too, lest the burden of undone work weigh me down. My analyst told me at an early stage that I had to work on this immaturity, because it had seriously limiting, if not incapacitating, consequences for creativity. He was right. Yet I never lost my deeply rooted desire to shy away from involvement, nor did I lose my desire to be special. After all, I was "Robertche," fragile, special, the only child, who also wanted to be admired, catered to, even in my adulthood.

With the organizations I joined during the period of time we lived in Englewood, I would steep myself in the substance but try to avoid the social chitchat. I always felt happy and relieved when a meeting was over, when the guests had gone or the lunch broke up. Once we moved back into New York City in 1976, the anonymity I craved came easily. Somehow, during more than forty years of marriage, Eva and I had learned to fulfill different needs: she is social, on the phone, at lunches, giving or accepting party invitations; I became used to it, sometimes even enjoyed her way with people, and she respected my reluctance. How much easier and enjoyable my life could have been but for that "how could you?!" and "special" nonsense with which I grew up and old!

In the early 1980s, partly influenced by Andrea's religious observance, partly as a natural complement to my Zionist-secular involvement, I looked for a synagogue I could join. It took more than five years (leaving aside the two years of residence in Paris) before I found one where I felt comfortable. I wanted a Conservative ritual, because that is what I was brought up with in Frankfurt before my father became more Orthodox. I wanted a rabbi who would not make me feel guilty if I did not appear every Saturday for services. I was not interested in being uplifted by sermons that were bound to fall short of this laudable rabbinic objective; I wanted a place to worship, without duties or commitments, in the way that I chose. After a long search and several tryouts, I found a congenial small congregation on the East Side that suited my needs. We hold Seders and observe the High Holy Days, but otherwise take religious ritual lightly.

Throughout the 1970s and early 1980s, while at Ford, I had maintained contact with European, especially German, institutions and kept up on European developments through imported newspapers and magazines. Eva and I had taken many European vacations, in addition to working trips. My interest in working with Germany, as a Jew and as an American, remained alive and well. In 1986, when the job of European director, with an office in Paris, fell vacant, I was excited by the possibilities. I was sixty-five by then, not an age to start a new career and make a complicated move, but also an age that for me was light years away from retirement. I was offered the job.

There was much to argue against the move. To Eva, music, and especially the piano, had meant much all her adult life. Since the children left home, she had resumed regular lessons, and was practicing every day and accomplishing a good deal. Would she have to interrupt it all in Paris? And there were other concerns: her close and extended family here, and both Peter and Judy, now married, lived in or near New York. A year-old grandchild was growing up in Brooklyn, and others would come soon. But then, Andrea's twins were due just as our move to Europe would happen, and we would be five and a half hours nearer! Everyone, including myself, made this argument to an understandably move-reluctant Eva, who replied, "Yes, but where I'll be I'll have nobody close!"

Family consultation eventually yielded a unanimous judgment: the Paris offer was too good to be rejected. Good not because it was Paris, romantic, and whatever the conventional American connotations of "Paris" imply, but because it was so right for me! It would not have mattered if the office had been located in London, the Hague, or wherever in Western Europe; what mattered was that after a lifetime of search, happenstance, and partial job satisfaction, the three components of my intellectual and personal development—Judaism, European and especially German influences, and American culture—would be needed to make me successful in my work.

We moved in mid-1986, and happened on a lovely apartment of friends of friends. The owners lived in America and were subletting their sunny, large furnished place opposite the Parc Monceau. A walk across the park led me to my exercise club, which was only a five-minute metro ride away from the office. I inherited the most skilled, intelligent, and loyal assistant I have ever had; found my way into reasonably manageable, yet far from fluent and still farther from perfect French; and began work. London, Brussels, Rome, Madrid, and Frankfurt were on my "route." Israel, attitudes toward Jews, and work with Jewish community organizations were the agenda.

We stayed for two years. The experience had crammed decades worth of new knowledge, sensitivities, and above all contacts with people into me. I made new friends—friends, to be sure, as I define them: with the needed measure of distance between us. What I found was that this distance, the reluctance to become deeply involved, was much more readily accepted and practiced in Europe, especially France, than in America. It was just fine with me, though painful for my sociable spouse.

Some of the closest friends I acquired and with whom I stay in regular contact were in Germany. No doubt language is responsible for helping bring people closer to each other. Time and again I have found that language is so much more than a means of communication: it opens not just minds but psyches, steps up candor, and yields "togetherness," even amid substantive disagreement. People who expect an American or other foreigner and hear him greet them not just in the local language but in the vernacular and the tone that resembles their own invariably change expression. It has nothing to do with citizenship or actual "belonging"; it is a spontaneous ethnic-cultural feeling that bursts forth.

What I was doing in my Paris assignment—and what I still do today via phone, fax, and periodic visits—is to work on Jewish and other minority problems as an American with Europeans, especially Germans. It has been in Germany where, because of a history-conditioned conscience, I found the clearest and most helpful responses. I felt it was right and good, and I felt qualified to do the work.

What had come about I had articulated earlier, in Colombo, Sri Lanka. As part of my development work for the Institute for Ethnic Studies, I had made contact with British and German foundations as supplementary funding sources. In the course of these efforts, I had met and worked with the Federal German ambassador in Colombo. On one of my visits, a group of us were invited to dinner at the embassy. A larger group had been invited, including some visiting German scientists and members of the diplomatic corps. At one point, the ambassador rose, raised his glass, and made appropriate comments, especially about the institute's agenda of trying to help mediate, work out, and find new ways of grappling with ethnic conflicts.

A response was due from our side; the natural candidate to make it was the institute's chairman, who sat across from me. I signaled to him to respond. He shook his head, signaling back that it was my assignment. The pause became embarrassing. He sat tight and I knew he would not move.

I got up, glass in hand, experiencing one of the most difficult and tense moments of my professional life. What could I say, as an American Jew in a German embassy in Southern Asia, about ethnic conflict? I had no time to plan; I had to say whatever came to me.

I spoke of how appropriate were place, subject, and speaker. Ethnic conflict in its worst form, deadly persecution, shaped the beginning of my life. Germany was the source of evil then. Germany was trying to be a source of help now. An American foundation was funding the initiative. And who better than a German Jew who suffered should be present now, when some small concrete steps could be taken so that what happened then would never happen again. I raised my glass to our joint efforts, toasting the "closing of the circle."

There was no applause. There was silence. But the response in the faces around that table said more than words. The threads had come together.

❧

Jewish Lives